D1551753

AMERICA'S FEW

OSPREY
PUBLISHING

BILL YENNE

AMERICA'S FEW

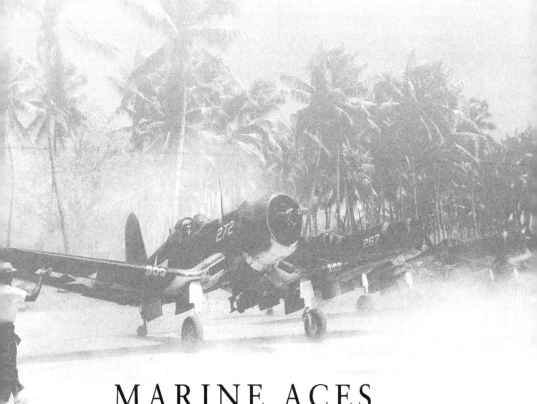

MARINE ACES
OF THE SOUTH PACIFIC

OSPREY PUBLISHING
Bloomsbury Publishing Plc
Kemp House, Chawley Park, Cumnor Hill, Oxford OX2 9PH, UK
29 Earlsfort Terrace, Dublin 2, Ireland
1385 Broadway, 5th Floor, New York, NY 10018, USA
E-mail: info@ospreypublishing.com
www.ospreypublishing.com

OSPREY is a trademark of Osprey Publishing Ltd

First published in Great Britain in 2022

A catalog record for this book is available from the British Library.

ISBN: HB 978 1 4728 4749 2; PB 978 1 4728 4750 8; eBook 978 1 4728 4748 5;
ePDF 978 1 4728 4746 1; XML 978 1 4728 4747 8

22 23 24 25 26   10 9 8 7 6 5 4 3 2 1

Maps by www.bounford.com
Index by Zoe Ross

Typeset by Deanta Global Publishing Services, Chennai, India
Printed and bound in Great Britain by CPI (Group) UK Ltd, Croydon CR0 4YY

Osprey Publishing supports the Woodland Trust, the UK's leading woodland conservation charity.

To find out more about our authors and books visit www.ospreypublishing.com. Here you
will find extracts, author interviews, details of forthcoming events and the option to sign up
for our newsletter.

Contents

List of Illustrations

Loren Dale "Doc" Everton scored the first of his dozen aerial victories while on loan to VMF-223. (USMC)

William Pratt Marontate scored his 13 aerial victories while flying with VMF-121. (USMC)

Joe Foss received the Medal of Honor on May 18, 1943. (USMC)

The first Marine Vought F4U-1 Corsairs of VMF-124 arrived at Guadalcanal on February 12, 1943. (USMC)

Kenneth Ambrose Walsh became the fourth highest-scoring Marine ace of all time, with 21 victories. (USMC)

A view from the cockpit of Marine SBD Dauntlesses over the Solomons, circa early 1943. (USMC)

Wilbur Jackson "Gus" Thomas of VMF-213 scored four aerial victories in his first engagement with the enemy. (USMC)

Edward Oliver "Bud" Shaw of VMF-213 scored three aerial victories in his first taste of combat in June 1943. (USMC)

James Norman Cupp was one of a trio of double-digit aces in VMF-213. (USMC)

On August 14, 1943, VMF-215 became the first Marine fighting squadron to operate from the former Japanese airfield at Munda on New Georgia. (USMC)

Flight operations began at Barakoma airfield on Vella Lavella in September 1943. (USMC)

Harold Leman "Hal" Spears scored 15 aerial victories with VMF-215. (USMC)

Jack Eugene Conger scored eight victories with VMF-212 and two when he was on loan to VMF-223. (USMC)

A Marine F4U-1 Corsair takes off Barakoma airfield on Vella Lavella. (USN)

James Elms Swett of VMF-221 earned a Medal of Honor for downing *seven* Japanese aircraft on a single day. (USMC)

Harold Edward "Murderous Manny" Segal downed a dozen Japanese aircraft. (USMC)

F4U-1 Corsairs of VMF-222 on the flightline at Barakoma airfield. (USMC)

The aviators of VMF-214 pose with a Corsair on Espiritu Santo. (USN)

An F4U-1D of VMF-124 aboard the USS *Essex*. (USMC)

Major Marion Carl and USN Commander Turner Caldwell with
    a Douglas D-558-1 Skystreak. (USN)

In the years after he left the Marine Corps in 1945, Joe Foss
    served as a brigadier general in the Air National Guard.
    (Arlington National Cemetery)

Brigadier General Robert Galer commanded VMF-224 in the
    Solomons in 1942. (USMC)

Lieutenant Kenneth Walsh retired as a lieutenant colonel in
    February 1962. (USMC)

Major General Marion Carl in August 1967 after commanding
    the 1st Marine Brigade at Danang in Vietnam. (USMC)

Maps

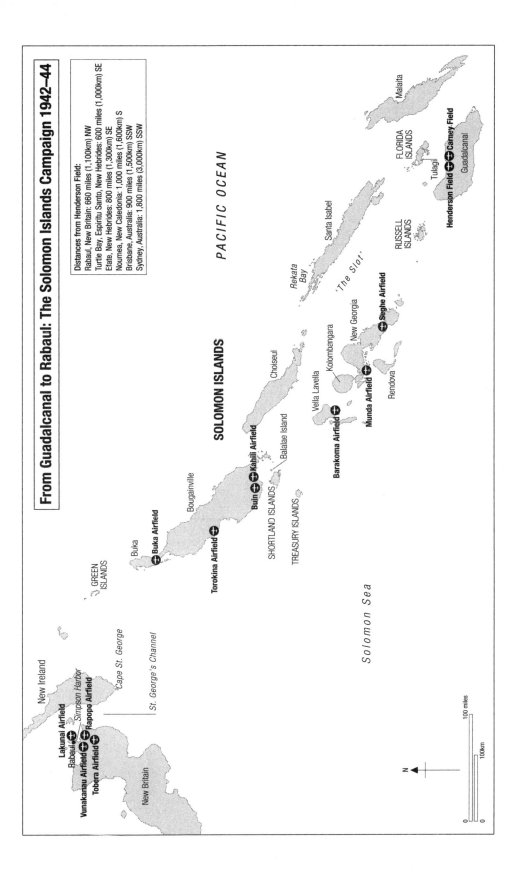

From Guadalcanal to Rabaul: The Solomon Islands Campaign 1942–44

Distances from Henderson Field:
Rabaul, New Britain: 660 miles (1,100km) NW
Turtle Bay, Espiritu Santo, New Hebrides: 600 miles (1,000km) SE
Efate, New Hebrides: 800 miles (1,300km) SE
Noumea, New Caledonia: 1,000 miles (1,600km) S
Brisbane, Australia: 900 miles (1,500km) SSW
Sydney, Australia: 1,800 miles (3,000km) SSW

PACIFIC OCEAN

Malaita

FLORIDA ISLANDS
Tulagi
Henderson Field Carney Field
Guadalcanal

RUSSELL ISLANDS

Santa Isabel

Rekata Bay

'The Slot'

New Georgia
Seghe Airfield

Kolombangara

Vella Lavella

Munda Airfield

Rendova

Barakoma Airfield

Choiseul

SOLOMON ISLANDS

Balalae Island

Kahili Airfield
Buin

SHORTLAND ISLANDS

TREASURY ISLANDS

Bougainville

Torokina Airfield

Buka
Buka Airfield

GREEN ISLANDS

New Ireland

Cape St. George

St. George's Channel

Simpson Harbor
Lakunai Airfield
Rabaul
Vunakanau Airfield Rapopo Airfield
Tobera Airfield

New Britain

Solomon Sea

N

0   100 miles
0   100km

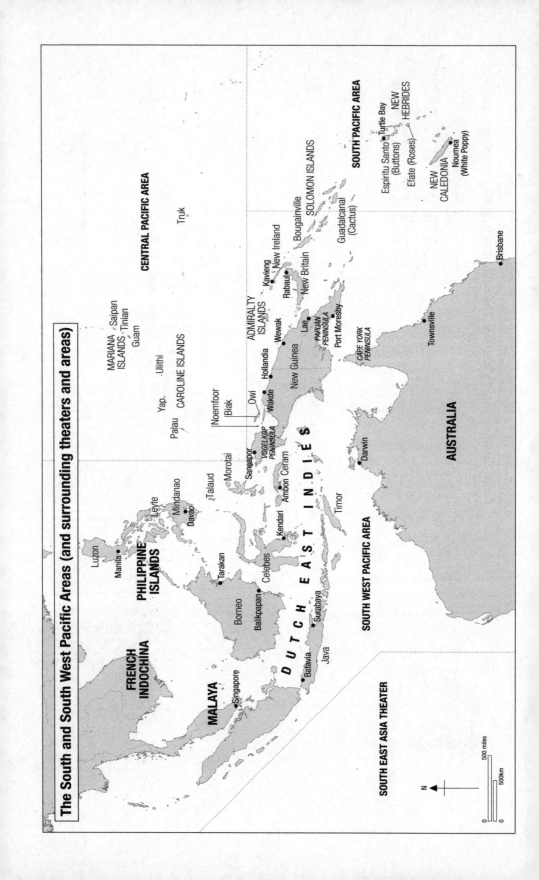

The South and South West Pacific Areas (and surrounding theaters and areas)

CENTRAL PACIFIC AREA

SOUTH PACIFIC AREA

Turtle Bay
Espiritu Santo
(Buttons)
NEW
HEBRIDES
Efate (Roses)
NEW
CALEDONIA
Nouméa
(White Poppy)

Truk

MARIANA Saipan
ISLANDS Tinian
Guam

Ulithi

Yap
CAROLINE ISLANDS

Palau

Bougainville
SOLOMON ISLANDS

Guadalcanal
(Cactus)

New Ireland
Kavieng
Rabaul
New Britain

ADMIRALTY
ISLANDS
Wewak
Lae
PAPUAN
PENINSULA
Port Moresby

Noemfoor
Biak
Owi
Wakde
Hollandia
New Guinea

CAPE YORK
PENINSULA

VOGELKOP
PENINSULA
Sansapor
Morotai
Talaud
Mindanao
Davao

Ambon Ceram
Kendari

D U T C H   E A S T   I N D I E S

Darwin

Leyte
Luzon
Manila
PHILIPPINE
ISLANDS
Tarakan
Borneo
Celebes
Balikpapan
Surabaya
Batavia
Java

Timor

AUSTRALIA

Townsville

Brisbane

FRENCH
INDOCHINA

MALAYA
Singapore

SOUTH WEST PACIFIC AREA

SOUTH EAST ASIA THEATER

N

0   500 miles
0   500km

Introduction

They were America's Few, a handful of Marine aviators who were in the right place at the right time.

The right place was a small, obscure South Pacific island called Guadalcanal, familiar to almost no one in the outside world, and which no one could have predicted would be the venue of a turning point in world history.

The right time was the darkest hours of 1942 when the armies of Imperial Japan raged unchecked across the Far East and the Western Pacific.

The term "Few" is, of course, borrowed from Winston Churchill's iconic characterization of the outnumbered fighter pilots of the Royal Air Force who saved Britain from Hitler's war machine in 1940.

There were differences between Churchill's Few and those whom we describe with that name. The Few of the RAF fought to save their own land from a rumbling Blitzkrieg that was literally within sight of their doorstep. The Marine Few fought a rampaging monster thousands of miles from their own doorstep.

On the other hand, these American Few were much fewer than the RAF Few. There were days when their total number of available aircraft could be counted on the fingers of one hand—while they faced enemy aircraft that numbered in the dozens. Meanwhile, they operated in the most primitive of conditions at the end of a long and unimaginably fragile supply line.

Strategically, the stakes were high. For Churchill's Few, it was Britain's survival offshore from a continent under the shadow of the swastika. For America's Few it was stopping the advance of an Axis enemy that already controlled the lives of around 500 million people—by virtue of Japan's occupation of much of China, virtually all of Southeast Asia and the East Indies. A failure to stop Japan's advances in 1942 would have meant the virtual isolation of Australia and a status quo of brutal Japanese imperial rule across Asia that might well have prevailed unchallenged for decades.

WHO WERE AMERICA'S FEW?

They were a generation of young men who had grown up never having heard of Guadalcanal. Most of them had heard, because these men had a predisposition to an interest in aviation, of the term "ace," as it relates to pilots who do battle with one another and score five or more aerial victories.

They each may well have heard of Roland Garros, the great French aviator who is often identified, albeit erroneously, as the world's first ace. They may have known of Adolphe Pégoud, who actually was the world's first ace. However, it is safe to say that they all knew the name of Eddie Rickenbacker, America's "Ace of Aces" in World War I.

Neither Garros nor Pégoud survived World War I, but Rickenbacker was around to inspire a new generation of American fighter pilots, and to send congratulatory messages to many of them as they matched his accomplishments during the early 1940s.

Aces present an image of the lone warrior that is unique to the twentieth century. It is an image that arouses the imagination and paints warfare not as hell but as glorious. The ace, like the knights of European legend or the gunfighters of American legend, is not lost among the anonymous dead, but preserved as an individual for posterity.

While the US Army Air Forces had aces that did battle in theaters of operation throughout the world during World War II, the aces of the US Marine Corps flew only in Pacific skies. The highest-scoring among them saw action mainly in the intense battles of 1942 and 1943 high above the myriad islands that lie between Guadalcanal and New Britain, though a second generation of Marine aviators achieved ace status against the dreaded kamikaze threat in 1944 and 1945.

The American Fighter Aces Association notes that the USAAF boasted 735 aces in World War II, the US Navy 381, and the Marine Corps 122. Of these, five men achieved 20 or more aerial victories, and just over a dozen scored between 10 and 19. Considering the relatively small overall pool of Marine aviators from which these aces were derived, and the relatively narrow geographic area in which they operated, their record is extraordinary.

Having written a dual biography of the top USAAF aces of the war—Dick Bong and Tommy McGuire—and another biography of the top female ace of all time—Lidiya Litvyak of the Red Air Force—this author turned to the Marines.

I have always been intrigued by the comparisons and contrasts between the three men often recognized as the Marines with the highest tally of aerial victories.

Gregory Boyington and Joseph Jacob Foss were both born in the West when it was barely out of its Wild West phase of development. Robert Murray Hanson was born in India, the son of missionaries. Each of the trio earned the Medal of Honor. Foss and Boyington became household names during the war and remained as such for years afterward. Hanson, who was killed in action in 1944, never had a postwar career that would help to define his legacy, and he is today largely forgotten.

I have always felt a certain attachment to Foss and Boyington, because of a family connection to the geography of their origins and mine. My mother was born in South Dakota a few years before Foss, and while he was growing up outside Sioux Falls, she was growing up a half day's drive away on a gravel road in Highmore. While Boyington was in his teens in St. Maries, Idaho, my father was working as a packer for the US Forest Service in the St. Joe National Forest. St. Maries was the hub of activity for the Forest Service in that part of Idaho. They may well have crossed paths.

In the pantheon of aces, no substantial gulf separates the top three from the next tier. Kenneth Ambrose Walsh, Donald Nathan

Aldrich, and John Lucian Smith had confirmed scores of 21, 20, and 19 respectively, and both Walsh and Smith earned the Medal of Honor.

Next, there were two aces tied at 18.5 (including shared victories). They were Wilbur Jackson "Jack" Thomas—better known as "Gus"—and Marion Eugene Carl, who was the first Marine Corps ace in 1942, and a legendary test pilot after the war.

Among the highest scoring within the succeeding tiers, there were fascinating stories. In researching the exploits of aces, one occasionally comes across "ace in a day" pilots who scored five victories in a single day. The Marines' Archie Donahue was almost an "ace in a day" twice. He got five on April 12, 1945, having scored four plus a probable on May 13, 1943.

In discussing the final scores, especially in the context of the razor-thin margins between them, it is important to remember that these numbers, now enshrined in the permanent record, were originally compiled in the immediate aftermath of battle. Most were observed by wingmen or other observers, but as aviation historian Barrett Tillman told this author, the Marine Corps had "no victory assessment board as with the Army Air Forces so claims and credits had to be on the honor system."

In discussions of warriors who died too young, talk often turns to conversations that include the phrase "what if." Take Medal of Honor recipient Harold William "Indian Joe" Bauer, who graduated from the US Naval Academy at Annapolis in 1930 when most of the other top aces were still in elementary or high school. He scored just 11 aerial victories, but he was killed in action in November 1942 before the combat careers of most of the other aces had really begun. The only Annapolis man among the double-digit Marine aces, Bauer is certainly an example of someone whose potential went unfulfilled.

By 1943, the Few gradually became no longer a few, but those among the Few who had become double-digit aces continued in action, so we will follow them through their careers, and in many cases through their intriguing later lives.

In telling these stories, I was both surprised and delighted by the depth of material in the various after-action reports that were maintained by the squadrons, and by the fact that this material still exists. Having been typed on fragile onion skin and preserved for over three quarters of a century, it still exists.

These after-action documents, including squadron war diaries and aircraft action reports, contain not just raw data, but the words of the Marine aviators themselves as they were debriefed, recorded and typed just hours after their aerial battles. With this, I am pleased to include herein these words, spoken as they sat beneath canvas tarps, with the smell of oil, cordite, and the sweat of battle still in their nostrils, and the images of those battles still fresh in their minds.

This is not an encyclopedic work, though statistical details are provided throughout. Nor is it about all Marine aces, and because it focuses on double-digit aces, we do not cover the majority of the 1944–1945 aces, who are a topic for another time.

This is not a story of grand strategy. These have been written, some of them magnificently. This is a story of individual battles, one-on-one battles, battles of the most personal kind. This is a story of individual lives, the individual lives of a unique group of men.

Double-Digit US Marine Corps Aces of World War II

Joseph Jacob Foss (26)
Robert Murray Hanson (25)
Gregory "Pappy" Boyington (22–28)*
Kenneth Ambrose Walsh (21)
Donald Nathan Aldrich (20)
John Lucian Smith (19)
Marion Eugene Carl (18.5)
Wilbur Jackson "Gus" Thomas (18.5)
James Elms Swett (15.5)
Harold Leman Spears (15)
Edward Oliver "Bud" Shaw (14.5)
Archie Glenn Donahue (14)
Robert Edward Galer (13)
William Pratt Marontate (13)
Kenneth DeForrest Frazier (12.5)
James Norman Cupp (12)
Loren Dale "Doc" Everton (12)
Harold Edward "Murderous Manny" Segal (12)
William Nugent Snider (11.5)
Phillip Cunliffe DeLong (11.16)†
Harold William "Coach" Bauer (11)
Jack Eugene Conger (10)
Herbert Harvey Long (10)
Donald Hooten Sapp (10)

---

*Boyington's exact total is complicated. On January 3, 1944, he "officially" brought his total from 25 to 26 just before being shot down himself. This total included his claim of six while flying with the American Volunteer Group in China. However, AVG records give him only two aerial victories, which if true would reduce the 26 to 22. After his release from a POW camp in 1945, he claimed two more for January 3, which were unverified. If all claims were verified his total would be 28. If all unverified claims are excluded, his total would be 22. Therefore, Boyington's actual score is somewhere between 22 and 28.

†DeLong scored two additional victories in the Korean War to bring his final tally to 13.16.

Squadron Names

In addition to their numerical Marine Fighting Squadron (VMF) designation, the squadrons had squadron names which were used day-to-day to varying degrees. For the sake of clarity and to avoid confusion in the narrative, we have decided to use only the numerical designations in telling the stories. An exception herein is the name "Black Sheep" as applied to VMF-214. From just a half-dozen in 1942, the number of overseas deployed fighting squadrons grew six-fold by the last months of the war. The names of the squadrons among these upon which we focus most of our narrative are as follows:

VMF-112 Wolfpack
VMF-113 Whistling Devils
VMF-114 Death Dealers
VMF-115 Joe's Jokers
VMF-121 (had no name during the war, but much later became the Green Knights)
VMF-122 Werewolves
VMF-124 Wild Aces (or Death's Head)
VMF-212 Hell Hounds
VMF-213 Hell Hawks
VMF-214 Black Sheep (previously Swashbucklers)
VMF-215 Fighting Corsairs
VMF-221 Fighting Falcons
VMF-222 Flying Deuces
VMF-223 Bulldogs
VMF-224 Fighting Wildcats
VMF-451 Blue Devils

PART I

Origins

I

Marine Corps Aviation from Flanders to Wake Island

The idea of marines as a naval infantry force dates back to before Roman times, though the Romans refined the doctrine of routinely using such forces to board and capture opposing naval vessels.

The British Royal Marines were formed in 1664, and the US Marine Corps dates its lineage to 1775 with the creation of the Continental Marines. Disbanded in 1783 at the end of the Revolutionary War, they were reconstituted as the Marine Corps in 1798. They distinguished themselves during the early nineteenth century in such battles as those commemorated by the first two lines of "The Marines' Hymn"—"The Halls of Montezuma" (Mexico City's Chapultepec Castle in 1847), and "The Shores of Tripoli" (at Derna, Libya against the Barbary Pirates in 1805).

Though they maintain a command structure separate from the US Navy, the Marines have been a component of, and administered by, the Navy Department since 1834.

Long proud of its mandate to operate on both land and sea, the US Marine Corps added "air" to the operational mix in 1912, only two years after US Navy Lieutenant Theodore Gordon "Spuds" Ellyson learned to fly from aviation pioneer Glenn Curtiss and became the US Navy's Naval Aviator No.1. Marine aviators did not see combat until World War I. Major Alfred Austell Cunningham

(Marine Aviator No. 5) reached France with the 1st Marine Aviation Force on July 30, 1918, and soon he and his aviators were in action.

On September 28, 1918, while flying a bombing mission with RAF No. 218 Squadron in a two-place DeHavilland DH-9, Marine Lieutenant Everett Brewer and Gunnery Sergeant Harry Wersheiner downed a German fighter over Belgium, scoring the Corps' first victory in aerial combat.

By October, the 1st Marine Aviation Force had four squadrons, 149 officers, and 842 enlisted men in France. On October 14, Captain Robert Lytle led the first operational Marine Corps mission utilizing Marine aircraft, dropping more than a ton of bombs on a German-held rail yard in Belgium. They were on their way home when they were jumped by a dozen German fighters. Two aircraft, including Lytle's, were damaged and forced down, with Lieutenant Ralph Talbot killed. For their heroism that day, Talbot and Corporal Robert Robinson were awarded the Medal of Honor.

In 1920 the Navy Department introduced a designation system for aircraft and aviation squadrons, a form of which is still in use today. Squadrons of heavier-than-air aircraft bore a core designator of "V," while those with lighter-than-air craft, such as dirigibles, were designated with "Z." For example, Navy fighting squadrons had a "VF" prefix followed by a numeral. Marine fighting squadrons were the same, but with an "M" tagged on at the end after a numeral. By World War II the prefix had been formalized as "VMF."

As World War I receded into history, the downsized Marine Corps saw more combat in the 1920s than any of the other scaled-back services. There was extensive unrest in the Caribbean and Central America, where central governments were weak and where regional warlords ran gangs that were essentially private armies. Bandit attacks on American civilians and property brought calls to "Send in the Marines!"

Indeed, beginning as early as 1912, the Marines were sent. Alfred Cunningham himself led the Marine aviation contingent into Santo Domingo in the Dominican Republic in 1920.

The major campaign for the Marine Corps in the region came in Nicaragua between 1927 and 1930 in an operation against the bandit leader Augusto Sandino, who became infamous for harassing civilians, for attempting to disrupt elections, and for his death's head battle flag. It was during these operations that Lieutenant Christian Schilt earned the third Medal of Honor awarded to a Marine aviator when he evacuated 18 wounded men under fire.

The role of the US Marine Corps as an amphibious landing force—for which they would become famous during World War II—was formalized as a doctrine in 1933 with the creation of the Fleet Marine Force. This supplanted the previous organization by merging the two Marine expeditionary forces that had existed on the east and west coast. An important landing operations manual published in 1935 laid the foundation for operations in the following decade. The role of Marine airpower was defined as supporting the surface actions during and after the landings. To paraphrase "The Marines' Hymn," it was "air in support of land and sea."

On December 7, 1941, World War II began inauspiciously for Marine aviation. All 48 of the aircraft at Marine Corps Air Station Ewa, five miles west of Pearl Harbor, were destroyed on the ground by Japanese attackers.

Three days earlier, and 2,300 miles farther west, the stage had been set for Marine aviators to be the first Marines to do battle with the enemy. As part of their overall strategy, the Japanese coordinated the Pearl Harbor strike with simultaneous attacks all across the Far East—from Malaya to Hong Kong to the Philippines—where it was across the International Date Line and therefore December 8. This operation also included an air strike on Wake Island by three dozen Imperial Japanese Navy Air Force (IJNAF) G3M bombers flying from Kwajalein.

Eight of the dozen Marine F4F Wildcats on Wake were destroyed on the ground, but the other four, then on patrol, survived and became part of a vigorous and heroic defense. On December 9, two F4Fs, piloted by Lieutenant David Kliewer and Sergeant William Hamilton, intercepted a second air strike and downed the first two

Japanese aircraft to be claimed by Marines. Captain Henry Elrod shot down two more the next day in a single-handed attack against a bomber formation.

The Marines ashore on Wake, under the command of Major James Devereux, successfully repulsed the first Japanese landing attempt on December 11, with their five-inch guns damaging several ships and sinking a destroyer. Five days later, the Marine Wildcats played the key role in sinking another Japanese destroyer, but one by one, the F4Fs were lost in action until there were none.

The Japanese finally launched a successful landing on December 23, and the battered American force surrendered after a bloody defense that lasted many hours. "Hammerin' Hank" Elrod was killed on December 23 while leading a ground defense action. This and his heroism in the air resulted in him being awarded a posthumous Medal of Honor. It was the first Medal of Honor action by a Marine aviator in World War II.

2

Who They Were

The leading Marine Corps aces of World War II all came of age during that first gilded epoch of American aviation that was capped by Charles Lindbergh's solo flight across the Atlantic in 1927. This feat, which electrified a nation, was especially energizing for a new generation thrilled by aviation and anxious to see the world from a cockpit.

The majority of these future aces were born after the birth of Marine aviation in 1912, most of them still toddlers or not yet born when Ralph Talbot and Robert Robinson became the first Marine aviators awarded the Medal of Honor. There was one notable exception. The oldest of the leading aces was Harold William Bauer. He was born, the middle of five siblings, on November 20, 1908 when Lindbergh was only six and none of the American military services had acquired their first airplane.

Both of his parents, John Thomas Bauer and Anna Martha Hoff, were ethnic Germans who had been born in Russia in the 1880s, and who were part of a diaspora of "Volga Germans," descendants of an eighteenth-century emigration from Germany to Russia at the invitation of German-born Russian Empress Catherine the Great.

When Harold was born, his father was a telegraph operator with the Chicago, Burlington & Quincy Railroad at Woodruff, Kansas, near the Nebraska state line. Harold and his siblings grew up in an apartment above the station, and just a few steps from the tracks.

By the time that the older Bauer siblings were in high school, Thomas was a station manager in Alma, Nebraska. Harold played football and helped lead the basketball team to the state finals three years running. According to Kent Brown, Coach Bill Bogel said that Harold was "probably the best natural athlete I ever saw."

Also a good student, Harold set his sights on a higher education. Given the family's financial situation, he set those sights on a service academy, where there would be no tuition costs. Having passed the entrance exam, he received an appointment to the US Naval Academy from Congressman Ashton Shallenberger in 1926. The family had moved again, and he is noted in the Annapolis yearbook as having entered the school from Holdrege, Nebraska, 25 miles north of Alma.

While Harold Bauer was heading for Annapolis in June of 1926, young Gregory (Greg) Hallenbeck was growing up in the Idaho panhandle not knowing who he really was. Greg was born on December 4, 1912, the only son of Grace Gregory Boyington and Charles Barker Boyington, in the town of Couer d'Alene, one of a series of Idaho lumber towns along the route of the Northern Pacific Railroad that snaked through the heavily wooded and treacherously steep mountains of the panhandle.

Charles Boyington was a rolling stone, not one to be tied down long. He bounced around the Midwest and West for a number of years before graduating from the Northwestern University Dental School in Evanston, Illinois. He landed in Couer d'Alene, where he married his second wife, Grace Barnhardt Gregory, on New Year's Day in 1912. Charles Boyington soon demonstrated himself to be an abusive husband, lashing out at Grace with both tongue and fists. This only got worse after Greg was born.

Ellsworth Hallenbeck, a married man from Spokane, Washington, entered the picture in 1914 as a paramour of Grace Boyington. A ne'er-do-well in his own right, Hallenbeck drifted from job to job and had connections to criminal gangs. Charles was furious and sued for divorce. Well before this was finalized in 1915, Charles had gone and Grace and little Greg were living with Hallenbeck.

In early 1917, they moved to remote St. Maries, Idaho about 60 twisting, hairpin-turning road miles south of Couer d'Alene. Here, young Greg, just turned four, would grow up in the wooded hillsides on the banks of the St. Joe River firmly under the illusion that Ellsworth and Grace Barnhardt Hallenbeck were legally married to one another, that his younger brother Bill was not merely a half brother, and that his own name was really Gregory Hallenbeck.

Greg's introduction to aviation came when he was only six. Clyde Pangborn, a fellow Idahoan and a former US Army flyer turned barnstormer, passed through in his Curtiss JN-4 Jenny offering airplane rides. Greg talked Ellsworth Hallenbeck out of five dollars and his mother into letting him do what would today be unthinkable for a first-grader. He paid the famous aviator and took the ride that changed his life. Over the next few years, he attended as many air shows as he could. "I had always loved the idea of flying," he later told Colin Heaton of *Aviation History* magazine. "I used to read all of the books about the World War I fighter aces, and I built model planes, gliders and things."

By 1926, when Greg was in his early teens, Ellsworth Hallenbeck, his life tortured by alcohol, had been fired by nearly all the potential employers in St. Maries. He moved the family west to Puget Sound, where they settled in Tacoma. It was then a dirty smelter and mill town where opportunities for gainful employment were abundant, but so was the availability of vice, and both Ellsworth and Grace were abusing alcohol. By the time that Greg was passing through his years at Lincoln High in Tacoma, Ellsworth had become a bitter and abusive man, but unlike Charles Boyington, he did not run off—at least not yet.

In high school, Gregory Hallenbeck was an average student, and as an athlete, he gravitated toward individual sports such as wrestling and swimming, in which he did reasonably well. The Depression struck the nation when Greg was a senior, and in 1930, after he graduated, the family moved north to Seattle, where he enrolled at the University of Washington.

Greg worked part time parking cars in downtown Seattle and spent his college summers back in Idaho, working in the mines and forests in a world familiar from his youth. At the university, he narrowed his interest in engineering to aeronautics.

Another student in the engineering program, a year behind Greg and less than a year younger, was Robert Edward Galer, who had been born in Seattle on October 13, 1913. He would also go on to become a Marine Corps ace, and would command VMF-224 on Guadalcanal in 1942.

Greg Hallenbeck continued wrestling at university level and earned the Pacific Northwest Intercollegiate middleweight title. He also joined the Reserve Officer Training Corps (ROTC) program on campus. A future job as an army officer—even a reserve officer— was better than the uncertainty that faced most college graduates during the depths of the Great Depression.

Though he would not receive his engineering degree from the University of Washington until December 1934, he completed his ROTC course and was commissioned as a second lieutenant in June. Assigned to the US Army's Coast Artillery Reserve, he was sent for a short active duty tour to Fort Worden at the mouth of Puget Sound.

———

Joseph Jacob Foss was born on April 17, 1915 in Sioux Falls, South Dakota and, like Greg Hallenbeck, he grew up in the rural, gravel road environment of a West that had still not fully shaken off the cloak of its Wild West identity. Both of Joe's parents were born in Minnesota. On his father's side, the family were recent Norwegian Lutheran immigrants, while his mother's family were Catholics who had migrated from Scotland and Ireland.

Joe's father, Olouse "Ole" Foss, went by the name Frank, though many people called him "Foxy" because he was a snappy dresser. He had worked a variety of jobs before he settled down and married Mary Esther Lacy in 1914. He had been an engineer with the Great Northern Railway, an automobile dealer, and he had toured with the Ringling Brothers Circus. He even had his own traveling show for a while. Mary, who had inherited 160 acres four miles east of Sioux Falls from her family, convinced Foxy to set aside his wanderlust and become a farmer. In fact, Mary did at least as much of the farm work as her husband. "Pop was gregarious and loved an audience," Joe remembered. "My mother was dead serious. She had absolutely no sense of humor."

"My father could do anything," Joe recalled in his memoirs. "I still regard him as the most fascinating person I've ever known and the greatest influence in my life."

Joe was the first-born, with Clifford and Mary Flora coming later. While Cliff took to farming naturally, Joe's head was elsewhere: exploring, fishing, trapping gophers for a nickel bounty, or hunting. When he was seven, his father gave him a .22 rifle and he soon discovered that he had extraordinary vision and was an amazingly good shot. At fourteen, Joe had a .410 shotgun and always got his limit during bird season.

Often, Joe's head was in the clouds, especially as the mailplanes routinely droned over the farm. In 1931, four years after the papers were first filled to the brim with the daring feats of Charles Lindbergh, Joe and his father each paid a dollar and a half to board a Ford Trimotor for their first airplane ride. From that date, Joe knew what he wanted to do in his life.

Frank's own days were numbered; in the midst of a driving rainstorm one night in March 1933, the wind brought down a billboard, which brought down a power line. As Frank Foss drove past, he hit the power line, which shorted out his ignition and stopped his car. As he stepped out to investigate, he was fatally electrocuted. Joe arrived in another car shortly thereafter and saw his father's body. As he wrote in his memoirs, he had lost "the one person who was always there when I needed him. I had lost my best friend."

Joe's carefree days were over. It was the depths of the Depression and the threshold of the Dust Bowl years when he shouldered a bigger part of caring for the farm. In the fall of 1934, though, his mother insisted that he attend college, so he enrolled at Augustana in Sioux Falls, financing his tuition with a job at the Morrell packing plant. Things did not work out. By 1937, he had to drop out of Augustana because of poor grades.

Undaunted, he enrolled at the less challenging Sioux Falls College. He not only turned his abysmal grade point average around, but he was able to finish his college career with a year at the University of South Dakota.

In the meantime, another outlandish scheme entered his head and he spent a month's wages from his gas station job to learn to fly at the Sioux Skyways flight school. When Joe told his mother that he was thinking about joining the Army Air Corps, she was furious that he would leave college and "goof it up to run off and fly airplanes."

The third member of the trio at the top of the statistical pantheon of Marine aces, Robert Murray Hanson, did not share the experience of the texture of life in early twentieth century America with Foss, Boyington, or Bauer. He was born in Lucknow, India and spent his early years nearly 8,000 miles due east of the contiguous forty-eight states.

Bob's parents, Harry Albert Hanson and Alice Jean Dorchester Hanson, were married in Southborough, Massachusetts in 1916 and became part of the Methodist mission to India. The Methodists had first come to India in 1856, and had established a substantial presence there that included colleges and medical schools.

Bob Hanson was born on February 4, 1920, one of four Hanson sons born in India between 1916 and 1927. Their sister was born in 1939 when their father was 50 and Bob was almost 20. The boys attended the American-operated Woodstock School in Landour, near Mussoorie, a hill station about 400 miles north of Lucknow in the Himalaya foothills. Because average temperatures in India's major cities exceed 90 degrees Fahrenheit for much of the year, India's British ruling class, as well as the expat community, tended to spend as much time as possible in the cooler hill stations. The

Woodstock School still exists and is described on its own website as "Asia's oldest international boarding school."

Sent to the United States for junior high, Bob Hanson had a brief taste of the homeland of his parents in the early 1930s, but he returned to India for high school. Like Greg Boyington—then still Greg Hallenbeck—back in the States, Bob was a good athlete who gravitated toward wrestling. He is even recalled as having been the heavyweight champion, presumably among expat schools, in the United Provinces of Agra and Oudh.

His parents returned to the United States during World War II, so Hanson's home address would be listed in wartime dispatches as being at a modest two-story home on Brooks Avenue in Newtonville, Massachusetts.

Marion Eugene Carl was born on November 1, 1915 on a farm near Hubbard in Oregon's Willamette Valley farm country, about 20 miles north of the state capital at Salem. The fertile Willamette had been the end of the rainbow for immigrants on the 2,200-mile Oregon Trail since the 1830s, and thus it was for Herman Lee Carl who had made his way there from Poweshiek County, Iowa. He married Ellen Ellingston in 1902, and their son Leland, Marion's older brother, was born in 1907. Herman and Ellen were living in a tent cabin while building their farmhouse on the cold, wet November day when Marion arrived.

As they were both born in the same year, there were numerous similarities between the early lives of Joe Foss and Marion Carl. For both, farming was the all-consuming occupation. In the memoirs which he wrote with aviation author Barrett Tillman in the 1990s, Carl remembered that milking the cows was an all-day affair, and of course there was also the pitching of hay and corn fields to tend.

Both men developed an early interest in aviation, and grew up in a place where mailplanes were routinely visible in the skies above. Carl called his fascination with aircraft a "powerful attraction."

As was the case with Foss and most farm boys, then as now, Carl learned to use a .22 rifle and a shotgun during his preteen years and used these to hunt game birds and deal with predators. For Foss, Carl and many others—including top USAAF ace, Richard Ira Bong in Wisconsin—the rifles helped hone marksmanship skills that would come into play in the skies over the Pacific.

Like Foss, Carl idolized his father, noting that he was "recognized as the hardest-working Human in the area [who] probably never rose later than four o'clock in the morning." Both Foss and Carl would lose their fathers in 1933, the elder Foss to electrocution and Herman Carl in the aftermath of a double mastoid operation.

Despite the challenges of running a farm without a patriarch, the mothers of both boys insisted that their sons go on to college, and both did so in 1934—coincidentally the year that Greg Hallenbeck graduated from the University of Washington. Marion Carl enrolled in the engineering program at Oregon State in Corvallis, and like Hallenbeck, he also signed up for ROTC.

———

Another leading ace was John Lucian Smith, who commanded VMF-223 during the anxious moments of the bloody Guadalcanal campaign in the fall of 1942—and who was, at that time, *the* leading American ace of any of the services.

He was born on the day after Christmas in 1914 in Lexington, Oklahoma where his father, R.O. Smith, was a rural route mail carrier. Like Joe Foss and Marion Carl, Smith grew up as a hunter. The day that he was supposed to be graduating from high school, he was off hunting. He graduated from the University of Oklahoma in 1936 with a degree in accounting and an ROTC commission as a field artillery lieutenant, but he quit two months later to join the Marines and apply for flight training.

———

As was the case with these men, briefly sketched above, the majority of the double-digit Marine aces were from the West or the Great Plains states. Three were born in Seattle. In addition to Bob Galer, who attended the University of Washington with Greg Hallenbeck, there was William Pratt Marontate and James Elms Swett, born in December 1919 and June 1920, respectively—although Swett grew up in San Mateo, California.

Among the others from the West and Plains states was Edward Oliver "Bud" Shaw, who was born in January 1920 in Bloomer, Wisconsin, but he called Spokane, Washington home. Wilbur Jackson "Gus" Thomas was born in El Dorado, Kansas in October 1920; Archie Glenn Donahue in Casper, Wyoming in October 1917; and Loren Dale Everton in Crofton, Nebraska in July 1915.

Two were from Iowa—James Norman Cupp was born in Corning in March 1921, and Jack Eugene Conger in Orient, 20 miles to the northeast, in April 1921. Conger grew up in Sioux Falls, South Dakota, where he had a job as a movie theater usher during his high school years. It was in this role that he once had to kick Joe Foss and his cousin Jake out of the theater for sneaking in through the back door.

Four others were born in the upper Midwest. Donald Nathan Aldrich was born in Moline, Illinois in October 1917, but grew up in Chicago; Phillip Cunliffe DeLong was born in July 1919 in Jackson, Michigan; and Harold Edward Segal was born in Chicago in September 1920. William Nugent Snider, born in Cairo, Illinois, would consider Memphis, Tennessee, 160 miles downriver on the Mississippi, as his home.

There were four from East Coast states on the double-digit roster. Two were from New Jersey: Kenneth Ambrose Walsh, who grew up in Jersey City—though he was born in Brooklyn in November 1916—and Kenneth DeForrest Frazier, born in Florence, New Jersey in October 1919. Donald Hooten Sapp was born in December 1916 in rural Center Hill, Florida, west of Orlando, but grew up in Miami. Herbert Harvey Long was born in New York City in April 1919, but called Florida home.

One reason for the preponderance of country boys among the leading aces may have been their long and routine experience as hunters, especially of game birds. Joe Foss certainly believed so. In his memoirs, he theorized that "standard military target practice did not automatically produce expert sharpshooters, especially in crisis situations. Men who had had little or no experience with firearms found moving targets a frustrating challenge. They'd aim where the target was before it moved, whereas those of us who had done field shooting knew the importance of proper lead on a moving target. There were exceptions to the rule, of course—city boys who excelled in combat and farm kids who didn't."

Among those exceptions were the three urbanites from the West, Galer, Marontate and Swett from Seattle as well as the pair of Chicago boys, Aldrich and Segal. Ken Walsh was born in Brooklyn, and though he moved to Jersey City by the time he was in high school, he always considered Brooklyn his home.

3

Taking to the Air

When Harold William Bauer, the oldest of the future double-digit Marine aces, entered the US Naval Academy in 1926, only Greg Hallenbeck among the others had even graduated from high school.

In the 1930 edition of the *Lucky Bag*, the Annapolis annual, Bauer was cited for his "ever-present cheerfulness and overleaping enthusiasm." He excelled as an athlete. He boxed, played lacrosse, made the football team all four years, and captained the varsity basketball team for three. The yearbook recalled that "possessing grit, determination, and untiring energy, Joe has made good in three major sports and earned the coveted awards." In addition it said, "Nor have Academics, on the other hand, been an obstacle for him. He conquered them easily, and with much merit, by means of earnest, conscientious application."

Bauer's Annapolis nickname evolved gradually. The chaplain was known as "Holy Joe," and somehow, Bauer came to be called "another Holy Joe." This was shortened simply to "Joe," but later he picked up a prefix and became "Injun Joe," or "Indian Joe." In the *Lucky Bag*, it was said that the sobriquet was "in compliment to his war-whooping ability and his lean sinewy appearance." Indeed, his dark eyes and high cheekbones gave him an American Indian appearance, and he occasionally claimed such heritage with tongue firmly in cheek.

After graduating 135th out of a class of 405 in 1930, Bauer picked the Marines over the Navy, completed Student Basic School in Philadelphia and was assigned to the 6th Marine Regiment at Quantico, Virginia. Given his academy record, he spent much of the next few years coaching Marine Corps teams, and in 1932, he was recalled to Annapolis as lacrosse coach and assistant basketball coach. And here, Joe picked up yet another nickname that would still be with him in the South Pacific—"Coach."

In December 1932, the Coach took a wife, tying the knot with Harriette Hemman. By this time, he had decided that he wanted to become a Marine aviator, but it was not until December 1934, after he had completed his required sea duty aboard the USS *San Francisco* (CA-38), that he was able to report to flight school at NAS Pensacola. Coincidentally, the *San Francisco* was to be one of the ships most heavily involved in the sea Battle of Guadalcanal in 1942 while Bauer was distinguishing himself in the air battles high above.

Naval Air Station Pensacola, the center for naval flight training since it graduated its first aviators in 1914, had trained around a thousand during World War I, but in the postwar years, it averaged only about a hundred annually, which gave it a certain exclusivity. According to the Naval History and Heritage Command, it had come to be known as the "Annapolis of the Air," because the majority of its trainees were graduates of the Naval Academy.

While this was still true when Joe Bauer arrived at the end of 1934, things would change dramatically just a few months later when the Aviation Cadet Program brought in a flood of candidates from all quarters.

At Pensacola in the late 1930s, as the future aces of World War II passed through, training was conducted in a variety of aircraft, notably the ubiquitous Stearman Model 75 Kaydet biplane, of which more than 10,000 were built to serve the US Navy under the NS and N2S designations, and with the US Army Air Corps as the PT-17.

Prior to 1939, when World War II began in Europe, Marines at Pensacola each passed through five separate squadrons so as to learn the basics in a variety of aircraft from bombers to observation planes. Fighter training at Pensacola was conducted with the Boeing F4B, and Bauer logged time in this aircraft before he earned his wings and graduated to the Grumman F3F-2 biplane. It was the front-line Navy and Marine Corps fighter before being superseded by the monoplane fighters that would be in service as World War II began—the Brewster F2A Buffalo and Grumman's own F4F Wildcat.

In June 1940, after a tour as the flight officer in charge of operations with VMF-1 (formerly VF-9M) at MCAS Quantico, Joe Bauer went west. He and Harriette, with their three children, moved to San Diego, where he was assigned to NAS North Island at Coronado in San Diego Bay. Here, while flying Grumman F3F-2 fighters with VMF-2, Bauer crossed paths with future aces, such as Bob Galer and Dale Everton.

In July 1941, Bauer became operations officer for VMF-221. Formed at North Island, VMF-221 was part of a series of new "three-digit" squadrons that were being created in an expansion of Marine aviation. He would later command VMF-221 in battle.

Greg Hallenbeck was commissioned as a US Army second lieutenant in June 1934 after completing his ROTC course at the University of Washington. After a short reserve deployment with the US Army Coast Artillery Reserve, he was back in Seattle, and where he used his engineering degree to get a job as a draftsman with Seattle's own Boeing Aircraft Company. In the meantime, he had met and married Helene Clark, who used the surname of her married sister, Wickstrom, on the marriage license.

In April 1935, Hallenbeck took advantage of the newly enacted Aviation Cadet Act, in which the Navy and Marines sought to increase the number of reserve aviators within their ranks. They would pay new applicants to attend flight school with the possibility of a full-time job and a commission at the end of it. Having been taken with the sight of a Marine fighter aircraft that he'd seen a Boeing Field a few years earlier, Greg picked the Marines.

Just as the trajectory of his life might have been seen as moving in the right direction, things began to unravel. In the background, Ellsworth Hallenbeck had just left Greg's mother and had moved to Okanogan, halfway across the state. Grace was alone, and Helene was now pregnant. Having to worry financially about his wife, as well as his abandoned mother, meant a mounting financial strain for Greg. Then came worse news: married men were ineligible for the Aviation Cadet Program.

However, things were about to become even more complicated—and downright weird. As he had begun working with Boeing and applied for the Aviation Cadet Program, he had written to Idaho for his birth certificate. This seemed rather routine until he learned that there was no record of Gregory Hallenbeck having ever been born.

When he asked his mother about this, she tearfully admitted that he was really Gregory *Boyington*. He had no idea. He had graduated from the university, gotten married, been commissioned into the US Army, and had gone to work for Boeing under the wrong name.

There was, however, a silver lining. As far as the Aviation Cadet Program and the Marine Corps were concerned, Gregory *Boyington* was unmarried, and therefore eligible for the program. In June 1935, he was still at his Boeing drafting table when he was invited for "elimination" training at NAS Sand Point on Lake Washington in Seattle. The Navy had Elimination Air Bases, or "E-Bases," located at air stations and airports throughout the country to weed out applicants with no aptitude for flying—before they reached primary training facilities.

After several flights, Boyington passed on July 3 and was recommended for continued training. Because of the backlog now ensuing at Pensacola, and the shortage of spaces for Marines among the Navy pilots, Boyington was not officially appointed as an aviation cadet until February 1936. With him as he departed for Florida to join Class 88-C for flight training was his old University of Washington engineering classmate and future Marine ace, Bob Galer.

Boyington did more poorly than Galer in his training, though he was able to squeak by in the bottom tier of their class, finally earning his wings in March 1937. He was ordered to report to VMF-1 at MCAS Quantico, but in the meantime he was given 30 days' leave. He needed it.

When Boyington tried to conceal his marital status in order to stay in the cadet program, things could not have been worse. His mother, who had helped to look out for Helene and the baby, left for Okanogan to rejoin the abusive Ellsworth, and Helene moved in with another man. Nearly three thousand road miles away, Greg Boyington was powerless to intervene in any way until April 1937, when he was able to use his leave to retrieve his wife and son and move them across the country to Fredericksburg, 20 miles south of Quantico, where he would keep them out of sight and still using the Hallenbeck surname.

During the next two years while he was hiding his family, the rest of Boyington's life was a mixed bag. He had plenty of opportunity for flying in various aircraft types, and in May 1939, he graduated from Marine Corps Basic School in Philadelphia, albeit almost last in his class. As would be the case for the next quarter century, his time in the air was exciting and successful, while on the ground, it was dominated by drinking, brawling, and spending more money than he made.

Not known as a drinker before Pensacola, he had begun on the road to alcoholism that would complicate the rest of his life. While drinking and getting into fights was a common practice for the aviators at Pensacola and other training bases, it became the defining aspect of Boyington's lifestyle.

He did not bring his family out of the shadows until November 1939, half a year after he had been assigned to NAS North Island in California. By that time, there were two children and a third on the way, so he pretended that he had recently married a widow with children.

At North Island, many of the people he knew, including Bob Galer and Joe Bauer, were flying Grumman F3F-2 fighters with VMF-2, while Boyington was flying Curtiss SOC-3 Seagulls with scouting squadron VMS-2. He finally made the move to VMF-2 early in 1940 just before it went to sea. As the Navy wanted Marine Corps aviators to be carrier qualified, VMF-2 was sent on a two-month tour of duty aboard the USS *Yorktown* (CV-5).

It was during the aerial exercises and competitions of the summer of 1940 that the man whose best moments were always in the air proved himself. In mock combat scenarios, Greg Boyington emerged as an extraordinary pilot with an uncanny aptitude for dogfighting.

Early in 1941, Boyington and his family moved again, this time back to Pensacola, where Greg was assigned to become a flight instructor. As had become a pattern, his conduct in the air was laudable, but his escapades while off duty were ignoble at best. His debtors were starting to complain to the base commander about bills that were beyond past due, he was routinely seen in the company of women other than his wife, and finally, he slugged a senior naval officer in a barroom brawl.

Though he got off easy in the latter incident, Helene left him and went back to Seattle. By the early part of 1941, Boyington's life and career had not so much reached a crossroads as the edge of a precipice.

In the spring of 1940, as Greg Boyington was flying F3F-2s off the decks of the USS *Yorktown* in the Pacific, Joe Foss was in Vermillion, getting ready to graduate from the University of South Dakota—and itching to become a Marine aviator himself. He had decided on the Marines based on stories told by a former college roommate who became a Marine pilot.

In June 1940, he reported to the E-Base at Wold-Chamberlain Field in Minneapolis. Though his flight training was not without mishap, Foss showed great skill as a pilot, thanks to his having first learned to fly on his own dime back in 1936. In the meantime, he quickly demonstrated his uncanny marksmanship, honed by years of putting grouse and pheasant on the dinner table.

Six weeks later, Foss was among nine of twelve in his class who passed and he set out for Pensacola, hitchhiking 1,200 miles.

———

Like Joe Foss, Loren Dale "Doc" Everton was one of those kids who was enamored with flight during the Lindbergh years, and he was a trained pilot before he ever climbed into a military aircraft. In a 1966 conversation with Eugene Valencia, a World War II double-digit US Navy ace, he related the story. "Back in the real barnstorming days, a pilot came in and landed in an old clover patch outside of town, so I put my old legs to work and I ran all the way out there. A businessman in town was looking the thing over … he knew me well … and he asked if I wanted to go for a ride. I said, 'Sure.' So we climbed in and away we went. And from there on, I was sold. I have never gotten this out of my system."

In 1931, when Everton was a 16-year-old kid, he had a job at an airport about 30 miles from his home in Crofton, Nebraska. He explained that "I'd get up before dawn and hitchhike over to work around the hangar, push airplanes, clean hangars, clean engines … and with an allowance I got from my parents, I managed to buy some flight time. Not very much, but I soloed in five hours … Aviation had really been in my blood."

He went on to say that his parents did not know that he was doing this, but that his mother had her suspicions. When she finally confronted him and wanted to know what he was doing, he told her. She asked how he was getting along, and about the dangers; he "assured her there wasn't any danger."

Everton had wanted to take a commercial aviation course when he got out of high school, but his father, like a lot of businessmen, was hard hit by the Depression and had lost money in the banks. Walter Allen Everton was a druggist who wanted his son to go into the family business, so Dale, as he was known, went off to the University of Nebraska, then graduated from the School of Pharmacy and became a registered pharmacist, hence his nickname, "Doc."

Everton continued to fly all through his college years, and even after he began working as a druggist in Wayne, Nebraska. In 1939, he decided that he was "going to get rid of this bug one way or the other, once and for all, so [he] just asked for time off and went down to Kansas City and took a flight physical and that was it."

Having passed the physical, he reported to the Kansas City E-Base, having decided to keep quiet about his previous flight experience.

I wasn't going to dangle it out in front of the instructor and say, "Well, I already know how to fly and I've been flying here for eight years." I know that people take a dim view because you pick up bad habits. I just went in with a completely open mind and if they wanted to tell me I didn't know how to fly, I didn't know how to fly ... the instructor, who was a Marine Reservist on active duty, said after about an hour in the air, "You catch on awfully quickly."

The instructor down at Pensacola made the same remark.

In 1940, Everton was assigned to NAS North Island to fly SBD Dauntless scout bombers. He was there around the same time as Bob Galer and Greg Boyington, but ahead of Joe Foss and Marion Carl. Everton departed for Pearl Harbor on January 3, 1941. He would remember the date because that was the year that the Cornhuskers of his alma mater were in the Rose Bowl. Everton had tickets to the game, but could not go because he was busy getting ready to ship out. Nebraska lost to Stanford 13–21.

In Hawaii, he was based first at Ford Island and then at nearby MCAS Ewa. Over the coming months, he was involved in a great deal of training, almost half of it at night. One of many training missions he flew involved staging out of Maui and making simulated bombing attacks on Pearl Harbor.

Not all the Marine aviators who graduated from flight training at Pensacola in the late 1930s were officers, nor were they college graduates. There were a few "flying sergeants" in the Corps during World War II, but in April 1937, Kenneth Ambrose Walsh earned his wings at Pensacola as a private.

Destined to be the fourth highest-scoring Marine Corps ace ever, he joined the Marines when he graduated from Dickenson High School in Jersey City, New Jersey in 1933. After two years as an aviation mechanic at Quantico, Walsh was selected for flight training in March 1936. He served as a pilot aboard three separate aircraft carriers before Pearl Harbor, and would not earn his second lieutenant's commission until October 1942.

Marion Carl had graduated from the University of Oregon in 1938, four years after Boyington at the University of Washington and two years ahead of Foss at South Dakota. Having been enrolled in ROTC, Carl, like Boyington, was commissioned as a second lieutenant in the US Army Reserve.

He was assigned to the Corps of Engineers because of his engineering major, but he really wanted to go to flight school, so he applied for the Army Air Corps training program at Fort Lewis, Washington. When he was told that their quota was full, Carl used a little-known loophole that allowed 10 percent of Army ROTC graduates to transfer to the Marines. In August 1938, now a Marine private first class, he reported to the E-Base at NAS Sand Point in Seattle, where Boyington and Bob Galer had been three years earlier. Given his flying experience, he was the first of his class to solo.

On January 5, 1939, Carl was again first in his class at Pensacola to solo. In his memoirs, he bragged that he "had been overqualified the day [he] drove through the main gate."

Not immune to the Pensacola high jinks that accompanied the careers of the Marine aviators-to-be, Carl participated in some unauthorized simulated dogfights that earned him a reprimand,

and a reputation as someone with an aptitude for combat. As a result, immediately upon his earning his wings in December 1939, Lieutenant Marion Carl was invited to join VMF-1 at Quantico.

January 1940 found him flying F3F-2 fighters over the Caribbean during the annual winter gunnery exercises, but in May 1940, he was reassigned to Pensacola as an instructor. It was here that he first crossed paths with Joe Foss, then a student pilot. Usually, being taken out of an operational squadron for a training job is considered undesirable, but Carl took it in his stride. He noted in his memoirs that he found truth in the axiom that "the best way to truly learn a subject is to teach it."

Nevertheless, he lobbied long and hard to be reassigned back to fighters. In August 1941, Carl's long exile in Pensacola finally ended and he was assigned to fly Brewster F2A Buffalo monoplane fighters with the newly formed VMF-221 at NAS North Island in San Diego Bay.

At North Island, Carl learned that the squadron operations officer was a man considered to be what would later be referred to in naval parlance as the "top gun." The man was Joe Bauer, now a venerable 33 years of age, seven years older than Carl. In his memoirs Carl described a dogfight duel with Bauer over the desert east of San Diego. Carl did not name a winner, but said that "from then on, we regarded one another with mutual respect." He also added that Bauer was "perhaps the finest pilot and officer I ever knew."

John L. Smith earned his wings at Pensacola in the summer of 1939 and was assigned to MCAS Quantico. While many men went by nicknames, it is generally noted that one of Smith's idiosyncrasies was that he did not. As recalled by Marion Carl, who served under him with VMF-223 on Guadalcanal, "it was peculiar how he was usually called by his full name, like J. Edgar Hoover." Some people, including Carl, called him "Smitty," but to most, he was always John L. Smith.

It was while he was in Virginia that Smith, now 27, met and married Louise Maddox Outland of Norfolk, a 1937 graduate of the College of William and Mary, who was on the threshold of a lengthy career as a school teacher. In marrying into the family, Smith was in blue-blooded company. Louise's younger sister, Jean, would later be the second wife of Walter Percy Chrysler, Jr., the son of the founder of the Chrysler Corporation.

By December 1941, Bauer, Carl, and Smith, now all assigned to VMF-221 in San Diego, were ready to embark on their routine carrier trial, and their aircraft were loaded onto the USS *Saratoga* (CV-3). They were scheduled to depart San Diego for Pearl Harbor on the Monday morning, December 8, 1941.

4

First Combat

Gregory Boyington was the first of the future double-digit Marine Corps aces to see combat in World War II—but *not* as a Marine. In his baptism of fire against the Japanese in the Far East in 1941, Boyington flew as a bounty hunter.

When 1941 began, Boyington's life was—as so often it would be over the next four decades—teetering on the edge. His professional and financial circumstances were a hair's breadth away from disaster when he sat down with a man named Richard Aldworth in a suite in Pensacola's San Carlos Hotel. Aldworth worked for the Central Aircraft Manufacturing Company (CAMCO), then being used as a front for an elaborate scheme to help China in its war with Japan.

At the time, China was also on the edge. Imperial Japan had invaded and occupied Manchuria in 1931, and had invaded most of China's populated coastline in 1937. The Japanese captured Shanghai, Peking (now called Beijing), and the Chinese capital at Nanking (now Nanjing), precipitating the infamous Nanking Massacre. Though much of China was ruled by a myriad of competing regional warlords (including the Communists), it had an internationally recognized central government under Generalissimo Chiang Kai-shek of the nationalist Kuomintang Party.

The brains behind Chiang's rule was his wife, the brilliant, American-educated Soong May-ling, best known at the time as

"Madame Chiang." Being aware of the importance of airpower to modern warfare, she and her financier brother, T.V. Soong, became active in soliciting American investment in Chinese aviation. CAMCO was one of many examples used to funnel American aviation expertise into China. It had been set up in 1933 by American entrepreneur William Douglas Pawley as a joint venture between Chinese interests and the Curtiss-Wright Corporation of Buffalo, New York, a leading manufacturer of combat aircraft. The idea was to assemble Curtiss warplanes inside China.

Meanwhile, Madame Chiang recognized that the Chinese air force was no match for the Japanese, so she recruited an American advisor, Captain Claire Lee Chennault. He was a US Army Air Corps fighter pilot and a leading air combat tactician. When he left the service in 1937, he went to China to help overhaul China's air force. Chennault made several trips back to the States to solicit American aid for China's air force, long imagining a "foreign legion" of well-trained American pilots in China to fly missions against the Japanese. Whenever he mentioned this to military leaders in the United States during his visits, the reaction was uniformly and emphatically negative.

Early in 1941, after the passage of the Lend–Lease Act, Chennault took it up a notch and broached the subject to the commander-in-chief himself. President Franklin D. Roosevelt, who was very outspoken in his support of China, liked Chennault's idea. With his backing, Chennault was able to create the American Volunteer Group (AVG), staff it with 100 American aviators, and acquire 100 Curtiss-Wright Tomahawk fighter aircraft—the export variant of the US Army's P-40B—for them to fly.

"It took direct personal intervention from President Roosevelt to pry the pilots and ground crews from the Army and Navy," Chennault wrote in his memoirs. "On April 15, 1941, an unpublicized executive order went out under his signature, authorizing reserve officers and enlisted men to resign from the Army Air Corps, Naval and Marine Air Services for the purpose of joining the American Volunteer Group in China."

It was not so much an "unpublicized" executive order; it was just "unpublished." It never appeared in the Federal Register. Pilots would be hired as CAMCO "employees," with each man resigning from the service and signing a one-year contract effective July 4, 1941. The contract called for the men to receive monthly salaries—ranging from $250 for ground crewmen to $750 for flight leaders—plus expenses routed though a Chinese bank account. The latter sum, for pilots hired as flight leaders, is worth around $12,500 in current dollars, and exceeded the price of a new car.

Chennault explained that "there was no mention in the contract of a $500 'bonus' for every Japanese plane destroyed. Volunteers were told simply that there was a rumor that the Chinese government would pay $500 for each confirmed Jap plane. They could take the rumor for what it was worth. It turned out to be worth exactly $500 per plane." This, in effect, turned the former military officers into a cadre of bounty hunters. In addition to aircraft destroyed in air-to-air combat, the AVG bonuses were paid for aircraft destroyed on the ground.

It was widely believed, and mentioned by Greg Boyington in his memoirs, that the resignations of those who had resigned from regular—as opposed to reserve—commissions were under lock and key and would simply be torn up when the man returned to seamlessly rejoin his branch of the service. It proved not to be so simple.

Boyington tendered his resignation from the Marine Corps on August 8, 1941 and shipped out for Rangoon, Burma from San Francisco on September 24 among the last two dozen AVG "volunteer" pilots.

In addition to Boyington, among the Marines joining the AVG were Edmund Fryer "Ed" Overend and John Richard "Dick" Rossi, who had once been a roommate of Joe Foss at an off-base boarding house in Pensacola.

Operationally, the AVG was to be based at Kunming in China, with staging bases in Burma, and a supply line that ran from Burma's port of Rangoon across the mountains into China on the Burma Road, China's own lifeline. In December 1941, when Japan began its Southeast Asia offensive into Malaya and Burma, the air defense of Rangoon took on an importance for the AVG that was equal to its intended mission defending China.

The AVG has long been best remembered as the "Flying Tigers," a term that the pilots did not coin themselves and which is of unknown origin. In November 1941, they started painting shark's teeth on their engine cowlings—an idea borrowed from the RAF in North Africa—and the phrase "Flying Tigers" began appearing in published reports a month later.

The Flying Tigers proved extremely effective in their role in the air defense of Rangoon during early 1942. On February 6, Air Vice Marshal D.F. Stevenson, the RAF commander in Burma, had sent a congratulatory telegram to Chennault, noting that the AVG had now destroyed 100 enemy aircraft in the defense of Rangoon. Including those downed in actions over China, the AVG could now claim around 120 total aerial victories.

Compared to what the pilots had experienced in the American services, discipline at the AVG bases was lax, though Chennault demanded the opposite in the air. The men played hard, drank hard and were not strangers at Rangoon's bars and night clubs. Few men played or drank harder than Boyington, but he seemed to have managed to maintain a high level of discipline while in the cockpit, at least in the early months of 1942.

On February 6, the same day that Stevenson congratulated Chennault, success finally visited Greg Boyington. He was one of seven Allied pilots who intercepted a strafing attack by a gaggle of Nakajima Ki-27 fighters that outnumbered them five to one. Boyington did everything right. Instead of trying to outmaneuver the more nimble Japanese fighters, he used the Tomahawk's superior power to overtake the enemy aircraft, which were, as Boyington recalled in his memoirs, "not paying attention," and blasted two of them at close range. Two victories—and a thousand dollars in "bonus payments"—were his.

Boyington's next payments would come as a result of a daring and dramatic March 24 mission that was made by the AVG against the big Imperial Japanese Army Air Force (IJAAF) air base at Chiang

Mai (Chiengmai), which was so deep into northern Thailand that the Japanese were unlikely to expect an air strike.

In his memoirs, Boyington wrote that "the plan was to arrive over the Chiang Mai airstrip in the morning at the exact instant—and it lasts for only a minute or so—when one can see the ground from the air and they cannot see you." The plan succeeded.

The attackers claimed at least 25 Japanese aircraft destroyed, while the Stateside headlines reported as many as 40. Boyington claimed seven himself. However, after a detailed debrief, with duplications weeded out, the number for which bonus money would be paid was reduced to only 15, and a decision was made, possibly by Chennault himself, to divide the money equally. Boyington was furious that his claim of seven had withered to just one and a half.

This marked Boyington's second and final AVG payday. His final tally stood at three and a half, though he dug in his heels with a claim of six—which later came to be "officially" added to his Marine Corps total.

On March 31, when he cranked up his Tomahawk taking off on an alert mission, he blamed engine trouble, but there were rumors that he had been hungover or drunk. He never flew another operational AVG mission. On April 21, he resigned from the AVG after a week-long drinking jag and walked out with a briefcase full of money from his back pay and bonuses—most of it Chinese currency.

"I became so anxious to get out of Kunming, and all that it meant to me, that I damn nearly would have volunteered to walk back to the United States," he wrote in his memoirs. He caught a commercial flight to India and essentially hitchhiked from there. "The only reason I had hung around this long was that one of Chennault's stooges in my squadron claimed that some of our Rangoon combat reports had been lost, but they would straighten it out for pay purposes later [but] that never did fully happen."

One other former and future Marine aviator who was flying with the AVG was Edmund Overend. Having scored a confirmed

five victories, he remained with the Flying Tigers until they were
disbanded in July 1942 before returning Stateside.

During the early months that Greg Boyington was in combat
with the Flying Tigers in China, Doc Everton was on the island of
Midway. He did not know, of course, that in June 1942, Midway
would become a turning point in the war, but by that time, he
would be gone and heading for the South Pacific. What he did
know was that in December 1941 he had barely missed being
among the first Marine aviators in combat—at Wake Island.

On November 20, 1941, Everton was among the Marine
flight crews and ground personnel who boarded the USS *Wright*
(AV-1), a seaplane tender used for delivering Marine aircraft and
equipment. Some of the Marines would disembark at Wake, while
others would travel on to the ship's second stop at Midway. When
the *Wright* reached Wake on November 28 and dropped off its
cargo and Marines, Everton was among them.

He had already begun to help set up tents and to get ready when
word reached Wake Island that the Marine scout bombers had
been rerouted to Midway. The aircraft that were to arrive a few
days later aboard the USS *Enterprise* (CV-6) included only fighters.
This meant that all of the supplies and personnel for the bombers
had to be reloaded aboard the ship.

"We worked all night under lights and separated all the fighter
gear that we had ashore," he later recalled. "We got loaded onboard,
shoved off and headed for Midway. We got there [on December
4] just before this thing cranked off, this war. There were a few
Marines [at Midway], a few defense workers, and thousands and
thousands of gooney birds [albatrosses]. And that was it."

The Marine aircraft would not arrive on Midway until after Pearl
Harbor was attacked.

"On the morning of December 7, I had finished breakfast when
an Army warrant officer came in to the mess hall with a paper in his
hands looking for the Marine Major that headed up the defense for

[Eastern Island, one of the two major islands comprising Midway Atoll]." Everton recalled. He got a look at the paper and knew immediately what had happened at Pearl Harbor.

"I got all my Air Marines together and told them to break out the tin hats, break out the weapons, dig some holes and get ready," he recalled. His senior ordnance man arrived with a big ring of keys and explained that they did not work on the machine gun chests. After he told the man to break the locks, the man replied, saying "I think they're having the same trouble down at Wake Island because these are all the keys for the Wake Island chests."

———————

Joe Bauer, Marion Carl and John L. Smith departed San Diego with VMF-221 aboard the USS *Saratoga* on the morning after the Pearl Harbor attack, and arrived on December 15 as the damage was still smoldering. Their mission as briefed was to continue westward as part of Task Force 14, commanded by Rear Admiral Frank Jack Fletcher, and aid in the defense of Wake Island. Progress was slow because of the need to zig-zag to avoid Japanese submarines, and the task force was recalled on December 23, the day that Wake fell to the enemy.

"The only place left for VMF-221 was Midway," Carl wrote in his memoirs. They flew ashore on Christmas Day and the *Saratoga* returned to Pearl Harbor. Doc Everton recalled their arrival as "a pretty good Christmas present."

Nevertheless, circumstances on the atoll were hardly something to put anyone in the holiday spirit. "So began the drab, monotonous existence that we would endure for the next six months. Living conditions were dank and unpleasant, consisting of dugouts whose floors were barely above the water table."

Watching the gooney birds was a source of amusement, and the boredom was broken by plenty of flying time in their Brewster Buffalos, patrolling a mostly empty ocean. The Japanese occasionally sent a long-range flying boat to snoop. The Marines damaged a

Kawanishi H6K with ground fire on March 10, but it disappeared into a cloud and its destruction was not confirmed.

Over time, many of VMF-221's aviators were pulled back to MCAS Ewa near Pearl Harbor to become part of newer squadrons now being formed. Joe Bauer left Midway in March to take command of newly formed VMF-212, and Doc Everton left to join this squadron as well.

John L. Smith departed Midway in late April to lead VMF-223. Bob Galer, who had been with VMF-211 at Ewa when the Japanese had attacked, was now given command of VMF-224.

Marion Carl stayed behind, wrapped in the boredom of life on desolate Midway, but in late May things grew more ominous when reports of an impending Japanese attack began to circulate.

When the sun came up on June 4, 1942, VMF-221 had 28 aircraft on the roster, including seven recently arrived F4F-3 Wildcats, but only 25 were flight ready. News that more than 100 Japanese aircraft were inbound from carriers about 150 miles offshore came at 0545hrs. VMF-221 had 25 planes in the air 15 minutes later. Marion Carl was in the seat of one of the Wildcats.

With a 2,000-foot altitude advantage, the Marines dived on the Japanese bombers only to be set upon by escorting Japanese Mitsubishi A6M Zero fighters. Marion Carl lined up one of the bombers, pressed the trigger and sliced through the bomber formation with a Zero on his tail. When he rolled out of his dive, the A6M had moved away to stay with the bombers.

When Carl leapt back into the fray, the bomber formation was widely separated. As he looked for a straggler to attack, he heard the sound of bullets striking his F4F-3. Taking evasive action, he managed to elude the Zero, which dived past and chased after someone else.

By this time, the Japanese bombers had departed Midway, leaving huge columns of black smoke. A few Zeros remained in the area and Carl dived on one of them. As he wrote succinctly in his 1994 memoirs, co-authored with historian Barrett Tillman, "the first man I ever killed never knew I was there."

Unseen by his target, Carl closed in tight and cut loose a stream of .50-caliber fire. The Zero went into an uncontrolled spin and spiraled into the Pacific.

Returning to Midway to refuel, Carl found himself one of only ten pilots to come back. An hour later, he was one of only two to answer the call when the air raid siren announced an impending second attack—which turned out to be a false alarm.

Though inflated numbers circulated on both sides—the Japanese claimed 40 and the Americans 11—VMF-221 had lost ten and shot down seven Japanese aircraft. VMSB-241, the Marine scout bomber squadron on Midway, had lost a dozen of its 27 aircraft.

As we know from the hindsight of history, Midway was a fantastic American victory, the tipping point of the Pacific War, but this was not apparent to the Marine aviators that night. Marion Carl called it a "calamity," and from the perspective of VMF-221, he was right.

PART II
The Few

5

That Place Called Guadalcanal

Had any of the Marine aviators introduced thus far in this book—
or anyone, anywhere in the United States for that matter—been
asked in 1941 to pick it out on a map, or even recognize the strange
word as a place name, no more than one person in a thousand
would have reacted with more than a blank stare.

Guadalcanal is a 2,047-square-mile island named in 1568 after a
town in Andalusia by passing Spaniards who came, looked over the
thousand-island archipelago they called the Solomons, and kept
passing by. In the late-nineteenth century, it was claimed, albeit
unenthusiastically, first by Germans and later by Englishmen,
almost all of whom had seen it only as a speck on a map.

A strange story from 1892 relates the island to the minutiae of
World War II. In that year, the three-masted Austro-Hungarian
corvette SMS *Saida* was on an extended show-the-flag cruise to
the South Pacific. In Sydney, Australia they picked up the Austrian
geologist Baron von Foullon-Norbeck, who was surveying various
south sea islands, looking for minerals. On this trip he went ashore
on around 30 of the Solomons. Escorting him on these excursions
was a young naval officer named Miklós Horthy. On Guadalcanal,
they found traces of both gold and nickel.

This man, whose career began with him literally *prospecting for
gold on Guadalcanal*, had then gone on to serve as the last admiral
to command the Austro-Hungarian Navy, and was later named

as Hungary's regent—the ruler in lieu of the banished Hapsburg monarchy—of the Kingdom of Hungary. In 1940, Horthy had accepted an invitation from Joachim von Ribbentrop, Hitler's foreign minister, to have Hungary anointed as the *fourth* Axis power.

It was in 1942 that Guadalcanal abruptly leapt from obscurity— thanks to the ambitions of the *third* Axis power—Japan. Like Gettysburg, it became a one-word phrase for a desperate turning point in American history, a once-obscure point that would later be seen as the high-water mark of ambition. As Gettysburg was for the Confederacy, Guadalcanal was for the Japanese Empire.

In 1942, Guadalcanal was a space on the vast chessboard of the Western Pacific, on which a one-sided game had been going on since December 1941. The armies of Imperial Japan had moved quickly, gobbling up more territory in less time than Hitler's legions had in Europe.

In five months, the Imperial 14th Army had conquered all the Philippines (except teetering Corregidor); the 15th Army had defeated Thailand overnight and occupied most of Burma; while the 16th Army had added the oil-rich Dutch East Indies to Japan's Empire. The 25th Army, meanwhile, captured all of Malaya in less than two months, and had subdued Britain's crown jewel of the Far East, the impregnable fortress of Singapore, in a week.

The Imperial Japanese Army—supported admirably by their rival service, the Imperial Japanese Navy—was, in the vernacular of a later time, on a roll.

Next, the Imperial 17th Army would tighten the noose around Australia. The farthest reach for this move on the chessboard was south into the Solomon Islands. Guadalcanal was to have been merely one of many Solomons stepping stones in this gambit—but it just happened to be the place where the heretofore invincible Imperial Japanese Army ran into the US Marines.

Located east of New Guinea, the archipelago of the Solomons consists roughly of two parallel lines of islands positioned at a 45-degree, northwest-to-southeast, angle. Bougainville island is at the top, and Guadalcanal at the bottom. The space between the lines was nicknamed "the Slot" by the Allied troops. The Japanese ocean supply lines ran through the Slot, and most of the naval battles of the Guadalcanal campaign took place there, especially at the southeast end. Several small island clusters, including the Florida Islands, the Russell Islands, and the Treasury Islands, are part of the Solomons.

Before 1942 was over, some of the fiercest naval battles of World War II would take place at the base of the Slot in the waters around Tulagi and between the Florida Islands and Guadalcanal. As a consequence, this area formerly known as Savo Sound would come to be known as "Ironbottom Sound" because of the dozens of ships and aircraft, including ten cruisers and more than 30 destroyers, that were sunk in battle here.

Strategically, the Japanese saw the islands of the Solomons, especially Tulagi, Florida, and Guadalcanal at the southeast end of the Slot, as ideal locations for air and naval bases from which to interrupt shipping between the United States and Australia.

They established a base on Tulagi in May 1942, and began building an airfield at Lunga Point on the northwest tip of Guadalcanal in July. They had been establishing bases and airfields all across the Western Pacific with impunity for half a year, so this was reasonably routine.

However, the Americans were now ready to draw a line in the sand, or in this case red dirt, on both Guadalcanal and on the eastern tip of New Guinea, 900 miles due west. On New Guinea, the confident Japanese 17th Army would face the Australian Army and the US Army. On Guadalcanal, the 17th Army would be challenged on the ground by the US Marines, thanks to the delineation of theater commands that originated in Washington, DC.

This delineation dated to March 1942, as the Americans reoriented their strategic thinking from desperate, isolated defensive actions to a comprehensive offensive plan. The vast Pacific Theater was officially subdivided into operational "Areas."

A South West Pacific Area (SWPA) was created. Here, all Allied forces were under US Army command, specifically that of General Douglas MacArthur, with Australian Major General George Brett as his deputy. Geographically the SWPA included Australia, the

Philippines, New Guinea, and the Dutch East Indies (except Sumatra)—although the Philippines and the Indies were by then Japanese-controlled. Farther west, the South East Asia Command (SEAC), under Britain's General Percival Wavell, had jurisdiction over operations in Burma, India, and Sumatra—though by then the latter was Japanese-occupied.

The rest of the Pacific from the Solomons to San Francisco became the Pacific Ocean Areas (POA), with all American forces under US Navy command, specifically that of Admiral Chester Nimitz, Commander-in-Chief of the US Pacific Fleet (CINCPAC). The POA was further subdivided into the North Pacific Area (NORPAC), the South Pacific Area (SOPAC), and the Central Pacific Area (CENPAC), which included Hawaii. Nimitz kept CENPAC, his largest area, under his direct command. SOPAC, which included the Solomon Islands, was commanded by Vice Admiral Robert Ghormley through October 1942, and by Vice Admiral William "Bull" Halsey thereafter. Under Halsey, the Marines in SOPAC were commanded by Major General Alexander Archer Vandegrift, a three-decade veteran of Marine operations from Haiti to China.

Supported by US Navy gunnery—as well as the naval airpower of three aircraft carriers—Vandegrift's opening move involved simultaneous August 7 landings on Guadalcanal, Tulagi and two smaller islands. The 1st Marine Division secured Tulagi in two days and, having caught the Japanese by surprise, established an American beachhead on the much larger Guadalcanal.

They proceeded to capture the nearly completed Japanese airfield at Lunga Point, which was finished by US Navy Seabees and renamed after Major Lofton "Joe" Henderson, commander of VMSB-241, who was killed at Midway.

Henderson Field began operations on August 12, with the landing of a US Navy PBY Catalina (aka "Dumbo") patrol plane. Next, the most heroic chapter in the annals of Marine aviation began on August 20 with the arrival of the F4F Wildcats and SBD Dauntlesses of VMF-223 and VMSB-232, launched from the USS *Long Island* (CVE-1).

The Marine aviators, true to their expeditionary force mandate, were initially the largest element among the combat units at the Henderson Field complex, but there would also be US Navy and Royal New Zealand Air Force (RNZAF) contingents, as well as US Army Air Forces (USAAF) units. The first of the latter was the 67th Fighter Squadron, flying Bell P-400 Airacobras, the export variant of the Bell P-39, which were sometimes referred to derisively as "RAF rejects." These were later augmented by the similar (except for armament detail differences) P-39 Airacobras. In the fall of 1942, the 67th was used primarily for ground attack missions in support of troops on the ground, rather than for air intercept missions. The latter were flown by US Navy and Marine Corps Wildcats.

The Grumman Wildcat, while less maneuverable than the Japanese A6M Zero, was a powerful and reliable machine. Best of all perhaps, it would soon develop a reputation for durability that would earn its manufacturer the nickname "Grumman Iron Works."

Because the Allied codename for Guadalcanal was "Cactus," this Allied aviation hodgepodge at Henderson became known—and ultimately legendary—as the "Cactus Air Force."

The Cactus Air Force was strategically important because, until November 1942, the Japanese were able to maintain naval superiority, running their routine "Tokyo Express" resupply missions through the Slot to their garrison on Guadalcanal by day. However, the Cactus Air Force rose to challenge them and deny their dominance, forcing them to make their runs at night.

The Cactus Air Force stood in the way of Japanese surface strategy, and for this reason, neutralizing Henderson Field became an important element of Japanese air strategy.

For the sake of simplicity we refer to Henderson Field as a single entity, but it was actually a complex of several airfields in the Lunga Point area, all of which, except the original Henderson Field, were completely American-built. In the context of Allied activities, the original Henderson Field was known locally as "Bomber One," because it mainly hosted offensive operations. Incidentally, it is today the site of Guadalcanal's Honiara International Airport.

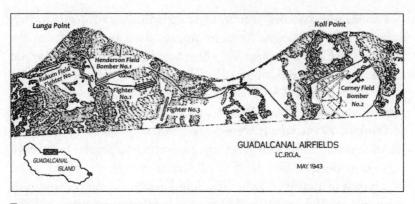

FIGURE I This map, issued by the Intelligence Center, Pacific Ocean Areas in
May 1943, shows the principal airfields on Guadalcanal. As other fighter fields
were added, the original Henderson Field was used mainly for bombers. The
distance from Henderson to Carney Field was about nine miles. (ICPOA)

Parallel to the main Henderson runway, and 500 yards inland to
the east, was "Fighter One," the principal base used by US Navy
and US Marine fighter units, including the squadrons with which
the Marine aces flew.

"Fighter Two," also called "Kukum Field," was located more than
a mile to the west, and was a secondary fighter field also shared by
USAAF aircraft. Carney Field, or "Bomber Two," was later located
on Koli Point, about nine miles east of Bomber One. There were
also several emergency landing fields within a 15-mile radius of
Henderson.

The Japanese Army on Guadalcanal made two major efforts to
recapture Henderson Field, but they were thwarted by the Marines
in the Battle of the Tenaru on August 21 and in the Battle of Edson's
Ridge, September 12–14.

The first fighters in the Cactus Air Force were the 19 F4F-4
Wildcats of VMF-223, led by Captain John L. Smith, who arrived
on August 20. The second contingent of 19 Wildcats arrived with
VMF-224, led by Bob Galer, Greg Boyington's old friend from
Seattle, which reached Guadalcanal on August 30.

These two fighting squadrons, along with two scout bomber
squadrons, comprised Marine Air Group 23 (MAG-23), commanded

by Colonel William Wallace. In turn, they were part of the 1st Marine Air Wing (MAW-1) under Brigadier General Roy Geiger, which had been Marine Aviator No. 5 before World War I. MAG-23 became a foundation block of the Cactus Air Force. Geiger's chief of staff, and eventual successor, was Lieutenant Colonel Louis Earnest Woods.

On August 31, Cactus was further reinforced when the Wildcats of the US Navy's VF-5 went ashore while the USS *Saratoga*, to which they were assigned, had battle damage repaired.

Marion Carl later noted that the F4F-4s that VMF-223 were flying at Guadalcanal had six .50-caliber machines guns, compared to just four in the F4F-3 that he had flown at Midway. He complained that the aircraft was 500 pounds heavier with no increase in power, and this made it "considerably slower." Both variants were powered by Pratt & Whitney R-1830 Twin Wasp, 14-cylinder radial engines rated at 1,200 horsepower.

It was at Guadalcanal that the Marine aviators and their Wildcats would have their first long, sustained contact with Japan's Mitsubishi A6M Zero fighter—though Marion Carl and others did have their brief encounter with them over Midway. Powerful and agile, the Zero entered service with the IJNAF in 1940 (2,600 in Japanese annual reckoning) and was identified as Type 0 because of the final digit of the year.

It was probably the best carrier fighter in the world in 1942, being as fast as a Wildcat and much more maneuverable in a dogfight. Its reputation preceded it, but American pilots were nevertheless surprised by its exceptional performance when they met it first hand.

Meanwhile, in 1942, the Allies developed a system of codenames for Japanese aircraft, with male names assigned to fighters and female names for bombers.

The A6M Zero was named "Zeke," though most Allied pilots still called it a "Zero." In this book, for consistency, we use the term "Zero" when referring to the A6M. Specifically, the type of Zero commonly encountered in 1942 was the A6M2 early standard variant. The A6M5 variant became standard by the fall of 1943, and more of these were produced than any other Zero variant.

To add to the complication, there were variants of the A6M Zero that were *not* codenamed "Zeke" by the Allies. The A6M2-N was a floatplane variant of the Zero that was developed by Nakajima and named "Rufe" by the Allies, though many Allied aviators called it a "floatplane Zero."

The Mitsubishi A6M3 Model 32 variant, with a more powerful engine, was originally codenamed "Hap," but USAAF Commanding General Henry Harley "Hap" Arnold naturally took exception, and the name was changed to "Hamp." Nevertheless, it occasionally appears in after-action reports as "Hap," and not infrequently the A6M3 is referred to as the "square-winged Zero," because the folding wingtips of the original A6M had been eliminated.

Sometimes, to distinguish them from Hamps and Rufes, basic A6M aircraft were referred to as "Zeke-type Zeros."

Finally, it should be added that there was a tendency in both formal and informal Allied reporting of Japanese air operations to use the term "Zero" for any Japanese fighter aircraft regardless of type. For example, the IJAAF's widely used Nakajima Ki-43 Hayabusa was codenamed "Oscar," but often mistakenly referred to as a "Zero." The two types *were* similar at first glance.

The Mitsubishi G3M and G4M twin-engine bombers, widely used by the IJNAF against the Americans in the Solomons, were called "Nell" and "Betty," respectively. Also part of the arsenal were Nakajima B5N single-engine torpedo bombers, codenamed "Kate," and Aichi D3A "Val" dive bombers. The latter were easily recognized by their fixed, non-retracting, landing gear.

While the Allies initially had few airfields from which to operate in the Solomons, the IJNAF had built them in many places nearby. The anchor point for the Japanese was their great naval and air base at Rabaul on New Britain, 660 miles northwest of Guadalcanal. Important Japanese air bases existed throughout the Solomons between Rabaul and Guadalcanal, notably in the Kahili–Buin area of Bougainville, and at Munda on New Georgia. These were 360 and 200 miles, respectively, from Guadalcanal.

Guadalcanal came to the attention of America suddenly and prominently in the late summer of 1942, thanks, in no small measure, to the reports from correspondents who were actually there, and who made the story of the Marines who fought there come alive for people in the States.

In the early days of August and September, they included Richard Wilcox of *Life* magazine and Richard Tregaskis of the International News Service. *Guadalcanal Diary* by Tregaskis, published on the first day of 1943, remains on the short list of the most important books published during World War II.

Both Wilcox and Tregaskis knew and interviewed the Marine pilots on Guadalcanal, and Wilcox wrote about John L. Smith in what became the *Life* cover story on the first anniversary of Pearl Harbor.

6

First Blood

August

On August 20, 1942, as the Marine aviators of VMF-223 bumped to a stop on the rough surface of Henderson Field, Marines swarmed out to greet them as answers to prayers. John L. Smith, who led them, told journalist Richard Wilcox that the voyage from Pearl Harbor to Guadalcanal aboard USS *Long Beach* was "a passage from one life to another ... on a jungle island none had ever seen and whose name few had ever heard."

In addition to Smith, there were four others among these 20 pilots who would become double-digit aces in the weeks to come. They included Marion Carl and Kenneth DeForrest Frazier of Smith's VMF-223 and Bob Galer of VMF-224.

The fourth man was Doc Everton, who joined them during a stop at Efate on August 18, 800 miles southeast of Guadalcanal. His time with VMF-223 was brief. He was officially assigned to VMF-212, which was under the command of Joe Bauer, who had been promoted to lieutenant colonel effective August 7.

Bauer had been in the SOPAC since the middle of May, several weeks before the Battle of Midway. He was expecting to get into action soon, but he was stuck at the staging base at Efate. He was sidetracked on his way into battle because of his organizational skills. Admiral John Sidney "Slew" McCain, the commander of naval and Marine aviation in the South Pacific (ComAirSoPac)—and the grandfather of the future presidential candidate—sidelined him as he passed through to help organize the flow of men and materiel into the South Pacific.

Air operations in SOPAC flowed through a series of staging bases, starting with Noumea, New Caledonia, the original SOPAC headquarters location, about 900 miles east of MacArthur's SWPA headquarters at Brisbane. From Noumea (codenamed White Poppy, and often called Poppy), the SOPAC line of communications ran in a series of northbound "hops" as follows:

(A) 350 miles northeasterly to Efate (codenamed Roses by the Allies) in the New Hebrides (now Vanuatu).

(B) 200 miles northwesterly from Efate to Espiritu Santo (codenamed Buttons), also in the New Hebrides, where the center of fighter operations was the busy airfield at Turtle Bay.

(C) 600 miles northwest from Espiritu Santo across the Coral Sea to Guadalcanal (codenamed Cactus) in the Solomons.

The airfields at Noumea, Efate and Espiritu Santo were being expanded to meet the needs of the flood of American aircraft and aviators—including USAAF and US Navy as well as Marine—that would be coming through, and Bauer played a major role in this activity.

Bauer had to have been jealous when VMF-223 passed through in hours while he had been stuck for months. As Everton recalled, "old John L. Smith came charging into the [Efate] harbor on a jeep carrier and he came up to our camp. We were having lunch together and John L. said that he had eight pilots that he didn't want to take into combat because they weren't trained far enough … [They had trained for] very few hours and Joe was building up their time and giving them some tactics."

When Bauer had reluctantly agreed to Smith's request, Everton recalled, "[I] opened my big mouth [and] I just asked Joe if he minded if I could go to Guadalcanal."

On Guadalcanal, the men of "Fighting 23," as Wilcox called their squadron, were issued with tents, blankets and mosquito netting that had been found among the large stocks of Japanese materiel that was captured when the Marines had come ashore unexpectedly two weeks earlier. The Japanese had been trying to evict them ever since and the aviators were serenaded during their first night by gunfire a few hundred yards from where they spent their first night on solid ground since the first day of the month.

On August 21, their second day, Smith was leading a four-ship patrol off the north coast of Guadalcanal when they were attacked by a half-dozen Zeros. Two of them made a pass at Smith, who was in the lead, and he rolled out to get below the second one. He later said that his mouth went dry when he saw the greenish aircraft in his sights, and recalled colorfully that as his tracers cut into it, the Zero opened up "like a split melon" and black smoke poured out as it careened into the deep blue water below.

In its baptism of fire on August 21, VMF-223 suffered no losses, though one Wildcat was damaged before the five remaining Zeros slipped away. It was on that day that Fighting 23 fought its biggest air battle to date. They tangled with a large strike force consisting of G4M Betty medium bombers and Nakajima B5N Kate torpedo bombers. Escorted by Zeros, they were inbound for the Marine positions around Henderson Field.

On August 24, Marion Carl had the best day of his career, claiming a Zero and a Betty, as well as a pair of Kates. Having now downed four Japanese aircraft over the Solomons to add to his single at Midway, Carl was now the first US Marine Corps ace.

However, a price was paid that day, as the squadron suffered its own first losses. Elwood Ray Bailey of Parma, Michigan had just celebrated his twenty-second birthday five days earlier. In San Diego on June 26, he had married Daisy Eunice Roberts, a fellow member of the Parma High School Class of '38. They had enjoyed exactly one day of married life before he shipped out for the Pacific. Bailey managed to claim a pair of Zeros before another one sent him spiraling into the sea. Including Bailey, four men failed to return that day, but one turned up a few days later, having bailed out and been recovered.

On August 26, Smith led an intercept of 16 G4Ms and a dozen Zeros. Among the six enemy aircraft shot down that day, Smith got a pair of G4Ms, and Marion Carl a Zero. However, another Zero shadowed him back to Henderson. With his landing gear down, Carl was vulnerable, so he lured the Japanese pilot close to an antiaircraft emplacement, which opened fire. The Zero got safely away, but then turned on Carl, who had cranked up his gear by now.

Carl watched as the Zero started to climb, outpacing his Wildcat. Carl made a quick deflection shot and his marksmanship was perfect. Hundreds of Marines on the ground watched the Zero explode and the pieces tumble into the sea.

Based on Japanese records that were accessed after the war, and the unique circumstances of this engagement, it is believed that the pilot whom Carl shot down that day was Lieutenant Commander Junichi Sasai, a 27-victory ace with the legendary Tainan Kokutai, the leading IJNAF fighter squadron.

Three G4M Bettys, and possibly a fourth, were downed that day by Doc Everton of VFM-212, on temporary duty with VMF-223 through the end of the month.

On August 29, VFM-223 intercepted another formation of medium bombers determined to attack Henderson. In this battle, Carl destroyed one bomber, while Smith downed a pair of Bettys to push his total with the squadron to five, making him the squadron's newest ace. The following day was a very bad day for the IJNAF, and Smith's best ever. He managed to down four Zeros, while Carl claimed three.

The following day, Bob Galer arrived with VMF-224, ready to join the fight. Little time was lost getting ready. On August 31, the new squadron launched 17 F4F-4s to join eight from VMF-223 on a combat air patrol. It was not an auspicious beginning. VMF-224 made no contact with the enemy, yet managed to lose three Wildcats. Apparently suffering from oxygen system issues, the aircraft piloted by Richard Anerine, Charles Bryans, and Gordon Thomson all disappeared. Anerine showed up a week later. He had indeed had a problem with his oxygen, as well as with his engine. He bailed out, landed at sea and swam ashore on Guadalcanal.

When accosted by a four-man Japanese patrol, he clobbered one with a rock, took his gun and shot the other three.

During his short time on detached duty with Smith's VMF-223, Doc Everton saw those target-rich skies first hand. As he recalled a quarter century later, "the hunting got so good there that about the first thing you did when you took off, you squeezed your trigger to shoot at a Jap that was in front of you, and the second thing you did was pull up your wheels because there was that many of them around. They were just like fleas out there."

These were chaotic times for the Marines on Guadalcanal, certainly for the Marines on the ground, but also for those fighting the Japanese high above. But through it all, they prevailed. As Richard Wilcox wrote, without really stretching the truth, they were, at least at the end of August, "always outnumbered in combat, but never beaten."

This was a reminder of how close the land battle of Guadalcanal was to Henderson Field, which was shelled often by Japanese troops or by Japanese ships offshore.

7

New Blood

September

As the first full month of Marine air operations out of Henderson Field began, Bob Galer and VMF-224 had their first contact with the enemy late on the morning of September 2, 1942. They were anxious to get into action alongside the ten-day veterans of VMF-223. For its part, the IJNAF was cooperating by providing both squadrons with plenty of targets, as well as sending large numbers of Bettys and Zeros to visit Guadalcanal almost every day.

When VMF-224 intercepted a Japanese strike force, Galer himself scored his own first victories, claiming a Betty bomber and one of the escorting Zeros. Future ace George Hollowell also downed a bomber, as did John Jones. This would be the only victory credited to Jones before he was killed in action a week later.

Including Jones, VMF-224 lost three men that week, but they claimed a half-dozen Japanese aircraft. These included Galer's third and the first two for future ace Charles Kunz. Galer became VMF-224's first ace on September 11, though he had to ditch his damaged Wildcat in the sea and wait to be picked up. He added a sixth victory two days later.

In the meantime, thanks to the journalists who had attached themselves to VMF-223, the exploits of its airmen continued to fill the headlines in American news reports datelined "Guadalcanal."

Legends of heroic aerial warriors began to take shape. Richard Wilcox wrote that with victory scores reaching double-digits,

"Smith and Marion Carl were the heavenly twins of Fighting 23. As their scores grew higher and higher, their legend grew among the Marine ground troops."

In his memoirs, Carl said that "heavenly twins" was "the sort of thing that takes months or years to live down."

In the pursuit of legends upon which to hang the Guadalcanal narrative, Wilcox wrote glowingly that Smith "would slide into his Grumman's cockpit like a man into an easy chair after a hard day's work. When he was airborne, his narrow, wide-set eyes were everywhere. And everything they saw, he destroyed."

Richard Tregaskis also fell under the spell of the man from Oklahoma. In a passage from *Guadalcanal Diary* first penned in early September when Smith's score stood at nine, Tregaskis wrote that "he has the steadiest eyes I have ever seen; they are brown and wide-set and you fancy they would be most at home looking out over the great plains of the West. Smith is a prairie type: tanned face, wide cheekbones, the erect head of a horseman, a thick neck set on square shoulders, a big, sinewy body. You get the impression that life must have a calm, elemental simplicity for him."

This larger-than-life man with the narrow, steady eyes had yet to see his twenty-eighth birthday.

On September 9, Marion Carl was flying his thirteenth Guadalcanal mission in a Wildcat marked with the numeral "13." As Carl himself observed, "maybe a numerologist could have predicted what happened next."

He had just shot down a pair of G4Ms to bring his score to a dozen when a Zero surprised him from behind and his Wildcat went down. Wilcox reported that "every Marine on the island mourned his loss" when the news reached Guadalcanal.

Though it was not known at the time among his squadronmates, Carl had popped his canopy at 22,000 feet and hit the silk. He landed safely near a tiny island about 30 miles south of Henderson Field, where he was picked up by a local man in a rowboat.

He was deposited with a friendly local doctor on Guadalcanal, but between this location and Henderson Field was a contingent of around 2,000 Japanese troops. The doctor had a motorboat, but the one-cylinder engine did not work, so Carl spent several days tinkering with it before it would start.

"My return from the dead caused something of a sensation," Carl wrote in his memoirs. They were glad to have him home.

Richard Wilcox recalled that "his first question, as the cheering Marines greeted him, was 'How many has Smitty got now?'"

When Carl learned that Smith was barely ahead of him in the victory tally, Wilcox reported that he asked General Roy Geiger, commanding the 1st Marine Air Wing, to ground Smith for five days so that he could catch up. In his memoirs, Carl noted that this "was not exactly how I remember it," but he does admit that the story did accurately "illustrate the feelings of rivalry between fighter aces."

Another future double-digit ace flying with VMF-223 that month was Jack Conger, whose official assignment was to Joe Bauer's VMF-212, but who had gotten himself assigned to John L. Smith's squadron. He scored his first aerial victory on September 13 on his first day of combat, though on his second combat mission. He took off on an uneventful patrol at 0945hrs, and went out again at 1320hrs as part of a bomber intercept mission. Approximately 27 bombers were intercepted by four Wildcats, with Conger and Robert Read each claiming an IJAAF Mitsubishi Ki-21 twin-engined heavy bomber, the type the Allies codenamed "Sally."

Jack Conger added his second aerial victory on September 27 on a bomber intercept mission with Marion Carl, Ken Frazier and a half-dozen others from VMF-223. Both Carl and Conger shot down a G4M Betty on that mission, and Carl shared a third with Kirk Armistead of VFM-224. This brought Conger's score to two, and Carl's to 14.5.

There had been a respite of sorts between September 14 and 17 when weather conditions precluded air operations by both sides. However, beneath the cloud cover, surface actions, both at sea and ashore, continued as the Japanese continued to pour reinforcements into Guadalcanal with an eye toward an offensive to recapture Henderson Field and push the Allies off Guadalcanal. At the same time, the Marines were bringing in more men to shore up the defensive perimeter on the contested island.

On September 22, General Roy Geiger of MAW-1 reorganized the Cactus Air Force by establishing two separate subsidiary commands that formally merged USAAF, Navy and Marine air combat assets into the same command structure. The Cactus Strike (Bomber) Command was under Albert Cooley, who headed MAG-14, while Cactus Fighter Command was created under Bill Wallace, the commander of MAG-23. Wallace was scheduled to depart SOPAC in mid-October, and Geiger already had it in mind that Lieutenant Colonel Joe Bauer would be his successor.

Bauer had yet to reach Guadalcanal, as he was stuck in the New Hebrides organizing the transition of fighting units to Guadalcanal. Doc Everton, who was with Bauer as VMF-212 lingered long at Efate, remembered in later years that Bauer was "very disappointed and, in fact, it just literally took the starch out of him, temporarily."

By October, Admiral McCain, albeit reluctantly, cut Bauer loose. In a September 21 memo to Geiger, McCain wrote that Bauer had "been instrumental in the selection of advanced flying fields; he has trained in his organization, at my instigation, pilots of Army and Marine Corps squadrons other than his own; he has done many other things too numerous to mention to support and forward the war effort in this area. In short, he has been a tower of strength and it is with sincere regret that our association is temporarily ended."

A week later, on September 28, Bauer landed on Guadalcanal in an R4D-1 Skytrain transport, walked up to Bob Galer and asked to borrow a Wildcat and to join VMF-224 for the day's intercept of an incoming IJNAF strike force. Galer agreed. The future Fighter Command boss needed combat experience, and he got it. A Mitsubishi G4M bomber fell to Joe Bauer's borrowed guns that day, as he began on his road to becoming an ace.

For Bob Galer, September 28 was also an especially good day, as he downed three G4Ms. Through the end of the month, Galer's score stood at nine confirmed, including six bombers.

At VMF-223, Smith and Carl, by this time promoted to major and captain, respectively, were still the leading aces in SOPAC. With this came an obvious competitiveness. By the end of September, only a hair's breadth separated them, as Smith now had 16, while Carl had 16.5.

On a rainy September 30, most missions had been canceled when an R4D-1 touched down at Henderson carrying Admiral Chester Nimitz. The Commander in Chief of the Pacific Fleet and of the Pacific Ocean Areas theater command, he was on a front-line inspection, a rarity for men of his rank.

"I really admired him," Marion Carl wrote many years later. "There weren't many four-stars who got within shooting distance of the enemy, and his concern for his people was genuine."

Nimitz also brought a Navy Cross—second only to the Medal of Honor as an award for valor for Marines and sailors—to pin on the top three Marine aces on Guadalcanal, Marion Carl, Bob Galer, and John L. Smith. Also receiving a Navy Cross was Richard Mangrum, who commanded VMSB-232, the first squadron of SBD Dauntless dive bombers to fly with the Cactus Air Force.

The fourth highest-scoring ace on Guadalcanal that day was Ken Frazier, whose total was 12.5, close to Galer's 13. He too received the Navy Cross, but not until December 1943. Both Smith and Galer were later awarded the Medal of Honor for their actions on Guadalcanal.

In a letter written a few days after he received the Navy Cross, Smith told his wife that "an Admiral pinned the Navy Cross on me the other morning. I am proud to get it, except that they think that it is good payment for seeing young pilots who are sharing my tent go down in flames day after day."

The losses were personal, and they were really getting to VMF-223's commanding officer.

8

Changing of the Guard

October

Richard Wilcox, the reporter who had hovered around VMF-223 since their first days on Guadalcanal a thousand years earlier in August, was on hand as they looked down the metaphorical tunnel toward the end of their tours of duty on October 10, 1942.

As the month began, their numbers were down to half the head count of the last week of August—and declining. Wilcox wrote that "some men started to brood and Smith began to worry. He couldn't blame them, they were going up every day and shooting down Japs, but the new ones came over with unfailing regularity the next day. They were facing excellent pilots who could shoot straight and fly well."

October 2 was a day that fell into line with the gathering darkness of melancholy. Shortly after noon, it was learned that an incoming fighter sweep involving as many as two dozen Zeros was on its way. Wildcats scrambled to meet them, including 14 from the Navy's VF-5 and 11 each from VMF-223 and VMF-224.

Sometimes incoming air strikes were detected by radar, but often reports were radioed to Henderson through the network of coastwatchers. They were Australians, New Zealanders, and Solomon islanders who operated out of jungle perches in barely accessible corners of remote islands—and sometimes right under the noses of the Japanese—where they kept tabs on enemy movements as they scanned the Slot with their binoculars, operated their clandestine radio transmitters, and tried not to get caught.

John L. Smith led a contingent that emerged from cloud cover at 25,000 feet to find themselves in the midst of more than a dozen Zeros from the deadly Tainin Kokutai. Smith shot down one, but by then, the luck of the flight he led began to run out. The Wildcat flown by Willis Lees III of VMF-223 was fatally damaged as he tried to slip back into the clouds. Lees was seen bailing out of his stricken aircraft, but he was never seen again.

Smith himself took a tremendous pounding from three Zeros, which damaged his wings and oil cooler. One of the three Japanese pilots, Tadashi Yoneda, claimed that he had shot down Smith's Wildcat, and indeed he had. With his overheated Twin Wasp screeching, clattering and billowing smoke, Smith dropped through the clouds and tried to get back to Henderson Field.

He didn't make it. He set the damaged F4F down in the brush about a half-dozen miles from the runway. As Marion Carl came over to check on him, Smith emerged and walked away from the wreck. Dodging Japanese patrols and jungle streams as he went, he hiked back to Henderson.

Also that day, the VMF-223 trio of Ken Frazier, Charles Hughes, and Charles Warren "Red" Kendrick engaged seven Zeros. Kendrick was somewhat of a prodigy who graduated from Harvard Law School shortly before he joined the Marines. By October, he had just downed his fifth Japanese aircraft to become an ace, but according to Richard Wilcox's description, he had become depressed.

Frazier, Hughes, and Kendrick attacked from above, but the Zeros eluded them in the clouds and Kendrick disappeared. The following day, the Wildcats flown by both Lees and Kendrick were located by ground parties as crumpled wreckage on Guadalcanal. Kendrick's body was buried at the site. After the war, Kendrick's father, the wealthy president of the Schlage Lock Company of San Francisco, mounted an expedition to Guadalcanal to locate his son's remains and to see him buried at home.

On October 3, Lieutenant Colonel Joe Bauer reappeared at Henderson and asked to fly a mission with Smith's VMF-223.

Smith suggested that he talk to Marion Carl about attaching himself to the flight that Carl was leading.

Bauer and Carl had gotten off to a bad start when they first crossed paths at San Diego a few years earlier, and they were never friends. However, as Carl pointed out in his memoirs, their relationship "eventually warmed to one of mutual regard and respect."

For Marion Carl, the bad luck experienced by VMF-223 on October 2 continued, but Joe Bauer found a silver lining in the clouds over the Slot. Carl's bad luck came in the form of an issue that was endemic to the Wildcat. The tight turns and negative G-forces caused the ammunition chutes to jam, and it was not always possible to unjam them. Carl had just downed a Zero with a difficult deflection shot, and had another align perfectly in his sights only to be hit with the empty silence of guns that refused to respond to his touch.

For Joe Bauer, flying with Carl's flight, October 3 was just the opposite. A day of cloud-compromised visibility was his big day. Carl remembered that the altimeter read 30,500 feet, the highest he had yet been, when they noted a gaggle of Zeros at 12,000 feet just before 1300hrs.

When they dived, Bauer was unable to communicate with the others because his radio was out. Carl, whose guns were silenced, watched him as he went after the Zero trailing at the end of the formation and shot it down. Suddenly, and in the metaphorical sense, Bauer had caught fire. All of his eagerness for combat, pent up over the previous months of touring construction sites armed with nothing more lethal than a pen and clipboard, exploded like a broken dam.

One by one, Bauer outfought and destroyed four Zeros. He seriously damaged another, but did not see him go down. He did not claim this as a victory, though his boss, Roy Geiger of MAW-1, later retroactively added it to his total score. His four confirmed on October 3, added to the one he scored with VMF-224, made Bauer an ace after just two combat missions.

On his way back to Henderson after this amazing combat action, Bauer happened—fortuitously—to pass Ken Frazier, who was hanging from a parachute high over the Slot.

Like Bauer, Frazier had been flying with Marion Carl's VMF-223 flight that day, and he had claimed a pair of Zeros before his luck ran out. He managed to pop the canopy, get out of his crippled Wildcat and yank the ripcord, when the Zero that destroyed his aircraft came back around to destroy *him*.

"My attacker had followed me down and was strafing me in my parachute," Frazier wrote in his after-action report. "After a few seconds of this, which seemed like a terrifying eternity, a lone F4F, piloted by Lt. Col. H.W. Bauer, closed in on this strafing Zero and drove him off trailing a large column of black smoke."

Frazier reported making a successful landing in the ocean several miles from the northeastern tip of Guadalcanal, where he was picked up by an American destroyer two hours later. He returned to base "none the worse for wear."

While Frazier was bobbing about in the water, Bauer and Carl landed back at Henderson. Carl, who scored his own last Guadalcanal aerial victory in the battle, remembered Bauer "jumping up and down" after the squadron had landed.

Elsewhere, the men of VMF-223 were no longer jumping up and down. The thrill was not exactly gone, but it was tempered by exhaustion and by loss.

John L. Smith scored the final two victories of his career on October 3 to bring his score to 19 and confirm him as the highest-scoring American ace of the war—to date. Back in the States, Smith was frequently mentioned in news articles datelined from the South Pacific.

October 10 was the last day in combat for Smith and VMF-223, the first Marine fighting squadron to see combat in the skies of World War II. The squadron was now down to just eight operational Wildcats. The mission for the day was escorting torpedo bombers that were out to intercept the enemy fleet and to put more Japanese iron on the bottom of Ironbottom Sound.

The Marine bombers and their covering fighters flew a northwesterly course, up the Slot toward the Florida Islands. Apparently assuming that both sections of aircraft were ordnance-laden bombers, not nimble fighters, a group of A6M2-N Rufe floatplane fighters dived to attack.

"A suicide squad," Smith told his pilots, according to Richard Wilcox's later description. "Follow me and we'll give them what they're looking for … pick your targets and we'll give the bastards something to remember [on] our last day."

Wilcox noted that in the waters of the Slot there were "nine splashes to mark the final tally of his squadron. It was a good last day."

Their work officially done, the men of VMF-223 waited a couple of days for transport, and Smith closed the log book on October 12. Peeking over his shoulder, Wilcox noted that they had shot down 95 enemy aircraft since August 20, though most later accounts, citing official sources—including Marion Carl in his memoirs and National Air and Space Museum historian Walter Boyne—put the number at 110. Smith had 19 and Carl had 16.5. This included 15.5 (though both he and Wilcox rounded this up to 16 in their later accounts) with VMF-223, plus one at Midway with VMF-221. Ken Frazier, the squadron's other double-digit ace, had 11.5.

VMF-223 had suffered a 60 percent casualty rate, with six killed and six wounded. Wilcox, who shared the flight back across the Pacific with the eight survivors, wrote that "they didn't bother to look back at Guadalcanal as they left."

———

On October 9, the day before VMF-223 flew their last mission, a new squadron arrived at Henderson Field—right on the original Henderson runway that was used operationally as "Bomber 1." John L. Smith drove out in a jeep and told them that they had to take off again and fly over to the nearby Fighter One airstrip.

The new squadron was VMF-121, untested and untried, but destined for big things. It was commanded by 29-year-old, Chicago-born Major Leonard "Duke" Davis. Like Joe Bauer, he was an Annapolis man—a rarity among Marine aviators—though he graduated from the Naval Academy in 1935, five years after Bauer, so the two had not crossed paths.

The executive officer of VMF-121 was Captain Joseph Jacob Foss. He had spent the spring of 1942 trying to get into the Advanced Carrier Training Group (ACTG) at North Island, but was told that it was a Navy program, and "we don't need Marines … Besides, you're too old." At the age of 27—he was much older than the average age of Marine pilots, at around 23—he would earn the nickname "Old Foos."

Persistence paid off and Foss got into ACTG. After he graduated on July 19, having logged 156 hours in the program, he began keeping his eyes open for a fighting squadron assignment. On the last day of the month, he was offered the post with VMF-121 at Camp Kearny (now MCAS Miramar) north of San Diego and he eagerly grabbed the assignment. Foss shipped out with VMF-121 on September 11, two days after marrying his high school sweetheart, June Shakstad.

At Noumea, they transferred to the escort carrier USS *Copahee* (CVE-12), which had brought their F4F-4s to the SOPAC. The ship then took them to a point about 200 miles due south of Guadalcanal where there was a series of remote coral atolls called "the Indispensable Reefs." It was here that they made their one and only in-theater carrier launch—and for many their first-ever catapult launch—for their flight to Guadalcanal.

In his memoirs, Foss recalled that "Guadalcanal was a rude shock for a guy from the plains of South Dakota … Between the rain and the humidity nothing ever dried out, including us. I'd never seen so much rain and mud in my life."

Bob Galer, the skipper of VMF-224, drove out to the flightline in his jeep to greet them. As Galer was pointing out the locations of the various airfields and other facilities, a shell exploded nearby. Galer explained that there was a Japanese gunner who had a cannon hidden up in the hills and, occasionally, he would slip it out and fire off a round or two.

The nightly artillery barrages that came from farther back behind Japanese lines were a far more serious matter, and the men of VMF-121 had one of these as part of their first day "welcome" package. Galer remembered that he and Foss spent the night in a slit trench that was "about 18-inches deep and was a little less in width than a twin bed, I'm sure. And our cover was a thin piece of aluminum that did nothing but hold the light of the bursting shells out. Fortunately, there was no shrapnel or anything else that hit us that evening. And I can tell you that the next day we spent a lot of time on improving our foxholes so that we had log barricades and sand on top and that they were deep."

On October 10, the day of VMF-223's final mission, Duke Davis and Joe Foss led VMF-121 on their first one, flying high cover for SBD scout bombers who were hitting Japanese shipping in the Slot.

What they found was more than the usual "Tokyo Express." It was a major Japanese naval action. The large reinforcement mission was accompanied by three heavy cruisers and two destroyers being sent to bombard and wipe out the Allied facilities and aircraft at the Henderson Field complex.

This force got under way from Shortland Island off Bougainville during the morning of October 11. Simultaneously, the IJNAF Japanese 11th Air Fleet launched air assaults against Henderson that involved 30 Zeros escorting 45 Betty bombers.

VMF-121 and VMF-224 rose to meet them, but it was Bob Galer and VMF-224 who owned the action, knocking down at least four Zeros and eight bombers. Among these, Galer himself claimed one bomber. The squadron had its biggest day of the war on October 11.

The costly air assault by the IJNAF failed to destroy Henderson Field or the Cactus Air Force, but it did succeed in centering the air battle over Guadalcanal and away from the naval force making its way down the Slot. Allied aerial reconnaissance did spot the IJN armada. Coincidentally, a US Navy task force had just entered the area. A force of four cruisers and five destroyers commanded by Rear Admiral Norman Scott were coming into view, escorting a convoy carrying US Army reinforcements to Guadalcanal.

Scott then moved to intercept the Japanese off Cape Esperance— the northwest tip of Guadalcanal—and the battle of the same name began shortly before midnight on October 11. Though there was considerable miscommunication and confusion among the American ships, the Japanese were caught by surprise.

Beginning at dawn on October 12, SBD-3 Dauntless dive bombers and TBF-1 Avenger torpedo bombers from US Navy and Marine squadrons on Guadalcanal, as well as from the carrier USS *Enterprise*, were able to join the battle. The US Navy lost one destroyer sunk, while the IJN lost a destroyer and a cruiser sunk and Aritomo Goto, commander of the IJN battle force, was mortally wounded. Meanwhile, the Japanese battleship *Hiei*, which had been incapacitated off Guadalcanal, became a sitting duck target for the Americans and it was sunk late on October 14.

The Americans emerged with a narrow victory in what came to be known alternately as the Battle of Cape Esperance, or the Second Battle of Savo Island. The latter name is derived from a 12-square-mile island that lies between Guadalcanal and Tulagi, and which was at the center of the four major naval battles near Guadalcanal between August and November 1942.

On October 13, in the wake of this battle, VMF-121 took the lead, scrambling 23 Wildcats to meet a Japanese bomber strike that came as a surprise because of a communications screw-up. The relentless IJNAF returned two hours later with 14 Bettys, escorted by 18 Zeros.

It was Joe Foss who led the intercept. As several Zeros dived on him, one overshot him and emerged into his sights. He recalled a "great flash" when the A6M exploded "into a thousand pieces."

Discovering that this maneuver had made him "a setup for three others," Foss took evasive action as oil poured from his oil cooler and his engine seized. He made a beeline back to Henderson for a dead stick landing and "came in like a rocket ship, sideslipping desperately at the last moment."

He had learned the fateful lesson to always "check six," to watch his six o'clock position, directly behind. As he recalled in his memoirs, from then on, he was known as "Swivel-Neck Joe," or "Old Swivelneck," because he was always looking back to check his six.

That night, the Japanese Navy treated the Cactus Air Force to the heaviest naval bombardment yet dished out, including the 14-inch guns of the battleships *Haruna* and *Kongo*. More than three dozen men were killed at the airfields.

Nevertheless, both VMF-121 and VFM-224, as well as the US Navy's VF-5, were able to launch Wildcats into the skies over Guadalcanal on the morning of October 14 to meet two waves of air strikes from the IJNAF. When the first alert came before breakfast, VMF-121 had only seven Wildcats flyable, so Duke Davis took out the first patrol, leaving Joe Foss to bide his time to take out a second contingent later in the day.

The flights that Davis and Foss led typically included the same aviators, and the latter group had become so well known for their aerobatic showmanship that they were called "Foss's Flying Circus." Foss remembered that it was Lieutenant Colonel Joe Bauer himself who had coined the nickname.

Among the early members of the Flying Circus were Andy Andrews, Casey Brandon, Cecil "Danny" Doyle, Bill Freeman, Thomas "Boot" Furlow, Roger "Hog" Haberman, and Gregory "Nemo" Loesch. On Guadalcanal since October, and with the Circus by November, was Frank "Skeezix" Presley from Encinitas, California, whose nickname came from a character in the popular *Gasoline Alley* comic strip.

While most fighter pilots were officers—lieutenants and captains, with majors commanding squadrons—there was a smattering of enlisted men among the Marine aviators, men who had come through the prewar Naval Aviation Pilot (NAP) program. The circus had Tech Sergeant Joe Palko.

Then there was an aviator who had gotten off to such a bad start with Foss that it is a wonder he ever became part of the Circus at all. In both his 1943 and 1992 memoirs, Foss makes no more than the occasional passing reference to William Pratt Marontate, which is remarkable because he would go on to become the second highest-scoring ace in VMF-121 after Foss himself, and the only other double-digit ace. However, in an interview with Jay Edgerton of the *Minneapolis Star-Tribune* in February 1949, Foss spoke about him at length.

> My first meeting with Bill Marontate was not too pleasant ... I had just arrived at Camp Kearny as executive officer of the squadron in the summer of 1942. We had eight planes at the time [and] on my first day as exec, Marontate took a plane and ran it right into a gun emplacement. Smashed up the wings and the prop badly ... I ate him up one side and down the other ... He just stood and took it. Never at any time, then or subsequently, did he show any signs of resentment. I guess he figured he had it coming. And he did. Later, we became good friends.

Marontate had several nicknames, one being "Guts" because of his peculiar habit of, in Foss's words "inflating his belly and protruding it amazingly." He was also called "Tate," the last syllable of his name, because, as Foss said, "he never learned to talk on the intercom. It always sounded like Donald Duck in the movies. Quack ... quack ... quack ... *Tate* ... a yell on the last syllable of his name."

Others, including Oscar Bate and Roy "Rudy" Ruddell, would be put on the roster of the Flying Circus as earlier Circus members were killed in action.

It was close to noon on October 15 when Foss led the Circus to meet the next wave, the typical strike package of G4M twin-engine bombers with an escort of Zeros. However, as the flight climbed into the sky, Foss's Twin Wasp began to cough and sputter. He managed to get it revving, but it cut out again, so he reported engine trouble and turned command of the flight over to Loesch.

Hanging back inside the edges of a cloud and fighting with his engine, there was nothing Foss could do but watch the air battle unfolding over Henderson. Suddenly, a diving Wildcat flashed by looking for cover inside the cloud, and on its tail, a diving Zero, both so close that they nearly rammed Foss.

For a split second, as the Japanese pilot maneuvered to stay on the Wildcat's tail, his Zero was directly aligned with Foss's gunsight.

A short burst of .50-caliber fire separated one of the Mitsubishi's wings from the rest of the aircraft and both tumbled away as Foss passed by with his sputtering engine.

When the day was over, Foss discovered that he was not alone in having had engine trouble, and the culprit turned out to be contaminated fuel. The Marines had hired some local people to fill a camouflaged storage tank in the nearby hills with fuel from 55-gallon drums by way of a wooden trough. They had discovered that if they dipped their feet in the fuel in the trough, the evaporation had a cooling effect. It also washed sand and coral off their feet and into the fuel. Procedures were then put in place to strain the fuel from the storage tank as it was put into the aircraft.

Fuel was a precious commodity on Guadalcanal. Cargo ships had to practically fight their way in with supplies, while Navy R4Ds and USAAF C-47s (both referred to in contemporary documents by their mutual civilian designation as DC-3s) flying up from Espiritu Santo could carry only a dozen drums of aviation fuel on each flight. On October 15, there was a bonanza of sorts when a huge stash of 450 drums of fuel was discovered hidden near Henderson Field. They had been concealed there by the Japanese when they were occuying that part of the island.

Still, the nagging fuel shortages combined with intensifying Japanese air attacks and nighttime artillery barrages made operations—never mind simply staying alive and making it through the night—difficult in the extreme.

The Japanese, who were becoming increasingly aggressive, made the audacious mistake of bringing troops ashore by landing craft during daylight on October 16. VMF-121 rallied for a series of low-level strafing attacks, a rarity for them. By some accounts, this was at Kokumbona (now Kakambona), less than ten miles west of the American perimeter around the Henderson Field complex, though in his memoirs, Joe Foss indicates something farther away.

"At the end of the field, where I normally would have climbed for height, our flight leveled out and turned," Foss wrote. "Skimming barely five feet above the treetops, the eight of us dropped into island valleys and all but brushed the hilltops as we hugged the contour of the land." As such, the Marines came in well below the altitude for which the antiaircraft guns were calibrated and so low that Foss was sure he could see rank insignia on the Japanese troops they were raking with their gunfire.

On October 17, VMF-121 was back to its usual workplace, closer to five miles above the treetops than five feet. Intercepting an incoming IJNAF strike force, Davis and Loesch, along with Joe Narr, Roger Haberman, and Wallace "Wally" Wethe shot down eight G4M bombers, while Bill Freeman downed a pair of Zeros.

Joe Foss did not score that day, but October 18 belonged to him. In his memoirs, he mentioned the sun being "almost straight up" when he led his Flying Circus off the runway at Henderson's Fighter One airstrip. The launch was disastrously interrupted when Andy Andrews, the sixth of the eight Wildcats, skidded off the runway and crashed into another aircraft in an enormous fireball, thus delaying the takeoff of the final two in Foss's flight.

The Zeros escorting the incoming IJNAF strike force were already over the field when Danny Doyle and Bill Marontate finally took to the air. Joe Foss watched as three of the Japanese fighters came in behind the two Americans as they were still trying to gain speed and altitude.

As Foss remembered it, he converted his turn to a dive, led the rest of the flight down and slid "gently" in behind the Zeros. One quick burst and the first enemy aircraft was a torch.

This action allowed Doyle and Marontate time to take evasive action, and the rest of the flight converged to destroy the two remaining Zeros.

No sooner had this happened when more Zeros piled on from above. Because they were diving while the Wildcats were pulling out of a dive, they had the speed advantage. As one of them twisted his trajectory to get behind Foss, he slowed down and Foss maneuvered to get on his six. He rolled and dived again to pick up speed.

"I began to recognize that I was not up against an inexperienced pilot," Foss recalled. "I'd seen plenty of good and bad Japanese fliers, and this was one of the best."

When these two experienced pilots rolled, tumbled, and jockeyed for advantage, they did so in a sky filled with more than a dozen other pilots doing the same thing. At last, Foss aligned the converging streams of fire from the guns on his two wings, placing the point of convergence on the enemy airplane. With smoke pouring from his engine, the enemy pilot gave it all he could and escaped to the north.

Rather than giving chase, Foss jumped back into the battle. Spotting a Zero in pursuit of another Wildcat, Foss dived on him. The Japanese pilot turned to face Foss head on. The Zero broke off first and as Foss was about to thumb his trigger, but he saw a Wildcat in his line of fire, so he had to maneuver again to set up another shot.

The Japanese pilot, thinking that Foss would be his kill today, obliged by turning into another head-on pass. He eagerly opened fire, but at too great a distance. He missed, and as they closed on one another, it was Foss's turn. His salvo was deadly accurate. As the two aircraft rocketed past one another, the Zero was already a ball of fire.

Foss wrote in his first book, published in 1943 when the war was still going on, that "I am not revealing a tactical secret when I say that we grew fond of going at the Zeros head on, as if attempting to ram them. The superior ruggedness of our Wildcats made this possible. Japs knew a collision was suicide and were also afraid of our devastating firepower. On a head-on approach we usually got a good shot, too, when the Zero slow-rolled, looped or made a climbing turn to avoid our attack."

Quickly after this first confirmed kill of the day, Foss next found himself looking directly into the formation of twin-engine G4M Betty bombers that had come to blast Henderson Field and the Marines below. He pulled back on the stick and jammed the throttle forward, climbing to get above the bombers. He picked one to attack, the right rear of the vee formation, but someone else blew it up before he could open fire.

Foss found himself diving past the formation, so once again he pulled into a climb. This time he picked out the left rear Betty and opened fire from below as his straining engine neared stall speed.

The G4M was an excellent aircraft in many respects, known for its speed, range, and reliability, but it had its Achilles heel. Like many other Japanese aircraft, it paid for its speed and range by dispensing with the weight of armor and self sealing fuel tanks. The latter made it a flying torch if struck by tracers in the right place. Such was the case for Joe Foss that day, shooting from below and directly at its tanks. He recalled "intense radiant heat" as the G4M tumbled past him. An explosion took off a wing before it hit the sea.

When Foss rolled to a stop after a dead-stick landing, he realized that the day's three victories now made him an ace. He would add two more on October 20, the second with a difficult "deflection" shot. Foss, like all of the best aces, became a master of "deflection shooting," or hitting an enemy at an angle other than head on or straight behind. As he later commented, deflection shooting "required good marksmanship. To a farm boy it was like shooting a pheasant on the fly."

As he watched his bullets hit the side of the Zero's cockpit that day, he recalled that the aircraft "went into a spin with no signs of smoke or fire, and continued to spin down with increasing momentum. I watched it twist downward for thousands of feet— on into the channel, where its impact raised a towering plume of water."

VMF-224, meanwhile, was packing up for their departure on the last day of October. According to the official history of VMF-224, the air battle of October 14 accounted for their final aerial victories. Five Japanese bombers were destroyed that day, one of them by

John Dobbin, while two Zeros went down, one of these being Bob Galer's thirteenth and final victory.

As they followed VMF-223 across the eastern horizon, they could claim 64 aerial victories, including 36 bombers, for their two months and two days in combat. Bob Galer, the only VMF-224 ace in double-digits, headed the list with his 13. In speaking about the double-digit aces Bob Galer, John L. Smith, and Marion Carl—as they all departed the theater—Joe Foss recalled that the trio had been called "The Three Flying Fools of Guadalcanal."

He added that "The enemy believed they could take the island back from the Allies like a piece of cake and move on to Australia and New Zealand. These guys had stopped them cold, and now it was our turn."

9

The Coach Takes the Field

October

On October 16, 1942 the reverberations from the Battle of Cape Esperance and the air battles of October 11–14 were still ringing in the ears of those on Guadalcanal when Lieutenant Colonel Joe Bauer, Slew McCain's tower of strength, finally led VMF-212 into Henderson Field.

And a dramatic entrance it was.

As the 19 Wildcats were coming in, low on fuel, after the 600-mile flight from Espiritu Santo, nine IJNAF Aichi D3A Vals were at work not far away. The dive bombers were attacking the destroyer USS *McFarland* (DD-237) as she was unloading cargo and embarking wounded personnel off Lunga Point. At least one bomb had hit and damaged the ship's stern, and another blew up a gasoline barge alongside. The ship's gunners had managed to down only one of the dive bombers.

Seeing that there were no other Allied aircraft in the area, Joe Bauer intervened—alone. Despite being almost out of fuel after the long flight from Espiritu Santo, he was able to engage and destroy *four* of the attackers before he finally had to break off and land at Henderson because of his critical fuel situation. His Medal of Honor citation would call it "above and beyond the call of duty," and it's hard to argue with this assessment.

By all accounts, this man who had been Slew McCain's tower of strength was a remarkable man and a remarkable leader. A quarter century later, Doc Everton, who arrived on Guadalcanal with Bauer and VMF-212 on October 16, sat down with Navy ace Eugene Valencia to talk about the war. Though he had begun his combat career on temporary duty with VMF-223 in August, Everton's permanent assignment on Guadalcanal began in October under Bauer. When the conversation with Valencia turned to Bauer, Everton had nothing but praise for the leadership of the man they called the "Coach." As Everton explained:

> He knew how to work with, and really handle people. He knew how to get the most out of them. He wasn't a driver, he was a leader. He was firm, and at the same time he was very fair. He was one that you can sit down and joke with, but when he got serious, you knew immediately between the two. Anybody that was brought up, so to speak, under Joe Bauer, [will tell you that] his attributes have been adopted by many, many people that work with men. There isn't a man that ever knew Joe Bauer and worked with Joe Bauer that wouldn't work 25 out of the 24 hours a day for him. That's the kind of a guy he was. He was a terrific man.

Beyond his leadership skills, there were several things that set Joe Bauer apart from other Marine aviators on Guadalcanal. First, there were not many Annapolis men in these ranks—Duke Davis being an exception—and second was the fact of his being older than them in an age group where a few years made a big difference. Among other squadron commanders, he was five years older than Galer and he had six years on Smith. He had been at Annapolis before either of them were in high school.

It was fitting that when the Coach at last assumed the leadership of Cactus Fighter Command on October 17, he had the credibility of a fighter pilot who had become an ace after two missions, and who had downed four enemy aircraft on each of two missions.

The Coach brought an aggressive new philosophy to Guadalcanal fighter operations. As Marine Major Timothy Clubb wrote in a 1982 Command and General Staff College thesis, Bauer was "considered one of the best fighter pilots in the Marine Corps at the time ... a man who was willing to take risks ... In contrast to previous tactics, Bauer espoused fighting Zeros under any condition. He believed that US pilots could defeat the Japanese pilots in one-on-one engagements and should not avoid them."

At 0720hrs on October 17, when 18 Zeros headed for Henderson Field, escorting 18 D3A Vals, ten of the strike force went down. Clubb quoted Bauer as having said "there's no way to make war safe. The thing to do is make it very unsafe for the enemy."

As was concluded in the Clubb study, Joe Bauer's "aggressive style of dogfighting caused an increase in Japanese fighter losses at a critical point in the campaign."

As Joe Foss put it more succinctly, Bauer "had a positive, hard-hitting philosophy of air combat that always tickled me."

With Bauer and VMF-212 on Guadalcanal that week were two future double-digit aces who were assigned to VMF-212, but who had scored their initial aerial victories while "freelancing" with John L. Smith's VMF-223 in August and September 1942.

Jack Conger scored his third and fourth aerial victories, a Zero and a Betty, on October 18, shortly after rejoining VMF-212. A Zero downed on October 21 would make him an ace.

Doc Everton, who had scored three with VMF-223, joined Joe Bauer among the aces of VMF-212 on October 20. Everton led his flight as they intercepted an inbound IJNAF strike force, and downed one G4M bomber and a Zero.

October 20 marked a sudden reversal of fortune for Everton. As he later explained, "we were just outnumbered and I didn't see the guy in back of me and he just laid some rounds into the cockpit and the engine. I made it back into the field, dead stick, and they carted me up to their bamboo hospital there on Guadalcanal and then evacuated me."

At first, they wanted to evacuate him in a USAAF C-47, but Everton, who had spent two years as an Army officer after he finished the ROTC course in college, refused to fly in an Army aircraft. "Take me back to the hospital," he insisted. "I'm not going to ride on that airplane. I'll take my chances up there instead of this airplane. The reason was that they were such damn poor navigators. They couldn't find their way inside of a hat on a bright day."

When his friend, Marine aviator Art Adams, happened to walk by, Everton found out that he was going to Espiritu Santo and asked him for a ride. They took off in the midst of Japanese shelling of the field, but made it to Espiritu Santo in fine shape. As Everton tells the story, the USAAF aircraft that he was supposed to be on was found to have crash landed on a reef about 200 miles north of the tip of New Caledonia after the pilot got lost.

That same week, wheels were turning behind the lines beyond the control of the Cactus Air Force. Just a few miles to the south and west, 20,000 Japanese troops were stirring, preparing for the long-awaited assault aimed at throwing the Americans off Guadalcanal once and for all. On October 23, the IJNAF sent an armada of G4M bombers and 25 Zeros to soften up Henderson on the eve of the planned ground attack.

Knowing that the Japanese had a big move in the offing, Joe Bauer had ordered the squadrons to push their maintenance crews to have the maximum number of fighters ready. VMF-212 launched ten Wildcats, while five were contributed by the US Navy's VF-71, which had joined the Cactus Air Force after their ship, the USS *Wasp* (CV-7), was sunk on September 15 by the Japanese submarine *I-19*.

From VMF-121, both Duke Davis and Joe Foss led flights to intercept the Zeros, which arrived in two layers at separate altitudes. Davis took his flight high, to where there were both Zeros and bombers, while Foss went after the other stratum.

One aggressive Zero pilot got on the tail of a Wildcat and Foss quickly blew him out of the sky. His Nakajima Sakae radial engine came off in what Foss described as "a crazy, lopsided whirl," and the pilot himself came out of the cockpit like "a pea that has been pressed from the pod."

When Foss turned hard to miss the cloud of debris, he quickly turned on another Zero pilot, who went into a loop to get away and behind Foss. Foss followed him and opened fire while both were upside down. Amazingly, his ammunition chutes did not jam, as they were prone to do in extreme maneuvering, and Foss scored his second for October 23.

Emerging out of his loop into target-rich skies, Foss saw a Zero in the midst of what may have been a victory roll and opened fire. As this aircraft exploded in a "lovely, blinding flash," he watched as its pilot "still buckled in his seat, popped out of the cockpit," only to be spattered by fragments of burning Zero. As Robert Leckie wrote in *Challenge for the Pacific*, "the Coach's theory was proved correct: Well-handled Wildcats could defeat Zeros in circling combat."

Foss's next encounter could have been his last. As Foss leveled out after his third victory for the day, he saw two Zeros converging on him, one from an angle and the other head on. Foss took the challenge of the second one and his game of "chicken." He felt the impact of the Zero's bullets just aft of his cowling, and saw tongues of flame. A split second later, he passed within a hair's breadth of a collision just as the A6M exploded off the Wildcat's wingtip.

As the other Zero moved in behind his crippled, smoking aircraft, Foss pushed the stick forward, "thanked the Lord for plenty of altitude," and escaped in a steep dive. He returned to Fighter One with a badly damaged F4F, having shot down four enemy fighters in a single mission, to raise his overall score to 11. For October 23, VMF-121 and VMF-212 had each shot down 11 Japanese aircraft, delivering a steeper than usual cost to the IJNAF.

Meanwhile, a thousand miles to the south in Noumea, Admiral Bull Halsey, who had just arrived to take command of SOPAC on October 18, met with General Vandergrift on October 23 to discuss the same thing—the American toehold on Guadalcanal. Should the Americans cut their losses and abandon the virtually untenable toehold on Guadalcanal? The Japanese controlled the sea lanes, at least by night, and they were close enough to the American perimeter that they could use both naval and land bombardment to pummel American positions, including Henderson Field itself.

As if to underscore Vandergrift's promise that he could hold Guadalcanal if Halsey sent him the reinforcements that he needed,

Bauer had aggressively scrambled every available aircraft, and VMF-121, VMF-212, and VF-71 had defeated the Japanese in the air that day.

The following day, President Roosevelt put his own stamp on the importance of this island in the Solomons. In a classified memo to the Joint Chiefs of Staff, he directed them to "make sure that every possible weapon gets into the area to hold Guadalcanal, and that having held in this crisis, munitions, planes and crews are on the way to take advantage of our success."

Notwithstanding their defeat overhead, the Japanese ground attack on the western side of the American perimeter came on the night of October 23. The plan had been for a coordinated attack from both the west and south, but Major General Tadashi Sumiyoshi got his wires crossed and jumped off a day too soon. This allowed the Americans to focus all their attention on his force, thwarting his assault and inflicting heavy losses.

The attack from the south was delayed until October 25, but it met the same fate as the October 23 debacle. By this time, the US Army troops that were offloaded at Guadalcanal from the reinforcement convoy on October 13 were able to join the Marines on Henderson Field and the Lunga Point perimeter.

Things went especially wrong when small Japanese units penetrated the Henderson perimeter and reports of this were magnified by Japanese miscommunication to suggest that the field had been captured. Overhead, Japanese carrier aircraft began circling in confident preparation for landing at Henderson as soon as they received the signal that the Japanese Army had taken it from the defending Marines.

Neither the Navy's VF-5 and VF-71 nor the Marine VMF-121 and VMF-212 had been briefed on the Japanese "capture" of the Henderson Field complex on October 25. Though operations were hampered by muddy conditions at the Fighter One airstrip, Joe Bauer's Cactus Fighter Command rose to deliver a rude surprise. All were in the air by 1000hrs to meet the Zeros.

The Flying Circus shot down three, two of which were claimed by Foss himself.

The huge air battle continued to thunder overhead, with a wave of a dozen Bettys and their fighters inbound to the American positions. Foss again took to the air, but was immediately attacked by a Zero. Foss outmaneuvered him into overshooting and quickly shot him down. Now short of ammunition, Foss decided to head back to Fighter One, but on the way he got into a scrap with another two Zeros. They ganged up on him, but he whipped his Wildcat around and went after them.

When the dust settled on October 25, the tally for the day at VMF-121 stood at 18 enemy aircraft shot down, the largest single day total in squadron history. Joe Foss had downed five Zeros in two missions, marking his own best day ever, and bringing his score to 16 after just 12 days.

Back in the States, Foss was beginning to be noticed. In an October 26 dispatch from "An Advanced South Pacific Base," F. Tillman Durdin of the *New York Times* compared him to John L. Smith, noting that Foss was "crowding" America's leading ace in "piling up ace scores."

"With several weeks ahead of him, Foss is gunning for a world American record of enemy planes destroyed," wrote Durdin. "Captain Foss is a 'natural' flier. He seems to know instinctively what tactics to use to get his man."

The journalist went on to provide a portrait from the field of America's budding hero, writing that "modest and fun-loving, he is the spark plug and joke master of the pursuit fliers on Guadalcanal. His favorite pastime is to sit around with his tentmates at night and act the role of a Japanese airfield commandant counting noses after the riddled remnants of Zero formations have returned from raids on Guadalcanal ... Foss, who sports a drooping, mandarin-type mustache, puts his audience in stitches as he gives his imitation of a purple-faced Japanese general."

October 25 was also a busy day for Jack Conger of VMF-212. During the intercept of a Japanese strike force, he found himself alone in a patch of sky filled with Zeros. He managed to shoot down two, and emptied his guns trying to down a third directly above Henderson Field.

Among those watching 1,500 feet below was Joe Foss, the man who had been kicked out of a Sioux Falls movie theater by Conger about a decade earlier.

As Foss related in his 1992 memoirs, Conger "turned his Grumman straight up as the Zero flew over, intending to use his propeller as a buzz saw to take off the enemy's tail rudder … Conger misjudged and hit halfway between the tail and the cockpit, chewing at least five feet of the Zero's tail before both planes started falling toward the water."

Conger escaped his falling Wildcat and pulled his ripcord, and looked out to watch the Japanese pilot coming down closer to shore beneath his own parachute.

Joe Foss recalled that he reached the beach in a commandeered jeep just as some sailors and Marines were headed out in a Higgins Boat to pick up the two pilots. The Japanese flier being nearest, they reached him first, but he waved them off, a gesture they took to mean that he was being chivalrous and wanting them to pick up the American first.

"Your friend back there said to pick you up first," the men in the Higgins Boat told Conger.

"He's a real sport," Conger replied.

When they circled back, the Marines wanted to shoot the Japanese pilot, but Conger insisted that he be rescued. Conger himself leaned down to grab him, but as he was pulled up over the side, he pulled his Nambu pistol and tried to shoot Conger at point-blank range. However, when he squeezed the trigger, the waterlogged 8mm ammunition misfired. He then put the gun to his own head and tried unsuccessfully to kill himself. Conger clobbered him with a gasoline can.

IJNAF Petty Officer Shiro Ishikawa was the first Japanese pilot captured in the Solomons, and he spent the remainder of the war in a New Zealand POW camp. In April 1990 he crossed paths with Conger once again at an aviation enthusiast event in the United States and the two men talked at great length. He thanked Conger for saving his life.

Halting the Japanese offensive on the ground was a serious boost for morale. While only a dozen of the 35 Cactus fighters were flyable at the end of the day on October 25, the job was done.

———

In a coordinated move, the Japanese Navy attempted to draw the US Navy into a decisive battle at sea. The two sides met about 400 miles to the east between October 25 and 27 in the Battle of the Santa Cruz Islands. The Japanese suffered serious damage to two carriers, while the Americans lost their carrier USS *Hornet* and one destroyer sunk. Both sides lost close to 100 aircraft. In the end, it was a narrow, but indecisive, Japanese victory. Both sides were compelled to retire, and the Japanese would not get their wish for a decisive battle until the middle of November. But then we should add the maxim, "be careful what you wish for."

To support their forces on Guadalcanal, the IJN depended on destroyers, which the Japanese favored as fast troop transports in their Tokyo Express operations. These were supported overhead by IJNAF floatplanes, which operated from the water, and thereby stayed in close proximity to the ships. These aircraft included A6M2-N "Rufes" and Mitsubishi F1M1 "Petes." The Rufe, which the Americans usually called a "floatplane Zero," was the Nakajima-built floatplane variant of the Zero. Though used as a fighter, the Rufe was less maneuverable than a Zero because of its floats. The Pete was a biplane floatplane designed as an observation aircraft, but it was used occasionally in combat. In addition to its pilot, the Pete carried a gunner with a rearward firing machine gun.

These floatplanes had a base at Rekata Bay on the northeast side of Santa Isabel Island, about 170 miles from Guadalcanal. On October 30, Joe Bauer led VMF-212 on an attack that destroyed a number of these aircraft. Among these were a Pete and a Rufe that brought Jack Conger to his final score of ten aerial victories. Conger would be awarded the Navy Cross, and would return to the Pacific in 1944, but his scoring days were over.

IO

Joe Foss Takes the Lead

November

After the frenetic action that culminated in the defeat of the great Japanese onslaught at the end of October, the American ground forces turned things around and began a methodical offensive against Japanese positions on the first of November. Overhead, there was a brief lull in the air action over Guadalcanal. Joe Foss recalled that "sitting and waiting began to get us down," so the Marine aviators of VMF-121 turned to strafing Japanese ground positions.

The inaction came to an end on November 7, 1942 when word came in that an especially large Japanese reinforcement effort was coming down through the Slot by daylight to deliver more ground troops to Guadalcanal. It included around ten fast transport destroyers, escorted by a cruiser. Joe Foss and his VMF-121 Flying Circus were tasked with taking on the IJNAF floatplanes from Rekata Bay that were protecting the Japanese convoy, while American dive bombers and torpedo bombers attacked the ships themselves.

As Foss's men reached the convoy, the Japanese floatplanes were already in action, having intercepted another flight of Wildcats. Foss closed in on a Rufe that was on the tail of a Wildcat, and destroyed him with one of his trademark short bursts at close range, while his wingman, Boot Furlow, flamed a second Rufe.

Meanwhile, Danny Doyle was out of sorts. He had been deeply depressed since Casey Brandon, his best friend and wingman, had been killed in late October. Foss had grounded Doyle for a while to give him time to pull himself together, but had allowed him back in the air that day. He wished that he hadn't.

Foss remembered that he watched Doyle line up for a head-on pass against another Rufe. Neither aircraft pulled out of the game of chicken and they collided in a deadly fireball. Foss recalled that Doyle's death "hit me harder because I let him fly when he was still upset." Ironically, this Rufe had been Doyle's fifth Japanese aircraft destroyed, making him a posthumous ace.

When Foss looked around, a flaming Rufe passed so close that he could see its pilot struggling to get out of his parachute harness so that he could die with his aircraft. The sky was filled with blossoming parachutes with empty harnesses. Foss wondered about "what strange vow they had taken" that cost the IJNAF the lives of trained pilots who might have survived.

With the Rufes out of the way, VMF-121 joined the bombers in attacking the ships. Foss dispatched the Flying Circus in reverse order so that he could cover their tails. As "Swivelneck Joe" scanned the sky above and behind, he spotted a slow-moving Pete coming out of a cloud behind him.

He circled up to attack, but misjudged the biplane's speed and overshot him. As he did so, his Wildcat presented a wonderful target for the Pete's rear gunner, who stitched a line of lead along Foss's forward fuselage—including one round through his cockpit canopy and another that knocked out his radio. Turning again, Foss made a second pass, pouring some of his own lead into the Pete's wing root and sawing off the wing.

As this aircraft went down, Foss spotted a second Pete. Attacking from below, where the gunner could not get at him, he made quick work of his third victim for the day.

When he leveled out, he saw his own Flying Circus in the distance. They had formed up and were heading back to Guadalcanal. Foss now realized that his radio was not working, so he could not tell them that he was still alive. As he tried to accelerate to catch up, his engine started to cough and smoke. At first he had thought no serious damage had been done by the rounds he had taken from the Pete gunner, but he had been wrong.

Foss calculated his position and headed for Henderson. As the sun went down and a rain squall loomed ahead, he struggled on while his engine sputtered and clattered—and finally quit.

Spotting a small island in the distance, Foss glided down toward it, hoping to find a sandy beach on which to land, but he ran out of speed and altitude faster that he would have liked, and he ditched into the sea. He had opened his canopy in preparation for a quick escape, but on impact, it slammed shut. To make matters worse, the Wildcat nosed over in the water and begin to sink like a rock.

Joe Foss was in a frightening predicament—trying to open his canopy underwater as the aircraft was plummeting toward the bottom of Ironbottom Sound. Struggling not to choke on salt water as he unfastened his leg straps, he fought to free himself from his aluminum coffin as it sank deeper and deeper. "The need to breathe was uncontrollable," he later recalled. "My craving for air was pure pain."

When he finally thought he was free, his foot got caught under the seat. He had to double over and go back into the cockpit to free it. When he finally did, he was abruptly jerked upward by the buoyancy of his Mae West lifejacket and his floatable parachute pack. He reached the surface head down and had to battle his own gear to get into a position where his head was above water.

This done, he thought to himself that all he had to do was swim five miles against the current through a raging storm—in the dark. This assessment came *before* he saw the circling shark fins.

After several torturous hours had passed, Foss heard voices that were not merely within his own head, and the slap of paddles. Someone was coming through the night in a boat. He was sure that it was the Japanese—until he heard an Australian accent. He called out, and lights came on. He saw that there were two canoes filled mainly with islanders, but among them were a Catholic missionary named Dan Stuyvenberg and an Australian mill owner from Malaita Island named Tommy Robertson.

They took him to the Catholic mission on Malaita, where he was treated to a warm fire and dry clothes. As he enjoyed the dinner they offered—his first fresh meat in weeks—he filled them in on the news of the world, about which they had heard very little since the Japanese occupied many of the neighboring islands.

After Mass the following morning, the sound of an airplane flying low over the island could be heard. Foss identified it as a Wildcat and began waving. Before the day was over, the Marine PBY flying boat belonging to General Roy Geiger, with Foss's old friend Major Jack Cram at the controls, landed in the small harbor and the islanders rowed Foss out to meet it.

Two days later, Foss flew over the island to drop a package to his friends. In addition to razor blades, candy bars and tobacco, it contained "the newest three-month-old magazines."

Fourteen years later, Robertson and Foss would meet one another again in the States on the set of the *This Is Your Life* television show.

When Foss reached Henderson Field late on November 8, the Associated Press wire service had already carried a story datelined Guadalcanal that told of the raid on the Japanese convoy, and had spoken of the four pilots who did not come back. One was Foss, and another was Jack Stub—but like Foss, he had survived and was recovered. Several days later, having spent time on Malaita himself, he walked into the operations building at Henderson to report back for duty.

In the meantime, there had been a changing of the guard on Guadalcanal. An exhausted Roy Geiger, now a major general, was succeeded by his chief of staff, Brigadier General Louis Earnest Woods, who took command of MAW-1 and of the Cactus Air Force. In his 1990 book, *Guadalcanal: The Definitive Account of the Landmark Battle*, Richard Frank said of Woods that this veteran Marine aviator was promptly recast from a "kindly colonel to a blood thirsty brigadier general." He would preside over the Cactus Air Force during its most grueling six weeks before turning the reins over to Brigadier General Francis Mulcahy on the day after Christmas.

On November 9, Admiral Halsey, three weeks on the job as SOPAC commander, arrived on Guadalcanal to see and be seen and to assess the situation first hand. His predecessor, the reticent Vice Admiral Robert Ghormley, had never been near Guadalcanal in his more than three months on the job. Halsey also carried with him Distinguished Service Crosses for Wally Wethe, Bill Freeman, and Joe Foss.

The citations were all for "extraordinary achievement" in aerial combat between October 13 and 20. The one awarded to Foss cited his "constant aggressiveness, skill, and leadership." When the citation was written, his score stood at seven, but that was out of date. The three aerial victories that Foss had claimed on November 7 brought his total to 19, matching that of John L. Smith when he had left the theater about a month earlier.

On November 11, Foss and Boot Furlow went out at sunrise on a strafing expedition up to the floatplane rookery at Rekata Bay, and they missed one of the biggest air battles yet seen over Guadalcanal. They returned to Fighter One as the battle was ongoing, but could not immediately refuel. When they finally did get airborne, it was over.

The Circus had done well without them. Nemo Loesch, Rudy Ruddell, and Wally Wethe were among the Marines that accounted for 11 Japanese aircraft shot down. Duke Davis, VMF-121's commander, also scored, but he took a face full of shrapnel when a 20mm shell came through his canopy. Foss reported that the corpsmen had to bandage his jaw carefully so that he could wear his oxygen mask for his next mission. Meanwhile, however, Roger Haberman took a bullet in the knee and had to be evacuated, while Tom Mann and Joe Palko were shot down. Mann later returned, but Palko had died.

Having missed the action on November 11, Joe Foss was anxious to be part of it the next day. The morning of November 12 brought low cloud cover and it was correctly predicted by the Americans that the Japanese bombers would arrive from the east rather than the north, using a slab of cloud cover hanging above Florida Island as a shield.

Diving from 29,000 feet, their canopies frosting up as they hit the warmer air, the Flying Circus tore into the first wave of G4M bombers and their Zero escorts.

The sky was filled with flak as the US Navy ships off Guadalcanal put up a wall of antiaircraft fire. A flight from VMF-112 under Paul Fontana also joined in the intercept, and the USAAF 67th Fighter Squadron had P-39s in the air.

Joe Foss picked out a Betty bomber, thumbed his trigger and watched its right engine burst into flames. As this bomber cartwheeled toward the sea, Foss looked for another and found it.

He was about to open fire when a Zero suddenly appeared on his six. He pulled out, let the enemy fighter overshoot him and the hunted became the hunter. After a short burst to the wing root and the fuel tank, he watched this fighter explode just a few feet above Ironbottom Sound.

Foss then roared back to the bombers and found what he thought to be the same one he had tried to target before the Zero had intervened. He made a first pass but missed, then came around for a second in which his guns found their target, shearing the left wing from this G4M.

Of the entire Japanese strike force, only two bombers survived the fusillade thrown at them by the American fighters and the antiaircraft guns of the ships below.

The great air battle of November 11 had, by Joe Foss's recollection, lasted eight minutes. In that space of time, he had increased his total score to 22, eclipsing that of John L. Smith and anointing him as the leading American ace anywhere.

11

Tipping Points

November into December

The battle was joined on Friday the 13th. The Imperial Japanese Navy had sought a decisive naval battle in the sea around the Solomon Islands since the Americans had interrupted their grand strategy for the South Pacific in August. Three months later, they got what they had asked for.

The battle was actually two battles 48 hours apart, mainly during the wee small hours of November 13 and 15, 1942. Often called the Naval Battle of Guadalcanal, it is also seen as the third and fourth battles of Savo Island, referring to the 12-square-mile rock between Tulagi and Guadalcanal around which the great seaborne clash would swirl. Arguably it should have been named after these waters, originally called Savo Sound, but renamed Ironbottom Sound. More iron was about to be added.

In the course of the Pacific War, the importance of the battle was substantial. As at Midway, it was not so much a turning point as it was a *tipping* point. As defined by the physicists, a tipping point is a threshold, the point at which an entity is displaced from a position of established balance into a new equilibrium significantly unlike what had existed previously. A tipping point is a moment of critical mass, from which previous momentum is interrupted and from which it cannot continue as it had done.

The battle began as an attempt by the Japanese to reinforce their garrison on Guadalcanal for the thus-far elusive battle that would push the Allies off the island. To support this effort, Admiral Isoroku Yamamoto, commander of the Japanese Combined Fleet and the infamous architect of Pearl Harbor, sent an overwhelming contingent of warships. To augment the ten cruisers and 16 destroyers commanded by Vice Admiral Hiroaki Abe, Yamamoto added the battleships *Hiei* and *Kirishima*, the former becoming Abe's flagship. The skies would be flooded with Bettys and Zeros. The air strikes interrupted by the Marines on November 11 and 12 were part of this plan.

As the Japanese descended the Slot, Rear Admiral Daniel Callahan, aboard his flagship heavy cruiser USS *San Francisco* (CA-38), brought five cruisers and eight destroyers to meet them. This confrontation began just before 0200hrs on November 13, only about 20 miles northwest of Henderson Field. In the ferocious battle that ensued—much of it at point-blank range—losses were steep on both sides, with four Japanese and six American warships put out of commission, and two American cruisers badly damaged. Several Japanese transport ships were sunk, and the rest retreated. The planned landing of Japanese reinforcements was postponed, and the scheduled bombardment of Henderson Field by Japanese warships did not happen.

When the sun came up on November 13, Marine torpedo bombers from Henderson laid into the badly crippled *Hiei* and maimed her further. At around 1000hrs on that Friday the 13th, Joe Foss led a Flying Circus vertical-dive strafing attack on the *Hiei*. He came out of his dive so low that he thought he'd almost hit the superstructure. By the end of the day, the once-great warship was so thoroughly damaged that she was scuttled by her own crew.

November 14 was the lull between the two storms of the Naval Battle of Guadalcanal. It was obvious that the fight was not yet over, and the opposing fleets sent in reinforcements.

Overhead, on November 13, future double-digit ace Archie Glenn Donahue and two other VMF-112 men took off on a combat air patrol at 0630hrs. They intercepted a half-dozen Zeros, one of which became Donahue's first aerial victory. His second, another Zero, came the following day. He would complete his road to becoming an ace in spectacular fashion in 1943.

Lieutenant Colonel Joe Bauer, the inimitable "Coach," was regarded by most Marine aviators who knew him on Guadalcanal as one of the best fighter pilots in the Cactus Air Force. With two four-victory missions to his credit, he had clearly proven himself.

However, he was the Coach. As the leader of Cactus Fighter Command, he had spent most of his time on Guadalcanal behind a clipboard, running a show in which he had not taken part.

Bauer's life was one of responding to the unending flurry of requests to "put me in, Coach." Finally, on November 14, the Coach decided that it was time for him to put *himself* in.

He told Joe Foss that he was going to join the Flying Circus as they took off around 1600hrs to escort SBDs to the area around the Russell Islands, where Japanese ships were licking their wounds after the night before.

All Foss had to say was "you lead, Coach."

Things began with a hiccup. As the Wildcats were started up to begin their takeoff roll, the one that Bauer was to fly had some engine trouble. Foss ordered Nemo Loesch to take the lead, while Foss and his wingman, Boot Furlow, stayed back to accompany Bauer when he was able to take off.

Finally, all three were airborne and headed northwest, up the Slot to where the Japanese ships were mustering for their planned movements that night. They were flying low to the water when they were jumped from above by eight Zeros.

Bauer engaged one Zero, quickly knocking it down, while Foss and Furlow each went on the attack against other Japanese fighters. The one that Foss was chasing flew so low over a Japanese destroyer that Foss had to pull up to keep from colliding with the ship. The Zero got away, but Foss found another and shot it down. Just as he watched Furlow down a Zero, Foss noticed that his radio had gone out—as the radios in the Wildcats often did.

Furlow formed up with Foss and they began looking for Bauer.

At last, they spotted an oil slick about a dozen miles due north of the Russells. Beside it, they saw Bauer floating in the water in his Mae West, unharmed. He waved to them and pointed to a nearby island, apparently indicating that he planned to swim to it.

Furlow radioed Fighter One and explained the situation. As he and Foss raced back, a Grumman J2F-5 Duck amphibian was made ready for a rescue mission. As soon as they returned, Foss crawled aboard the Duck, and Joe Renner began his takeoff roll before Foss had even climbed up through the aircraft to the rear cockpit.

By the time they got back to where the Coach had last been seen, the sun was down. The water was studded with burning wreckage from the Japanese troop transports that had been damaged in the naval battle and from the earlier air battle with the Zeros. Japanese destroyers, running without lights, were also in the area. Escorted by Wildcats circling overhead, Renner circled back, forth and all around with the Duck, frequently within a few feet of the water, but there was no sign of Joe Bauer.

As the sun was coming up on the morning of November 15, Renner was over the site again, escorted by Foss and the Flying Circus. They were interrupted by at least two Japanese Aichi E13A "Jake" floatplanes, which were probably in the area rescuing survivors from the ongoing naval battles. Oscar Bate downed one of them, and the other became Joe Foss's twenty-third aerial victory.

Again, the Marines scoured the surface of the water in a vain effort to find the needle of Joe Bauer in the haystack of the flotsam of the naval battle.

On November 24, Archie Donahue and three other aviators from VMF-112 escorted a J2F seaplane up to the island nearest where Bauer went down. The Duck landed and a team went ashore to query the islanders living there about anyone who might have seen the Coach. The VMF-112 war diary reports that "no survivors were picked up, but the natives reported two white men in the outlying villages." There was no mention of a visit to these villages.

In a February 1943 letter, Joe Foss told Bauer's parents of this frustrating search, and that the Marines did ask the local people to be on the lookout for him. One American pilot who had crashed five miles farther at sea than Bauer did show up, and he had been in the water for an excruciating 49 hours.

There have been numerous guesses as to what might have happened to Bauer. These once included the optimistic hope that he may have reached an island and survived, but they also included the possibility of a shark attack, and the probability that he was picked up by the Japanese. No specific evidence of any of those scenarios ever surfaced. The Coach disappeared without a trace and was declared KIA after the war. His total number of aerial victories stood at 11.

The main airfield on Efate, known as Efate Field or Vila Field, after the nearly town of Vila, was renamed Bauer Field. Still an operating airport, it continues to bear Joe Bauer's name.

It was on that night, November 14–15, the night that Joe Bauer was floating in the sea, that the other shoe of the Naval Battle of Guadalcanal dropped.

When the sun went down, the Japanese fleet, reinforced and reconfigured, moved again against the Americans at sea and on Guadalcanal. Commanded this time by Admiral Nobutake Kondo, the Japanese force included four cruisers, nine destroyers and the battleship *Kirishima*, a survivor of the previous battle. They were escorting four transports. The US Navy force under Admiral Willis Lee included none of the five cruisers of the previous battle, as one had been sunk and the others had withdrawn because of damage. The new force was spearheaded by four destroyers and backed up by the battleships USS *Washington* (BB-56) and USS *South Dakota* (BB-57), which Admiral Halsey had detached from the battle group of the USS *Enterprise* (CV-6).

The pivotal battle began before midnight and continued for several hours. Two American destroyers were sunk, two others put out of action, and the *South Dakota* damaged. The *Washington*, however, took on and sank the *Kirishima*.

The four Japanese transports reached Guadalcanal by 0400hrs, but they were destroyed by the Cactus Air Force and naval gunfire before they could offload more than a handful of troops, and almost no supplies. Again, the planned naval bombardment of Henderson Field could not be carried out. Yamamoto angrily ordered a withdrawal of the warships. All plans to attempt to dislodge the Americans from Guadalcanal were permanently shelved, although the Tokyo Express would continue to run. The forward momentum of the Japanese war machine in the Solomons had come to a halt.

That week, another end was marked. The curtain had come down on the first combat tour of the original cast of characters who came to Guadalcanal with VMF-121 on October 9. Some, like Joe Foss, would have a second act, but most of them began to travel back through Noumea on their way home, or to Australia for a stint of R&R. Nemo Loesch, Tom Mann, and Bill Marontate were among the first to go, and the others trickled south over the coming days as transportation aboard the hard-working SCAT Skytrains became available.

Oscar Bate, Bill Freeman, and Boot Furlow went south on November 19. Joe Foss was with them, but for him, it was a medevac flight. Several hours past midnight on November 16, he woke up in a pool of his own sweat. He was suffering from the aches and fever, as well as the delirium and double vision, of malaria. In his memoirs, he mused about what a mosquito had done to him and what the IJNAF had failed to do.

On December 7, 1942, the first anniversary of the Japanese attack on Pearl Harbor was marked with guarded optimism in the United States. John L. Smith, who had only just been eclipsed by Joe Foss as America's leading ace, was on the cover of *Life* magazine on that day. Bob Galer, Marion Carl and he had been awarded the Navy Cross in the field, and now there was talk of the Medal of Honor.

Yet this hopefulness was only in comparison with the first days of 1942. Back then, the Japanese juggernaut raging across Asia was unstoppable. Japanese armies were in Manila and Hong Kong. The Marines on Wake Island had been defeated and there was no place where the momentum was not on the enemy's side. Though this had been curbed by December 1942, the enemy was far from being defeated.

Those aggressive drives, the blood-red arrows on the situation maps, had now been blunted in New Guinea and on Guadalcanal, but the enemy war machine remained so sufficiently robust that few strategic planners on the Allied side could be sure that they would not gain the initiative once again.

Henderson Field, which had hung on by a thread since August, would never be retaken by the Japanese, and both sides now realized this. The Japanese troops who still occupied much of the island were the ones now hanging on by a thread—and many were dying of disease and malnutrition. The Japanese had already made their decision to abandon Guadalcanal and evacuate their troops, though this would not be fully implemented until February 1943.

Over Henderson Field, the systematic air raids by large numbers of Japanese aircraft gradually grew fewer as December wore on, though the artillery barrages from Japanese lines continued.

The skies, once routinely filled with swarms of IJNAF aircraft, were now generally quiet, except for an occasional nighttime visit from "Washing Machine Charlie," one of the lone, slow-moving aircraft with rickety engines that sounded like washing machine motors, which the Japanese sent over the American lines to harass the Marines while they were trying to sleep.

Phrases such as "routine local patrol ... no contact was made with the enemy and all returned safely," which were posted day after day that week in the VMF-112 log, were commonplace. On December 14, that squadron noted that "patrols have become very tiring and boring assignments."

At one point in December, there was great excitement when a coastwatcher reported a large four-engine, twin-tailed aircraft headed for Guadalcanal. Wildcat pilots scrambled eagerly, thinking it might be an IJNAF Kawanishi H6K flying boat, but to their disappointment, it turned out to be a USAAF B-24 Liberator.

There were changes in the command structure. On the day after Christmas, Brigadier Louis Woods handed over command of the Cactus Air Force to Brigadier General Francis Patrick Mulcahy, who had just arrived in SOPAC commanding the 2nd Marine Air Wing. As Marine Aviator No. 64, Mulcahy was an old timer who had flown in World War I, as well as in the Caribbean and Central America. In the 1945 Okinawa campaign, as a major general, he commanded the Tactical Air Force, Tenth Army, a joint-service command that included all American land-based airpower in the operation.

In December 1942, to accommodate the increasing number of its assets flowing into SOPAC—especially fighter squadrons equipped with P-38 Lightnings—the USAAF was also updating its own command structure. The new Thirteenth Air Force was constituted in December and activated in New Caledonia on January 13, 1943. Now under the command of Major General Nathan Farragut Twining, its headquarters moved forward to Espiritu Santo a week later.

The Thirteenth was to the SOPAC what the USAAF Fifth Air Force was for Douglas MacArthur's SWPA. A year older than the Thirteenth, the Fifth had grown into a substantial force under the command of "MacArthur's airman," General George Churchill Kenney. Unlike the joint service command structure in the Solomons, Kenney operated independently of the Navy and Marines.

Meanwhile on Guadalcanal, as the USAAF was beginning to play a more extensive role, Marine air was evolving organizationally. Lieutenant Colonel Samuel Sloan Jack, who had been the first commander of VMF-121 back before Foss and Marontate were in the squadron, had succeeded Joe Bauer as the head of the Cactus Fighter Command, a post he would retain until July 1943.

With the decisive battles behind them, and the general decrease in activity, many aviators were pulled out of Guadalcanal and rotated back to Espiritu Santo, Noumea, or even to Australia for rest and recreation. For the men who had been in the air on an almost daily basis for weeks, or even months, such a break had become imperative. As Duke Davis of VMF-121 later explained, "there was a very high fatigue factor in Guadalcanal … unless you've been subjected to it … you can't understand it."

By December, there was also a number of aviators who had become stricken with malaria. When Joe Foss left on November 19, he had been a mess. The sickness had wrapped him in its cloak of feverish delusion. Many other men would follow. Davis went so far as to say that

> most of the pilots that did a tour up there [Guadalcanal] ended up with dysentery and malaria. We couldn't take quinine because it gives you a balance disturbance due to a blood pressure change … And the result was that we took atabrine [mepacrine or quinacrine], which is nothing more than a deterrent and it will hold you for a while, but ultimately malaria will get you. I personally lost about 35 pounds in six weeks up there … due to the dysentery, I lived for about two weeks on bismuth and paregoric every four hours just … so [I] could fly.

Foss lost nearly 40 pounds, but he recalled that "Bill Freeman was so sick for a while he couldn't even talk." They were, however, among the lucky ones. Of those who survived malaria's wrath, some never returned to their squadrons. Others were out for months. Archie Donahue of VMF-112, who contracted malaria in December, did not return until April 1943.

Many malaria patients were evacuated to Noumea for hospitalization, where SOPAC had commandeered a hospital. As they recuperated the aviators convalesced in what they called the "aviatorium." A similar facility with the same name was established by the USAAF in Auckland, New Zealand. They were a sort of sanatorium that Foss described as "a garage for aviators who needed a rest and a tune-up."

12

Matching the Ace of Aces

January

As the sun rose on the first day of 1943, Joseph Jacob Foss, now America's foremost ace in the Pacific, returned to Guadalcanal, stepping off an R4D Skytrain at Henderson Field after an absence of six weeks, due to two bouts with malaria.

After a brief stint in Australia and a short relapse with the malaria that had crippled him in November, Foss was back at a Henderson Field he did not recognize. During his absence, roads had been paved, telephone lines strung, and muddy runways covered with Marston Mats, perforated steel planking (PSP), which dramatically improved operations.

While the raids by large numbers of Japanese aircraft had largely petered out by mid-December, occasional attacks did continue. However, the almost daily dogfights directly over Henderson Field were becoming a distant memory. Foss noted that he missed this action—to which he had become accustomed.

VMF-121 was now operating out of Fighter Two, or Kukum Field, located about a mile or so to the west of the main Henderson area. Several members of Foss's old Flying Circus, who had been pulled out to the aviatorium or to Australia during December, had also now returned. These included Oscar Bate, Bill Freeman, Boot Furlow, Roger Haberman, Nemo Loesch, Bill Marontate, and Skeezix Presley.

The situation had changed dramatically since the fall of 1942. Most of VMF-121's missions involved strafing the occasional Japanese transport ship. In his diary, Foss complained that "all the days seem the same," adding later that "I thrived on aerial combat and just wanted to get in there and win the war."

Aerial combat still occurred—Nemo Loesch led one four-Wildcat patrol that netted six enemy aircraft—but it eluded Foss until the middle of the month.

On January 15, Foss was able to note that "things are starting to look like old times," but the mission assigned to the Flying Circus that afternoon started out as a routine escort mission. Seven Circus F4Fs and some USAAF P-39s were escorting Marine SBD dive bombers against a pair of Japanese destroyers in the vicinity of New Georgia.

Suddenly, they spotted some "square-winged Zeros," the A6M3 Model 32 variant of the Zero, known as Hamp to the Allies. Foss sent three Wildcats to intercept the Hamps, while he and the others remained above, keeping an eye on a second cluster of enemy fighters that had appeared.

As the center of this air battle tumbled upward, Foss watched a Wildcat going down, minus a wing. He fired at a Hamp and missed, but a second one passed through his sights almost immediately, and was gone with a burst from Foss's guns.

A third Hamp passed him in pursuit of another Wildcat and Foss took him out as well. As Foss maneuvered out of this encounter, he spotted Oscar Bate with a Hamp on his tail.

Foss slid in close and opened fire. The Hamp maneuvered out of the way and turned against Foss head on. Both pilots fired, both pilots missed by inches, and they barely avoided a collision. Foss remembered clearly seeing the face of the enemy pilot.

This Japanese pilot made a wide turn and the two were at it in another head-on dash. When the enemy pilot broke off and turned slightly to the right, climbing to meet him, Foss poured lead into the enemy's cockpit area, but instead of going down, he made a wide circle to the right and came around for what seemed like a third pass. As he did so, two other Hamps entered on the scene, flying close to their comrade, so the outnumbered Foss turned away, ducking into a cloud. As he looked back, the Hamp that he had been fighting started trailing smoke, then it exploded and fell.

When the Wildcats regrouped and headed back, they found the Fighter Two field under attack, so they had to land under fire.

When the dust settled, the men of the Circus ascertained that the F4F that had gone down belonged to Bill Marontate. Bate and Presley had watched him in a head-on encounter with one of the Hamps—just as Foss had experienced twice that day—but the converging aircraft had not pulled out safely and the Hamp had clipped off Marontate's wing.

More than a year later, Foss ran into a man who had been a rear gunner in one of the SBDs that day. He remembered an F4F whose wing had been sheared off. He told Foss that the pilot had bailed out safely and he landed in the water near one of the Japanese destroyers. The men of VMF-121 knew that he had probably not escaped capture, but they held out hope that he had survived *after* he was picked up by the enemy.

"Some guys you remember for a long time," Foss told Jay Edgerton of the *Minneapolis Star-Tribune* in February 1949. "You can't seem to forget them. I always thought Marontate would come back. He was that kind of guy ... He was a good guy and a good pilot. I've always wished he could have come back."

With 13 aerial victories, Marontate was the second highest-scoring ace in VMF-121 and the only one other than Foss who was in double-digits. He was also one of the first Marine aces to be awarded a posthumous Navy Cross, the second highest award for valor given to Marines.

Though Marontate's loss dampened enthusiasm, January 15 marked the most successful day for the fighter pilots of VMF-121 since October 25, and its second best day ever, with a total of 17 aerial victories. As for Foss, his three victories in rapid succession that afternoon brought his total to 26. With this, he became the highest-scoring American ace, and the first to match the World War I total achieved by America's "Ace of Aces," Eddie Rickenbacker.

In his memoirs, Foss called Rickenbacker his "biggest childhood hero ... next to Charles Lindbergh," but he also claimed that he was "unaware of [his] record-setting accomplishment until [he] read about it in a newspaper article."

Perhaps this is true, but it is hard to imagine that the aviators on Guadalcanal, who kept meticulous tallies of aerial victories, had not been immediately aware of this milestone when it happened—and *celebrated* it. At home, the Associated Press wire service was aware of it, and it became headline news.

As he would when USAAF ace Richard Bong became the first American ace to *exceed* his World War I score in April 1944, Rickenbacker sent Foss a congratulatory letter and a case of whiskey. Both disappeared in transit. Foss later speculated that the letter wound up in the collection of a souvenir hunter. One cannot imagine what could *possibly* have happened to a case of whiskey passing through many hands as it made its way across rear echelon bases in the South Pacific.

On January 21, Foss was tasked with leading the Cactus Air Force in a massive escort mission for the highest level official delegation yet to visit Guadalcanal. Both Admiral Bull Halsey, the SOPAC commander, and Admiral Chester Nimitz, commander of the Pacific Ocean Areas, had visited Guadalcanal before, but today they arrived together. With them was Secretary of the Navy Frank Knox.

The VIPs spent four hours on Guadalcanal being given an extensive jeep tour of the island that was almost entirely cleared of Japanese positions. The visit was marred only by Knox being caught in official photographs with his helmet on *backward*.

The last missions flown by VMF-121 out of Henderson Field came four days later on January 25 when the Japanese mounted a major bomber attack against the Henderson Field area. Launching at 1245hrs, the Flying Circus F4Fs were joined by four USAAF P-38 Lightnings, a fast and powerful twin-engine fighter that had begun supplementing the inferior P-39s on Guadalcanal in November.

The scale of the Japanese strike force was best summarized in Foss's communication with Henderson after he'd seen it—"scramble everything!"

The IJNAF strike force included roughly two dozen G4M Bettys and almost as many dive bombers. They were escorted by more than 60 Zeros, of which a dozen were flying close to 12,000 feet, where the Circus was operating. Assuming that these were bait for a distraction to keep the Circus away from the American bombers, the P-38s successfully engaged the enemy, while Foss ordered his men to maintain their altitude and circle the enemy.

Foss later recalled noting that from his position, "waiting was almost more difficult than active combat, but if the Zeros were decoys, so were we."

The strategy seemed to work. As the additional fighters scrambled by the Cactus Air Force tore into the bombers, the Zero pilots high above grew suspicious when the Circus neither retreated from a superior force nor took the bait and attacked. They apparently assumed that more American fighters were nearby setting a trap, because they broke away and headed north, up the Slot, away from Guadalcanal. Foss likened it to bluffing in a poker game, commenting that "Old Foss had played the greatest empty hand of his life."

For Foss, the defining chapter of his life came to an end that day. On January 26, he and the long-time Circus veterans began the long trip back to the United States, to begin new chapters in their lives and careers. Two days later, VMF-121 was pulled out of Guadalcanal, back to Espiritu Santo, to regroup and reorganize. This would include the transition from their Grumman F4F-4 Wildcats to the new and more powerful gull-winged Chance Vought F4U-1 Corsair fighters.

In their four months of flying in combat with their Wildcats, the Marine aviators of VMF-121 had claimed, according to Robert Sherrod in *History of Marine Corps Aviation in World War II*, 165 aerial victories. After converting to Corsairs, the squadron would bring its final World War II victory total to 208, the most of any Marine Corps squadron ever—and it produced 14 aces. With 26 and 13 victories respectively, Joe Foss and Bill Marontate were the two double-digit men of VMF-121. Tom Mann had nine by the end of the war and Gregory "Nemo" Loesch of Foss's Flying Circus was next with 8.5.

13

The Long Season of the Dancing Bears

Who doesn't love a hero? In the winter of 1942–43, America desired, even demanded, heroes. The country was still reeling from the disaster of Pearl Harbor, the hopeless defeat of Bataan, and the dispiriting might and arrogance of the Axis.

Just as the British people, numbed by the devastation of the Blitz and by the bitter symbolism of Singapore, idealized the "Few" of the RAF, Americans saw larger-than-life symbolism in the leading Marine aces, who were at the time America's "Few," who stood up to the Japanese over Guadalcanal.

In that uncertain winter, even as Americans were being sent overseas in ever-growing numbers to battlefronts across the globe, others were coming home. Men like John L. Smith and Joe Foss came back to discover that they were no longer merely aviators among aviators, but inspiring lone warriors, like those from ancient literature— from Odysseus or Achilles to Lancelot or Galahad— and real heroes from American mythology such as Daniel Boone or Davy Crockett.

Theirs was the unique experience of thinking of oneself as average, yet discovering that they were being considered larger than life. Deemed by the media and Marine Corps as "heroic," men like Smith, Foss and others found themselves on tour, being used as recruiting tools and to help sell war bonds.

Joe Foss himself used the term "dancing bear act" in his 1992 memoirs, though not in those published in 1943. At that time, he still had stars in his eyes—or at least he was not about to reveal himself as a cynic while he was on tour.

John L. Smith had come home among an earlier wave in October 1942, and was celebrated for being America's leading ace. He was reunited with his wife, Louise, at her parents' home in Norfolk, Virginia, where the smiling couple—both appearing relieved—were photographed by the well-known photographer Nelson Morris for a spread in *Life* magazine. Morris also followed Smith to NAS Anacostia in the District of Columbia, where the Navy Department held a photo op with Smith, in flight gear, posing in a Wildcat cockpit. One of these became *Life*'s December 7, 1942 cover photo.

Guided by the deft hand of Brigadier General Robert Denig, the congenial and garrulous officer who was the Corps' first director of public information, the publicity machine was in high gear. On November 19, they presented Smith, along with Marion Carl and Richard Mangrum of VMSB-232, in a press conference at the Waldorf Astoria Hotel in New York City. The appearance was billed as "their first stop on a projected tour of the country to stimulate recruiting for the Marine Corps."

Smith, Carl, and Mangrum would spend the better part of a month as "dancing bears," making public appearances at recruiting and war bond rallies from Jacksonville to Chicago. The three men, at home in the dangerous skies over the Solomons, were noticeably nervous as they walked into the Waldorf Astoria ballroom, which was filled with shouting journalists and exploding flash bulbs. The unnamed author of a piece in the *New York Times* wrote that "each wearing the ribbon of the Navy Cross, [they] almost reluctantly recounted their experiences." Despite this, the writer added that "the three fliers parried questions skillfully."

Despite their boisterousness, the raucous reporters were a friendly pack, tossing out questions that provided the three aviators with a chance to shine. After all, readers wanted heroes, and they wanted to read about heroism.

"What was your best day?"

"The day we got 23 bombers 15 miles from our field," quipped Smith."

"Worst luck?"

"Getting shot down 30 miles south of the field and three miles at sea," Carl replied, recalling his experiences of September 9, and how he was rescued by an islander in a rowboat. "He also had a big machete and he looked me over carefully before he hauled me out of the water."

Smith and Carl were invited out to the Grumman Aircraft plant at Bethpage, Long Island, 30 miles east of New York City, where their sturdy F4F Wildcats had been built. In their own press release, the Grumman "Iron Works" called the two aces their "best customers." In Connecticut, on a later stop of their public relations tour, Carl test flew the Vought F4U-1 Corsair, which was to become the definitive Marine Corps fighter for the remainder of the war.

Back in New York City, the Marine aviators, being the "toast of the town," were wined and dined on the party circuit. To dress up the scene for the photo op cameras, the John Roberts Powers modeling agency sent in a contingent of fashion models to take the arms of the men in their dress uniforms. Carl, the only bachelor among the latter, found himself with 19-year-old Edna Kirvin of Brooklyn, and the sparks flew. After the photo op, they bar-hopped from the 21 Club to the Copacabana, closing down the Stork Club at three in the morning.

Marion and Edna stayed in touch, and on December 9 he was back in New York and took her for an all-day spin in an SNJ Texan trainer. His marriage proposal came eight days later. She said she'd think about it. Three days after Christmas, she said "yes," and their 55 years of marriage began on January 8, 1943. *Life* magazine sent a reporter and photographer to accompany them as Carl took his bride home to Oregon.

The awarding of the Medal of Honor, America's highest decoration for valor, had always been an important element in the recognition of heroes. Surprisingly, it was not when they first came home, but well into 1943 that the Marine aces of Guadalcanal began to be so recognized.

John L. Smith, who was working a desk job at the Navy Department in Washington, DC, was the first. On February 24, 1943, he was summoned to the White House, where he received his Medal of Honor personally from President Franklin D. Roosevelt. Bob Galer, who had commanded VMF-224 on Guadalcanal while Smith commanded VMF-223, received his medal from the president exactly one month later.

Marion Carl, who had received his Navy Cross on the same day as Smith and Galer, was recommended for a Medal of Honor, but did not receive one, a fact that is baffling to those familiar with his record and his standing. Perhaps it had something to do with balancing the number of such awards between the services at the time. In his memoirs, Carl shrugged it off by saying, tongue in cheek, that it might have had something to do with his having been shot down.

On May 18, 1943, Joe Foss became the third Marine ace to receive a Medal of Honor from Roosevelt.

Joe Bauer was awarded a well-deserved posthumous Medal of Honor, while nine-victory ace Jefferson DeBlanc would receive a Medal of Honor for being the first Marine "ace in a day." He had downed five of his total on January 31, 1943. Neither of these was awarded until 1946, though DeBlanc had earlier been awarded the Navy Cross for the same action, and this was upgraded to the Medal of Honor.

Foss began his own season as a dancing bear in April 1943. After departing Guadalcanal January 26, he and several members of the VMF-121 Flying Circus found themselves stuck for two weeks in Espiritu Santo awaiting onward transportation. Finally, Foss met a Navy transportation officer named Lieutenant Richard Milhous Nixon, who was able to get them a flight to Auckland, New Zealand. The two men crossed paths again after Nixon became President of the United States a quarter century later. Foss remained a while in Auckland, gobbling quinine to tamp down the lingering malaria and being debriefed by the brass.

From San Diego, Foss traveled on to Washington, DC, arriving in the same well-worn uniform he'd worn since Guadalcanal. Reunited with his wife, June, who had already been brought to Washington, Foss was formally greeted by Admiral Ernest King, Chief of Naval Operations, and Secretary of the Navy Frank Knox.

In his memoirs, a self-effacing Foss claimed that he did not realize he was a hero until he saw Robert Denig's glowing press releases and started reading the articles about him that were appearing. The *Saturday Evening Post* had done a spread on him a week before he reached the States. Placing him in their "Hall of Heroes," *Esquire* magazine called him the "ace of aces" and congratulated him for his graciousness in not exceeding Rickenbacker's World War I score— as though this had been deliberate.

As with Smith and Carl, Foss and his wife met the press at the Waldorf Astoria in New York and made a photo op visit to Grumman on Long Island. Denig and his team put Foss on a multi-city press and publicity tour from Connecticut to Florida to California—and "every major radio show in the country"—that was interrupted only by his visit to the White House to receive the Medal of Honor.

The publisher E.P. Dutton connected him with a ghost writer, Walter Simmons, and his wartime memoir, *Joe Foss: Flying Marine*, was on the shelves by the end of the year.

According to the last chapter, Foss's biggest thrill was his homecoming to Sioux Falls, South Dakota where "in this city of 41,000, a crowd of 75,000 turned out."

Eventually, the dancing bears managed to slip off stage and out of the limelight. John L. Smith and Bob Galer each turned to desk jobs, Smith at Marine headquarters in Washington, and Galer as operations officer at MCAS Miramar, near San Diego. Marion Carl, and eventually Joe Foss as well, would both return to their earlier jobs as Marine combat aviators. Initially, both were given command of Marine Fighting Squadrons filled with untested aviators preparing for their first deployments. These men would have benefited from the guiding hand of experience before going overseas.

In January 1943, Carl was reassigned to VMF-223, his and Smith's old squadron, now at MCAS El Toro near Irvine, California. He and Edna rented a bungalow in Laguna Beach, and he spent his spare time teaching her to drive. During that spring, Carl also had a one-line bit part during the filming at Camp Pendleton of the 20th Century Fox film based on *Guadalcanal Diary* by Richard Tregaskis, the journalist whom Carl had known on the island.

With Carl having assumed command, VMF-223 would finally return to the Western Pacific in November 1943.

In July 1943, meanwhile, Joe Foss took command of VMF-115 at MCAS Goleta near Santa Barbara. In addition to a great deal of new blood, Foss was able to pull in some of the VMF-121 aviators who were cycling through the system for their second tours and looking for squadron assignments. Nemo Loesch came in as VMF-115 executive officer and Bill Freeman as the engineering officer. When Loesch was killed bailing out after a midair collision over Goleta, John King, another veteran, took over as executive officer when the squadron finally went overseas in May 1944.

Other aces, who had been less heralded by the Marine Corps publicity machine, were also given squadron assignments, where they waited in the wings for their second act. Doc Everton, who had finally recovered from the injuries he had suffered in October 1942, took command of the new VMF-113, which was activated at El Toro in January 1943. The squadron finally went into combat in the Pacific one year later.

Of course, the vast majority of those returning from the global battlefronts that season were not made into national newsworthy celebrities. There was one man in particular among the roster of future double-digit Marine aces whose homecoming was the direct opposite of that accorded men such as Smith, Carl, and Foss.

Joseph Jacob "Joe" Foss scored 26 aerial victories while flying with VMF-121 between 1942 and 1943. A Medal of Honor recipient, he was the leading Marine ace of all time, and the first American ace to match the record of 26 aerial victories scored by America's leading World War I ace, Eddie Rickenbacker. (USMC)

Robert Murray Hanson scored 25 aerial victories, mainly while flying with VMF-215 over Rabaul in early 1944. Born in India, the son of missionaries, he earned the Medal of Honor and was one of the top three Marine aces of all time. (USMC)

Gregory Boyington was a colorful character who was undisciplined on the ground, but intuitively adept in aerial combat. He scored his first aerial victories with the Flying Tigers, and became one of the top three Marine aces of all time while leading the "Black Sheep" of VMF-214. (USMC)

A Grumman F4F-4 Wildcat takes off from Henderson Field on Guadalcanal in 1942. All the early Marine aces scored their aerial victories flying Wildcats from the airfields in the Henderson Field complex, notably Kukum Field (aka "Fighter One"). (USN)

The three leading scorers among the first generation of Marine aces from the fall of 1942 included (left to right) John L. Smith, the commander of VMF-223; Bob Galer, the commander of VMF-224; and Marion Carl, who flew with VMF-223. This photo was taken on September 30, 1942, when Admiral Chester Nimitz visited Guadalcanal to award the Navy Cross to each of these men. (USN)

Harold William "Indian Joe" Bauer was a Medal of Honor recipient widely regarded as the best Marine fighter pilot on Guadalcanal. The only Annapolis graduate among the double-digit aces, he downed 11 enemy aircraft, eight in just two missions. His career was cut short by his disappearance on November 14, 1942. (USMC)

This Marine F4F Wildcat marked with Japanese flags indicating 19 aerial victories could have belonged only to John L. Smith or Joe Foss, who achieved that number in Wildcats. However, this Wildcat may have been one marked up for a photo op. (USN)

A Marine F4F Wildcat taking off from one of the fighter airfields on Guadalcanal, circa 1942. After initially operating from Henderson Field proper, Marine fighting squadrons flew most of their missions from the nearby Kukum Field. (USMC)

This aerial photo of Henderson Field dates from August 1942, shortly after the arrival of the Marine aviators of VMF-223. Marine Wildcats can be seen at the far left. (USN)

Kenneth DeForrest Frazier scored 11.5 aerial victories while flying Wildcats with VMF-223 on Guadalcanal in the fall of 1942. He returned to the squadron at the end of 1943 and added one more victory while flying a Corsair. (USMC)

John Lucian Smith commanded VMF-223 on Guadalcanal in the fall of 1942.
He scored 19 aerial victories to become the highest-scoring Marine ace of the first phase of
Guadalcanal operations. This photograph was taken in October 1942 after he had returned
home to a hero's welcome. (USN)

John L. Smith (left) and Marion Carl (right) of VMF-223, along with Richard "Dick" Mangrum (center), the commander of VMSB-232—the first Marine scout bomber squadron on Guadalcanal. They face the cameras for a photo op at NAS Anacostia in the District of Columbia after their return from combat. (USN)

Loren Dale "Doc" Everton earned his nickname from his being a licensed pharmacist when he earned his wings as a Marine aviator. Assigned to VMF-212, he scored the first of his dozen aerial victories while on loan to VMF-223, and his last as commander of VMF-113 in the Central Pacific. (USMC)

William Pratt Marontate scored his 13 aerial victories while flying with VMF-121, and was the second highest-scoring ace in that squadron after Joe Foss. He disappeared while on a January 15, 1943 mission and was never seen again. (USMC)

Joe Foss received the Medal of Honor from President Franklin Delano Roosevelt at the White House on May 18, 1943. His medal is not visible in this official USMC photo that was possibly taken that day. (USMC)

The first Marine Vought F4U-1 Corsairs of VMF-124 arrived at Guadalcanal on February 12, 1943, and were flying operational missions the next day. (USMC)

Kenneth Ambrose Walsh, seen here in the cockpit of his Corsair, began his flying career as an enlisted pilot and went on to become the fourth highest-scoring Marine ace of all time, with 21 victories. The first "Corsair ace," he earned a Medal of Honor for his actions with VMF-124 in the summer of 1943, but scored his last victory in June 1945 with VMF-222. (USMC)

This expansive view from the cockpit of Marine SBD Dauntlesses over the Solomons, circa early 1943, would have been a familiar sight to the aviators of the Marine fighting squadrons. Escorting such aircraft on their missions to places such as Kahili was an integral part of the daily routine. (USMC)

Wilbur Jackson "Gus" Thomas of VMF-213 rose to prominence in June 1943, scoring four aerial victories in his first engagement with the enemy. By October, he raised his score to 16.5, frequently scoring multiple victories in the same day. He added two more while flying off the carrier USS *Essex* in 1945. (USMC)

Edward Oliver "Bud" Shaw of VMF-213 scored three aerial victories in his first taste of combat in June 1943. He brought his score to 14.5 by October when he returned home. He was killed in a training accident in July 1944. (USMC)

James Norman Cupp, seen here with the Corsair named for his wife, was one of a trio of double-digit aces in VMF-213. He began his combat career in June 1943, and had brought his score to an even dozen when tracers from a Japanese G4M bomber ignited a fire in his cockpit. He suffered horrific burns and was hospitalized for nearly two years. (USMC)

On August 14, 1943, VMF-215 became the first Marine fighting squadron to operate from the former Japanese airfield at Munda on the island of New Georgia, 200 miles northwest of Guadalcanal. Among the squadron's double digit aces were Don Aldrich, Bob Hanson, and Hal Spears. (USMC)

Flight operations began at Barakoma airfield on Vella Lavella in September 1943. A Navy F6F Hellcat and two Marine F4U-1 Corsairs are seen here in the foreground, with an SBD Dauntless by the tent on the left, and three RNZAF Kittyhawks at the edge of the field on the left. (USMC)

Harold Leman "Hal" Spears scored his 15 aerial victories with VMF-215 between August 1943 and February 1944, claiming multiple times in most of his engagements. He survived combat only to be killed in an accident in California in December 1944. (USMC)

Jack Eugene Conger scored eight victories with VMF-212 and two when he was on loan to VMF-223. On October 25, 1942, he collided with a Zero piloted by Shiro Ishikawa. Both pilots survived and were rescued, but in the process, Ishikawa tried unsuccessfully to kill Conger. The two met again on friendlier terms 48 years later. (USMC)

A Marine F4U-1 Corsair takes off from the crushed coral runway at Barakoma airfield on Vella Lavella in late 1943. In the background are several Marine and Navy aircraft. (USN)

James Elms Swett of VMF-221 earned a Medal of Honor for downing *seven* Japanese aircraft on a single day on April 7, 1943. Most of his victories were in 1943, but his last was off Okinawa in 1945. (USMC)

Gregory Boyington had come home not in uniform aboard a military ship or military aircraft, but as a civilian vagabond who had hitchhiked most of the way around the world. And his overlooked and unheralded homecoming occurred before any of the other aces—except Marion Carl at Midway—had even tasted combat. He quit the Flying Tigers, departed China for Calcutta by air on April 26, 1942, and waited a couple weeks to finally grab a British Overseas Airways flying boat to Karachi. From there, he found himself on a slow boat around the tip of South Africa, through the Atlantic.

Boyington finally reached New York on July 13, and traveled to Washington, DC to try to get back his Marine Corps commission. Having been led to believe that the process would to be as simple as someone just tearing up his August 1941 letter of resignation, he was stunned to learn that it was not going to be so easy—especially for someone with a disciplinary record as long as his.

At the Navy Department, the official response to his offering himself for duty was not a "no," because Brigadier General Ralph Johnson Mitchell, director of aviation at Marine Corps headquarters, took Boyington's side and recommended his reinstatement. However, because of the snarl of paperwork, it was "don't call us, we'll call you."

Discouraged, disappointed, and low on funds, Boyington went home to his mother, Grace Hallenbeck. He took the train to Okanogan, Washington, where the local press relished the novelty of the son of a hometown woman having been a Flying Tiger. Gradually, Boyington was invited to make speeches to local civic groups, and he had a taste of what the others would experience on a larger scale half a year later.

In August, Boyington moved on to Seattle, where he went to court to try to regain legal custody of his three children. Back in late 1941, he had finally gotten a divorce decree to end his troubled marriage to Helene, but she still had legal custody of the children, though none lived with her. Two were with Grace Hallenbeck and the other with Helene's sister in Seattle. On the grounds that Helene was an alcoholic, Boyington regained custody, but the judge insisted that the children should remain where they were, and that he make the child support payments to the court.

Boyington was broke, with debts piling up as they so often had done in his life, and he had been counting on a resumption of a regular paycheck. Finally, in desperation, he went to the parking garage in downtown Seattle where he had worked eight years earlier as a college student. His old boss was still there, and Boyington asked him for a job.

"You're kidding," the man said.

"No, I'm broke," Boyington admitted.

As Boyington wrote in his memoirs, "for two long dreary months, right in the heart of the war, I parked cars—and with only high school kids left on the job with me."

Military officers who came there to leave their vehicles with him often glowered at him disgustedly, assuming him to be a slacker not serving his country. He had to take it.

In the meantime, in Washington, DC, Mitchell pushed his recommendation that Boyington be reinstated up the chain of command, where it eventually reached the desk of Navy Secretary Frank Knox. On September 3, 1942, two days after the custody decree, Boyington learned that his reinstatement had been approved, but that it had not yet occurred. Again, it was "don't call us, we'll call you."

It was late November, when they finally *did* call. Boyington got the news he was waiting for—and a promotion to major as well.

Meanwhile, Boyington was not the only former Marine and alumnus of the Flying Tigers to rejoin the Corps. Like Boyington, Ed Overend came back in as a major, but while Boyington went overseas again in January, Overend was sent to MCAS El Toro in July 1943 to help organize VMF-114. Having moved to VMF-321, he did not go overseas until December. A five-victory ace with the AVG, Overend added three with VMF-321 over Rabaul in January 1944, but this came after Boyington's own meteoric Marine career had ended.

When Boyington stepped off the Matson Lines liner SS *Lurline* in the South Pacific in January 1943, he headed north to Espiritu Santo. Here, he crossed paths with Joe Foss headed south. It was the only time during the war that these two leading Marine Corps aces were in the same place at the same time.

This chance encounter was an illustration of a subtle but significant changing of the guard in early 1943.

PART III

No Longer a Mere Few

14

The Corsair and the Changing Game

As Foss and Boyington passed like ships in the night at the start of 1943, numerous changes were in motion across SOPAC that were setting the tone for a new era, both strategically and tactically, and from the command structure to the type of aircraft in which Marine aviators would score their aerial victories.

From Tokyo to Washington, the focus of grand strategy had changed. A year earlier, Japanese strategy had centered on a steady, incremental expansion of the Empire's perimeters. Now, this expansion had reached its high-water mark, from Midway to New Guinea to Guadalcanal. Allied strategy, meanwhile, had centered on stopping the unstoppable, and now it lay on rolling back the Japanese gains, on beginning the long road to Tokyo.

The watershed moment for both came in February 1943 when the Japanese finally withdrew from Guadalcanal.

Within the headquarters planning rooms of Douglas MacArthur's SWPA and Bull Halsey's SOPAC, all eyes were now on Rabaul— the keystone upon which the whole structure of the Japanese presence in the South Pacific was built.

Rabaul was a Japanese base complex on the island of New Britain, 660 miles northwest of Guadalcanal and 500 miles northeast of MacArthur's headquarters at Port Moresby on New Guinea. With its fine port of Simpson Harbor, it was a great naval and logistical base, as well as a headquarters for naval operations. Ringed by several major, well-developed airfields, Rabaul was also the center of IJAAF and IJNAF air operations throughout the region.

Between February and April 1943, a complex Allied plan called Operation *Cartwheel* took shape. It called for the neutralizing of the keystone of Rabaul, and thereby collapsing the structure of Japanese power across the region.

Within the Solomons, this would mean a steady, incremental amphibious landing campaign moving north out of Guadalcanal through 1943—to the Russell Islands in February, to New Georgia in June, to Vella Lavella in August, and to Empress Augusta Bay on Bougainville in November.

Against this backdrop came a reorganization of Allied airpower. Between February and April 1943, the ad hoc tactical airpower conglomeration known unofficially as the Cactus Air Force was gradually formalized as the joint-service Solomons Air Command (AirSols). Its first commander was the US Navy's Rear Admiral Charles Perry Mason, the naval aviator who took up the post on February 16. On April 4, Mason was succeeded as AirSols commander (ComAirSols) by Rear Admiral Marc Mitscher, who later in the war would command the US Navy's Fast Carrier Task Force.

As had been the case when the Cactus Air Force was patched together out of whole cloth in August 1942, the tactical situation demanded a unified command, and so it was. AirSols consisted of USAAF, US Navy, and US Marine units brought together under the same umbrella, and the Royal New Zealand Air Force (RNZAF) was also there.

In 1942, the Cactus Air Force had been on the defensive over Guadalcanal. By February 1943, the USAAF and the US Navy were bringing in four-engine heavy bombers to begin reversing the direction of the bomber offensive.

For Marine fighter aviation, perhaps nothing better symbolized the new era beginning in February 1943 than the Vought F4U-1

Corsair, the aircraft destined to supersede the F4F Wildcat as the standard aircraft of Marine fighting squadrons.

As with the old Cactus Air Force itself in 1942, the arrival of the Corsair in this place and time happened not by a carefully laid plan, but almost by accident. Just as the Marines were not supposed to have been the first line of air defense in the South Pacific in the first place, they were not intended to be the first to go into combat with the remarkable new Corsair.

The story of this aviation milestone began in May 1940 with the first flight of the XF4U-1 prototype. The aircraft was being developed by the US Navy as a carrier-based fighter, but with no immediate plan for it to go to the Marines. It was designed around the huge Pratt & Whitney R-2800-8 Double Wasp engine. In its production version, the 18-cylinder Double Wasp delivered 2,000 horsepower at takeoff (more in later variants), compared to 1,200 horsepower for the F4F-3 Wildcat's 14-cylinder R-1830 Twin Wasp.

Notably, the R-2800 engine drove a massive propeller that measured 13 feet 4 inches. This necessitated that the Corsair be designed with a bent, or "gulled," wing in order to provide ground clearance for the arc of the huge prop. The nickname "Bent-Wing Bird" for the Corsair would enter the lexicon. The engine–prop combination had a great deal of torque, which required special handling on takeoff. Applying too much power did not cause the aircraft to become uncontrollable, however.

The Corsair, like the Wildcat, was armed with three Browning M2 .50-caliber machine guns in each wing. These could be adjusted to shoot straight forward, but were often boresighted so that the streams of fire converged at a specific point ahead of the aircraft. In some cases, a squadron might boresight them to as close as 100 yards, which is relatively close for an aircraft flying at 300mph, and this in turn governed the tactics that a squadron might use.

As had been the case with those in the Wildcat, the guns were prone to jamming during violent or inverted maneuvering, though not all guns jammed simultaneously and they could be manually recharged from the cockpit.

In the production F4U-1 variant, which first appeared in June 1942, about half of the fuselage length was forward of the cockpit. This was partly because of the massive engine and partly because of the insertion of large fuel tanks. Fuel volume had to be moved from the wings to the fuselage because wing armament increased over the original specs from four to six .50-caliber machine guns.

Ultimately, more than 12,500 Corsairs were produced by three companies. Most of them were manufactured by Chance Vought in Stratford, Connecticut, but the Navy Department considered the program to be of a sufficiently high priority that two other factories were brought into the pool to aid production. Goodyear Aircraft of Akron, Ohio delivered more than 4,000 of the total under the designation FG-1, and Brewster Aircraft built 430 F3As in Pennsylvania.

The extended nose of the Corsair compromised forward visibility for take-off and landing, and this became problematic on aircraft carriers. This was where the plans for the Corsair abruptly changed. The US Navy decided late in 1942 to restrict the Corsair to land-based operations until techniques for carrier operations were figured out—and the aircraft, most promising in all other respects, was passed on to the Marines.

The compromised visibility in the earlier Corsairs was later addressed in the later F4U-1A and F4U-1D Corsair variants, in which the faceted "birdcage" canopy of the F4U-1 was superseded by a one-piece "blown Plexiglas" bubble canopy that provided much better visibility.

In service with the Marines in the Solomons, the Bent-Wing Bird turned out to be the right aircraft at the right time. It was fast—the second American fighter (after the USAAF's P-38 Lightning) to be capable of cruising faster than 400mph, making it roughly 100mph faster than the Wildcat and nearly twice as fast as a Zero.

It also had a range half again greater than the Wildcat, which greatly expanded the operational radius of Marine aviators within the Solomons. Unlike the Wildcat, the Corsair had the range to fly combat sorties all the way to Bougainville and to do battle with the Zeros there at the top of the Slot.

The first operational Corsair squadron was VMF-124, commanded by Major William Gise. They arrived at Kukum Field ("Fighter 2") within the Henderson Field complex on February 12, 1943, and flew their first mission, escorting a search and rescue PBY, on the same day. Over the next two days, VMF-124 and the Corsairs had their baptism of fire, but things did not go so well. They were caught up in what came to be known in the annals of SOPAC air operations as the "St. Valentine's Day Massacre."

In the missions of February 13 and 14, the Americans lost 15 aircraft, including two Corsairs, while Japanese losses were minimal, perhaps as few as two. The enemy may have abandoned Guadalcanal, but they were still a potent force in the Solomons. Gradually, VMF-124 evaluated how best to exploit the Corsair's advantages in combat with the Zeros.

Until the first of April, contact with the enemy was frustratingly rare for the Marine aviators on Guadalcanal. In contrast to the almost daily air-to-air combat in the fall of 1942, operations through the spring of 1943 saw more limited opportunities for such encounters.

Kenneth Ambrose Walsh of VMF-124, the first man to become a "Corsair ace," scored his first aerial victories on April 1. It was on this day that the IJNAF abruptly returned to the offensive—in a big way. Fleet Admiral Isoroku Yamamoto, commander of the IJN Combined Fleet and the architect of Pearl Harbor, initiated the operation known as I-Go Sakusen, a two-week air offensive against Allied positions from New Guinea to Guadalcanal.

Ken Walsh was airborne on that morning of April 1 leading a VMF-124 flight on a combat air patrol mission over the Russell Islands, ready to intercept an IJNAF strike force coming south.

A flight of USAAF P-38s was attacked by Zeros, who did not see the VMF-124 Corsairs above. Walsh led his flight in a diving attack, downing two of the enemy fighters. In another round of combat on May 13, he added three more, and the one-time "flying private" became the first Corsair ace.

For both Walsh and for the Corsair, these were merely the opening installments of remarkable stories.

15

Corsair Aces Over the Solomons

April into May

Though the F4U Corsairs had begun to make their appearance on Guadalcanal in February 1943, the F4F Wildcats continued to play a prominent role in air combat through the first quarter of the year. After the first week of April, though the transition would be rapid, Wildcats were not entirely superseded in Marine squadrons by Corsairs until August 1943.

When VMF-221, commanded by Captain Robert Burns, reached Guadalcanal early in 1943, it was a Wildcat squadron—just as it had been a year earlier when such legends as Joe Bauer, Marion Carl, and John L. Smith had flown with it on Midway.

After the decisive battle for that atoll in June 1942, VMF-221 had relocated to MCAS Ewa near Pearl Harbor to reorganize as its first wartime generation of aviators, who would be moved on to front line squadrons in the Solomons.

One of the men of VMF-221's second generation, as it reached the South Pacific, was James Elms Swett of San Mateo, California who earned his wings with the US Navy at NAS Corpus Christi in Texas, but transferred to the Marine Corps Reserve in April 1942.

One year later, Jim Swett had flown two uneventful combat air patrols over the Solomons with VMF-221 and was wondering when he'd get a taste of the air combat about which he had read so much the previous fall.

On April 1, when the Japanese launched I-Go Sakusen, VMF-221 was in the thick of things. The squadron's war diary opened with the phrase "April fool's day but not for us." Of the 19 Japanese aircraft claimed by the Marines, seven fell to VMF-221—but none to Jim Swett. He was not on flight duty that day.

A week later, on Wednesday, April 7, Swett finally had his chance. Yamamoto had plans for the aviators on Guadalcanal. According to then-Lieutenant Commander Masatake Okumiya of the IJNAF, who led units in this campaign and who later wrote the definitive Japanese history of the Zero, the maximum effort for which Yamamoto had prepared the IJNAF for this day was unprecedented in its striking power, including the best and most of IJNAF airpower from across the Pacific. The target of the day was Allied air and sea power throughout the area of Ironbottom Sound, on Guadalcanal, and at the US Navy's anchorage at Tulagi.

To augment his land-based airpower, Yamamoto even brought in aircrews from the carriers *Hiyo, Junyo, Zuiho*, and *Zuikaku*, repositioning them at land bases. In addition to 65 Aichi D3A Val dive bombers, there was a sizable number of Nakajima B5N Kate torpedo bombers and Mitsubishi G4M Betty medium bombers, the latter having been an almost constant fixture in the skies over Guadalcanal throughout the fall of 1942.

The Americans knew that something big was coming, as reconnaissance flights had detected a three-fold increase in the number of Japanese aircraft on Bougainville.

Jim Swett had been up since 0330hrs. He had flown with three others on VMF-221's dawn patrol over the Russell Islands and was back on the ground by noon when word came from radar and from the coastwatcher network that a sizable attack by nearly 100 Zeros and D3A Val dive bombers against Tulagi was imminent.

Swett was ordered to lead a four-ship division to intercept the enemy. Climbing to 16,000 feet, they spotted about 20 Vals at ten o'clock heading straight for the American destroyers at Tulagi.

Swett descended immediately to try to reach the Vals, watching them bank to go into their shallow dives against the ships. Suddenly, Zeros were in the sky, diving on the Wildcats. Swett, accelerating in his own dive, used his aircraft's superior power to outpace the Zeros and pressed his attack.

Closing in on one of the dive bombers to a range of 300 yards, Swett opened fire and the Val was quickly consumed by flames.

As bombs from the Vals were beginning to explode among the American ships, Swett lined up a second dive bomber at an altitude of about 2,000 feet, thumbed his trigger and watched it explode.

Continuing his dive to around 1,000 feet, he found a third Val now in his sights and again opened fire. Having scored hits on the enemy aircraft, he was surprised this time when it did not explode. Swett watched as it released its ordnance and began to climb up from its attack. Executing a high-G pullout, Swett nearly passed out, but caught himself and continued chasing the third dive bomber as it raced north across Florida Island at treetop level.

Noticing that he had damage to his left wing, including one of his six machine guns partially dislodged from its mount, Swett looked back at his six. He was relieved not to see any Zeros nearby, but mystified as to what had hit his wing.

Turning back to the low-fleeing Val, Swett opened fire again, this time at nearly point-blank range. Flames began pouring out of the enemy aircraft.

With a hole in his wing and half his ammunition expended, Swett climbed back toward Tulagi. By now the attack was over and the skies were full of swarming specks—Japanese aircraft mustering for their exit from the target area.

Picking out a cluster of Vals, Swett climbed into a nearby patch of cumulus, planning to use it as a blind for an attack on them. As he emerged from the darkness of the cloud, the enemy dive bombers were dead ahead and not expecting him. A short burst tore the first of these apart and it went down.

Picking out another, Swett closed in so tight that he could see the Val's rear gunner, realizing to his chagrin that he had forgotten that these aircraft had a Type 92 7.7mm machine gun pointing rearward to cover the six o'clock position while the bomber was in its attack. As he watched the rear gunner fumble with his gun,

Swett opened fire and soon saw flames pouring from the Val's wing roots.

When this aircraft plummeted into the water below, Jim Swett had now achieved his fifth aerial victory—and ace status in his first combat action—but his attention was on the next Val that found itself unluckily in his sights.

Checking his six and seeing no Zeros, Swett bored in on this Val, watching as it exploded before it even seemed to catch fire.

Dodging plummeting wreckage, Swett once again found a Val and put it into his sights. There was no explosion, but the fusillade of .50-caliber fire finally brought forth a trail of black smoke, and the enemy began to dive toward the wavetops below. As he later recalled, "I just took them one by one [with] two or three rounds per gun and flamed each and every one of them."

Banking hard to catch one more Val, Swett took a deflection shot into its left side and watched its forward fuselage shatter into shards. For some reason, the rear gunners of the first seven dive bombers that he attacked did not seem to be able to shoot back at him.

It was different on this eighth one.

Swett watched the muzzle flash from the Type 92 gun, felt the 7.7mm rounds hitting his own cockpit, tasted his own blood, and returned fire. At an estimated 100 feet of separation, he was in a deadly, point-blank shootout with the Japanese gunner.

At 50 feet, Swett could clearly see the gunner, his flying jacket and goggles sharply visible, as he slumped over, mortally wounded.

Then there was the ripping sound of hammers clattering within Swett's own guns, now empty.

Turning his attention to his instrument panel, Swett discovered that one of the enemy rounds had punctured his oil system and pressure was nil. The engine seized and his propeller abruptly stopped. Knowing that he could never reach Guadalcanal, he prepared to ditch in Ironbottom Sound off Florida Island.

With his left wing flaps not functional, he fought the Wildcat as he descended, his airspeed dangerously high. He jettisoned his canopy just as he sliced into the water at 125mph. Being thrown against the instrument panel with tremendous force left him stunned and suffering from a broken nose.

His stupefied condition cost him valuable seconds in trying to unfasten his harness to escape before the Wildcat sank. His aircraft went deep enough that he was enveloped in darkness before he finally broke free. He pulled the cord on his Mae West, and its sudden inflation propelled him to the surface before he inhaled water and drowned.

Having reached the surface, he inflated his life raft, fired a couple of rounds into the air from his service pistol to attract attention to himself, and sat down in the blistering sun to wait.

At last, a small US Coast Guard picket boat hove into view across the waves and somebody yelled, "Are you an American?"

To this, Swett replied, "You goddamn well right I am."

They took him to the small island of Gavutu, three miles from Tulagi, where he was greeted by a Marine colonel with a bottle of whiskey. From there, he was taken to a hospital in Tulagi, where he was given a shot of morphine. Then the mixture of the whiskey and saltwater in his stomach finally bubbled to the top and he puked his guts out.

The following day, Swett was picked up by a PBY and flown back to Guadalcanal. When debriefed, Swett claimed seven aerial victories with a probable eighth—which he had not actually seen go down.

There was abounding skepticism about this spectacular assertion of seven victories until Lieutenant (junior grade) Pete Lewis, a US Navy intelligence officer had spent five days on Tulagi and Florida interviewing witnesses. Though a Val presumed to be his eighth was later found on the ground, Swett's confirmed total of seven became official.

Of the 39 enemy aircraft that were shot down on April 7, VMF-221 accounted for 17 of them, though their war diary lists 18. Most were Zeros. In turn, the squadron had lost five Wildcats, including Swett's, but all the pilots survived.

As colorfully related in their squadron war diary for the April 7 battle, VMF-221 had done a disservice to Japanese plans, "pretty well messing up the raid." Nevertheless, the Japanese had destroyed three Allied ships. The minesweeper HMNZS *Moa*, the oiler USS *Kanawha* (AO-1), and the destroyer USS *Aaron Ward* (DD-483) all joined the lengthy roster at the bottom of Ironbottom Sound.

However, the price that the IJNAF had paid, especially in light of dwindling resources, was steep. Yamamoto knew that he could only repeat an air offensive like this one with difficulty.

Of course, Admiral Yamamoto did not have long to stew in his dissatisfaction. The Americans had cracked Japanese communications, and 11 days later, when he boarded a Mitsubishi G4M in Rabaul for an inspection trip to Bougainville, he would be intercepted by USAAF P-38s and shot down.

April 7, 1943 may have been a disappointing day for Isoroku Yamamoto, but a great day for Jim Swett. It was while he was in the hospital about a week later that he learned that Rear Admiral Marc Mitscher, ComAirSols, had recommended him for the Medal of Honor. The young man who had become an ace on his first combat mission was the only Marine, and the first American in World War II, to score seven in one day, and one of only a handful of aces in any air force to attain or exceed that number.

The medal citation credited Swett with having destroyed "*eight* enemy bombers in a single flight," though he remained credited with just seven. The eighth crashed Val was not found until much later.

These would not be Swett's last victories. VMF-221 was withdrawn from Guadalcanal on May 1, but the squadron—with Swett aboard—would be back in action on the last day of June. He would have a much later chapter in the annals of 1945.

———

On May 2, 1943, the war diary of Swett's VMF-221 contained the phrase "Our first siege is over! Everything is out of mind but Sydney." For others, Sydney was a receding memory. Among these squadrons returning from Australia were VMF-112 and VMF-124. Within each of these was an aviator who would become an ace during May, and who would ultimately push his score into double digits.

When VMF-221 departed, flying their F4F Wildcats south to Espiritu Santo as the first leg toward R&R in Australia, they crossed paths with the aviators of VMF-112, who were heading back from Noumea and now flying Corsairs. Archie Donahue, who had two aerial victories when he fell victim to a mosquito, was back with VMF-112 after battling malaria in Australia since December 1942.

VMF-112 settled into the Quonset hut quarters at the Fighter 1 field that were then being vacated by VMF-221. In the squadron war diary, VMF-112 commander Captain Robert Fraser would write of the improved conditions, especially the quality of the food. On May 9, he complained, tongue in check, that things were "getting too civilized for Marines—just about comfortable enough for the army now."

During the first two weeks of May, there was no air-to-air action for VMF-112. Their missions consisted of combat air patrols and strafing attacks against Japanese positions on islands in the mid-Solomons, such as Kolambangara, New Georgia, and Vella Lavella. They also flew missions escorting SBD, TBF and B-17 bombers in attacks against these targets and Japanese shipping. VMF-124, meanwhile, did not reach Guadalcanal until May 12.

On the morning of May 13, both of the recently arrived squadrons were airborne to meet a large IJNAF fighter force that was coming southeasterly through the Slot to probe Allied defenses.

Donahue led a six-man intercepting flight that took off around 0930hrs. The squadron war diary does not mention an exact time for Donahue's sortie, but does note a patrol launching at 0930hrs, so he may have taken off at that time too. Four others scrambled at 0945hrs.

Over Florida Island, VMF-112 made contact with the enemy—a recon aircraft escorted by 25 Zeros, which were scattered between 12,000 and 25,000 feet. Donahue led the intercept, relishing the Corsair's superior power as he picked off four Zeros, plus a probable.

The war diary is short on specific details of Donahue's four-victory day, but these, added to his previous two from 1942, had now made Archie Donahue an ace-plus-one in short order. Other VMF-112 aviators added three to the squadron total.

VMF-124 scrambled into the same air battle at 1210hrs, and shot down eight Zeros, including three by Ken Walsh. These victories, added to the pair that he scored on April 1, brought Walsh's score to five. Walsh now had the distinction of being the first Marine ace to have scored all of his aerial victories in a Corsair. Donahue had scored his first pair while flying a Wildcat.

The Japanese, meanwhile, also drew blood on May 13. Donahue came away with some gaping 20mm cannon shell holes in his right stabilizer, and another pilot had to make an emergency landing on the airstrip in the Russell Islands. Otto Seifert, Donahue's wingman, was listed as missing in action, having been last seen going down over the water, trailing smoke. Major William Gise, the commander of VMF-124, also went missing that day. Neither man was ever seen again, and they were declared KIA in 1945.

As bad as it had been for VMF-124, the Japanese had a worse day. Kramer Rohfleisch, writing in *Army Air Forces in World War II*, noted that May 13 was "a day of intense activity, one costing the Japanese sixteen fighters of a force of some two-dozen-odd out on a fighter sweep. But [the Japanese fighter sweeps as far south as Guadalcanal were] an intermittent business and the enemy's air effort would promptly subside after a period of effort, causing AirSols intelligence to conclude that Japanese air strength was increasing in New Guinea as it diminished in the Solomons. Perhaps the attrition was more than the enemy could support."

An amusing anecdote from the May 13 melee began with a report from the USAAF that some Marine Corsairs had fired on their P-40s, apparently mistaking them for Zeros. Neither VMF-112 nor VMF-124 took the blame. Robert Fraser responded by asking whether the P-40s were "shot up" or "shot down?" When the reply was the former, Fraser replied that "it wasn't VMF-112. We always shoot them *down*."

Apparently, P-40s were often mistaken for Zeros, despite their obvious dissimilarities.

Throughout the remainder of the month, both VMF-112 and VMF-124 continued to fly uneventful patrols through the central Solomons. The new aces Donahue and Walsh were in the rosters for VMF-112 and VMF-124 patrol or strafing flights, but since April 7, the big battle of May 13 marked the only day that carried a hint of the excitement of the days of 1942.

16

Slow Rolls and Victories Over the Slot

June into July

For VMF-112 and VMF-124, June 1943 began with a continuation of routine local patrols. Weather conditions delayed an escort mission for bombers headed north to Kahili on Bougainville for several days, but June 5 was anything but routine. The two squadrons, with a total of 32 Corsairs, took off from Guadalcanal around 0730hrs, topped off their tanks at the Russell Islands airstrip, rendezvoused with SBD dive bombers and TBF torpedo bombers, and headed north.

Around 0930hrs, as the bombers began attacking Japanese shipping in the Kahili and Buin area, the IJNAF welcomed them with an interception party of roughly two dozen A6M Zeros, A6M2-Ns, and F1M Pete float biplanes. Exiting the target area, the bombers scattered, making it difficult for the escorting fighters to provide cover. Nevertheless, the Corsairs tore into the Japanese fighters, and did some damage.

Including a seventh victory for recent ace Archie Donahue, VMF-112 claimed eight for sure, plus two probables. VMF-124, meanwhile, claimed four, including two for Ken Walsh, an A6M Zero and an A6M2-N Rufe.

The Americans lost just one bomber over the target, though several aircraft ditched near the Russells or made emergency landings there.

On June 7, the IJNAF returned the visit, launching their biggest fighter sweep since May 13, and possibly since the massive assault on April 7. Around 60 Zeros from the 204th and 251st Kokutais headed south through the Slot.

At 1020hrs, VMF-112 was ordered to launch all available aircraft. When two Corsairs suffered engine trouble, the count was an even dozen, divided into three flights. The third of these, with Archie Donahue in the lead, became separated while flying through a storm off Cape Esperance, so individual pilots attached themselves to the other flights as they emerged from the clouds near the Russell Islands.

When Donahue joined up with the flight led by squadron commander Robert Fraser, they observed Zeros at 20,000 feet. In the words of Fraser's after-action report, there were a half-dozen "doing loops and slow rolls—I guess to look around."

"They're behind us," Fraser heard over his radio, as six more Zeros dived out of the sun. The battle was on.

Two of the Zeros went down quickly, one of them claimed by Fraser, but the initial bounce turned into a swarming dogfight. As James Johnson was attacking a Zero, another got on his six, damaging his aircraft. James Percy attacked the Zero on Johnson's tail only to find himself in the sights of yet another Zero.

Johnson escaped and managed to shoot down a Zero on his way to an emergency landing on Guadalcanal. Percy was not so lucky. His controls gone, he bailed out of his Corsair 300 feet above Ironbottom Sound, but his parachute failed. He survived the fall with numerous injuries, including a broken hip, but he managed to reach land near the Russell Islands airstrip and was eventually rescued.

As all of this was playing out, Archie Donahue got separated from the others and found himself in the midst of several Zeros. Though one of them managed to hit his propeller with a lucky shot—causing the aircraft to vibrate terribly—Donahue downed a pair of the enemy fighters to bring his score to nine.

After a brief pause in the action, the two sides were at each other again. Fraser downed one, but was shot down himself.

After nearly drowning, he discovered how quickly an inflated Mae West could rocket a submerged man to the surface. He finally made it to land and was picked up by a US Navy LST four hours later.

USAAF and RNZAF fighter aircraft joined the fracas, and when the June 7 action was over, 23 Japanese aircraft had been shot down, seven claimed by VMF-112. The Allies lost five aircraft and one pilot.

Within a few days, VMF-112 began winding down its operations as it was being readied to rotate back to the States. By June 16, groups of aviators were beginning to be withdrawn to New Caledonia, en route Stateside or for a sojourn of R&R. Archie Donahue flew his last mission, an uneventful patrol, on June 12, and was among the first to depart for New Caledonia four days later. With nine victories, he was the top-scoring pilot in the squadron. Donahue would be back in combat two years later under very different circumstances.

VMF-124 missed the big air battle of June 7, but three days later, they intercepted three G4M bombers over Malaita Island, 75 miles east of Henderson Field, and shot down all three. It was their last combat action for the month. Beginning on June 16, the squadron's aviators departed for Australia via New Caledonia, many of them ferrying Corsairs out of Guadalcanal.

Ken Walsh, VMF-124's leading ace, would be back in action before the summer was over.

The last day of June 1943 was a remarkable one for two future aces of VMF-213. Edward Oliver "Bud" Shaw shot down four IJNAF Zeros in a single mission, while Wilbur Jackson "Gus" Thomas downed three. These victories of June 30 had been a long time coming for Shaw and Thomas. Along with James Nathan Cupp, they were two of three future double-digit aces who had arrived on Guadalcanal with the squadron back in April. None of them had scored an aerial victory until then.

Commanded by future ace Major Gregory Weissenberger, the squadron had begun its first tour of duty on Guadalcanal on April 3, two days after the great "April Fool's Day" battle. In the next big air battle, on April 7, VMF-213 had launched four flights, each with an average of four Corsairs, and downed the only Zero with which they made contact. The Japanese seemed to elude them on a day that was so busy for other squadrons. Their six-week tour consisted mainly of routine patrols and strafing missions, with their only other air-to-air engagement coming on April 25 during a bomber escort mission northwest of New Georgia island. The squadron downed six Zeros, while losing two Corsairs.

After a month in Australia, they returned in mid-June and finally saw combat on June 28, although when no one saw what happened to the lone Zero that was damaged by Sheldon "Red" Hall that day, it entered the log merely as a "probable." Against a backdrop of serious accidents, including two fatalities in as many days, VMF-213 seemed to be a bad-luck squadron.

Things changed on June 30.

The mission of the day was flying top cover for American forces conducting simultaneous amphibious landings on the north, west, and south coasts of New Georgia and on the smaller island of Rendova off its southwest coast. The objective of the surface operation was to push the Japanese perimeter in the Solomon Islands back 250 miles and capture their air base at Munda on the northwest coast of New Georgia.

VMF-213's morning patrol, including both Cupp and Shaw, covered the landings at Rendova, but the IJNAF did not appear. Gus Thomas took off at 1355hrs with Weissenberger's patrol. Arriving over Rendova about 45 minutes later, they had orbited northwest of the island at 20,000 feet for about a half-hour when they were alerted that radar had picked up enemy aircraft approaching from the northwest at an undetermined altitude. Soon, the Corsair pilots got a visual on 15 to 20 Zeros below and dived to attack.

Weissenberger scored first, downing two of the enemy aircraft, and then found himself being attacked head on by a third Zero. The two aircraft continued firing until they were at point-blank range with both trailing smoke. The Zero exploded as the Corsair burst into flames. Riding his aircraft down, Weissenberger was finally able to escape at about 800 feet. VMF-213's bad-luck streak avoided him. His parachute opened just above the waves, and the nearby destroyer USS *Talbot* (DD-390) picked him up 15 minutes later.

Gus Thomas, on Weissenberger's wing for the initial attack, spotted a Zero that was closing in on the major's tail as he was tangling with his first Zero. Thomas gave this one a "good burst at close range." As it burst into flames, Thomas saw tracers coming past his cockpit, dived to 7,000 feet, rolled to the right and saw a Zero in a steep climb.

Using the Corsair's superior power, Thomas easily closed in and opened fire on the climbing Zero. In the VMF-213 after-action report, Thomas recalled, "I saw bullets spray all through his cockpit and around the root of the wings. I could see ragged edges of his wing."

When Thomas pulled up, he saw another Zero passing from his left, so he "pulled up above him and porpoised down on him from his right. I fired at him, hitting him around the cockpit and he exploded in the air."

As he climbed up toward 10,000 feet, Thomas saw an F4F Wildcat on the tail of a Zero, with a second Zero on the six of the Wildcat. Though he was out of range, he opened fire on the latter Zero, which broke off his attack and dived away. The powerful Corsair easily overtook the diving Zero and Thomas gave him a series of short bursts. When the Zero crashed into the sea, Thomas was so close that he got a splash of saltwater spray on his windscreen.

When he arrived back at Guadalcanal, Thomas had four aerial victories and one probable. He landed with just 45 gallons in his fuel tank and a 7.7mm bullet hole in his Plexiglas canopy, just inches from his head.

Twenty minutes after Thomas landed, Cupp and Shaw were among eight aviators who took off in separate groups of four Corsairs each to cover the American ships supporting the Rendova landings. Cupp's patrol was uneventful, but Bud Shaw was in the right place at the right time. Orbiting above the vessels at 12,000 feet, he and the other three pilots in his flight watched nine A6M2-N Rufe "float-plane Zero" fighters closing in for an attack.

The Marines attacked with a vengeance, intent on making up for all those weeks of no contact with the enemy. All nine of the Zeros went down in flames. Shaw claimed three.

When the dust settled, it was learned that two other aviators from Thomas's flight, Greg DeFabio and Foy Garison, had each shot down a Zero, giving that division a total of nine victories for the day. It had been a good day for VMF-213. Their after-action report listed 20 enemy aircraft shot down. The following afternoon, a sound recording crew visited them in their ready tent, where they made preparations for their daily sorties, to make acetate disc recordings of the men describing the day's events for eventual broadcast in the United States.

Though June had gone out with the proverbial "bang" for VMF-213, July opened with ten days of routine patrols over Rendova and missions escorting SBDs, TBFs, and USAAF B-25 bombers that brought little in the way of aerial combat.

On July 11, though, when the squadron dispatched eight Corsairs on another patrol over Rendova, they were vectored north to Kolombangara island, where the IJNAF Zeros were tangling with AirSols P-40s. As the Corsairs intervened, diving on the Zeros from out of the sun, Weissenberger was the first to score, and DeFabio, on Weissenberger's wing, nailed a second Zero moments later. In an aerial battle that was over in minutes, Arthur "Ray" Boag also scored, downing two Zeros before most of the Japanese pilots raced north to get away.

For a total score of four, VMF-213 lost two Corsairs on July 11. Boag suffered serious engine damage and was losing oil, so he bailed out. Gus Thomas turned back with an oil leak before the fight, but had to make a water landing before he got back to base. Both aviators were rescued.

Four days later, VMF-213 again saw aerial combat. It was the first time that the squadron had encountered an enemy offensive air armada that included G4M Betty medium bombers, and the first day of combat on which each of the squadron's three eventual double-digit aces scored aerial victories.

The mission on July 15 was a patrol mission in the area roughly between northwestern Georgia Island and eastern Kolombangara. The eight Corsairs that took off at around 1330hrs were divided into two four-place divisions. Jim Cupp led the first, which included Gus Thomas. Bud Shaw was in the second division, led by Red Hall.

After an hour of flying, as the Marines passed over Rendova at 10,000 feet, they were told that a Japanese strike force was southbound over Kolombangara, heading toward the American positions on Rendova. Because the enemy was at 26,000 feet, the Corsairs could not rise to intercept them, so they climbed into a position from which they could hit them on their return.

The estimated 18 IJNAF bombers and their 20 Zero escorts crossed Kolombangara northbound toward Vella Gulf at 20,000 feet, making their way back to Kahili airfield on Bougainville, so Cupp's division moved on the Japanese aircraft over Vella Gulf, while Hall attacked the trailing section over Kolombangara.

Cupp charged his guns and waggled his wings to initiate the attack and the Corsairs pounced from 25,000 feet, coming down steep at almost 90 degrees so that the tail gunners in the bombers would have less opportunity to return fire. Nine bombers were arrayed in three vee formations of three. Cupp picked the left wingman of the lead Betty so that his own wingman, Theron Hart "Ted" Brown, could pick either the lead bomber or its right wingman. Brown took the leader.

As he was making a full deflection shot, Cupp put the pipper of his gunsight ahead of the bomber so as to lead its forward motion into the stream of fire. With the guns boresighted to just 100 yards, he made a close pass, barely missing the bomber's tail. It all happened so quickly that the bomber pilot had no time to take evasive action on Cupp's first pass.

The formation now started to break up as the other Corsairs piled on, and Cupp's bomber began to dive to get away, picking up speed. As Cupp chased the Betty, he came up on the tail, close enough to see the tail gunner's face, and opened fire, shredding the gunner's position. With no gunner to interfere, Cupp was able to stay on the bomber's six and follow it down until its right engine exploded into flame and it cartwheeled into Vella Gulf.

In the last moments of his pursuit of the bomber, Cupp was attacked by a Zero, which damaged his wing, but turned and flew away before finishing the job.

Now homeward bound, Cupp was nearing Rendova at about 1,000 feet when he saw a lone Zero circling fiery patches on the water where other Japanese aircraft had crashed—but this Zero had not seen the Corsair. It was a fatal mistake. Jim Cupp scored the second victory of his career.

In the initial attack on the bombers, Gus Thomas had gone after a Betty, but lost track of it after his first pass. He then found himself on the tail of a Zero, opened fire and watched it explode. It was his fifth confirmed victory. He was now an ace, but not ready to rest.

With a bomber in view—the one which he thought had eluded him earlier—he attacked again. The bomber was trailing smoke and heading downward as Thomas made his third pass at an altitude of only 1,500 feet. It was on fire as it sliced into Vella Gulf.

Thomas then made a climbing wing-over turn through a cloud and emerged with a Zero in his sights. Under fire, it exploded and tumbled into the water below.

Bud Shaw, meanwhile, had lost power earlier in the mission and had fallen behind the others. By the time he caught up, the battle was already on, but he found himself in a perfect position to intercept two Bettys below him that were escaping toward the west at 12,000 feet. Firing his guns, he dived on the one to the left, then pulled up and opened fire on its belly. As this one fell into the sea, Shaw made three passes against the remaining member of the pair and followed it down as it crashed west of Vella Lavella.

Separated from the rest of VMF-213, Shaw turned home, but ran into a dogfight between Zeros and P-40s off Vella Lavella's west coast. When a P-40 flashed past with a Zero on its tail, the Zero had the misfortune of aligning itself with Bud Shaw's gunsight.

A determined blast from his guns and the Zero disintegrated in the sky before him.

When VMF-213 regrouped on the ground back at Guadalcanal, the score that was tallied included six Zeros and ten Bettys. Cupp had shot down one of each, his first aerial victories, while Thomas and Shaw had each downed three aircraft that day, a Betty and two Zeros for Thomas, and the reverse for Shaw. Thomas was now an ace plus two, and the leading scorer of VMF-213.

After so long with aerial combat just a distant abstraction, July brought a Japanese onslaught which, counter to the IJNAF's intentions, now presented the Marines with opportunities rather than peril.

At 0730hrs on July 17, VMF-213 launched a dozen Corsairs in four divisions. Gus Thomas flew with Weissenberger in the first, while Cupp and Shaw each flew in separate divisions. The mission was to escort 18 TBF torpedo bombers against Japanese shipping in the area of Kahili and Buin at the southern tip of Bougainville. These fighters and bombers were part of a much larger operation that would involve 120 AirSols fighters escorting a total of 32 TBFs and 32 SBD dive bombers, with each component scheduled to approach the target area at a specific time.

VMF-213 made its rendezvous time at 0840hrs, and as the Corsairs followed the TBFs into the target area they were met by at least 20 Zeros. Four of them converged on Foy Garison, who was flying with Thomas in the division led by Major Weissenberger. As Garison's Corsair went down in flames, Shaw was shooting down a Zero that tried to attack the torpedo bombers. When Shaw pulled out of his attack, he was set upon by three F1M Pete float biplanes, one of which he destroyed. Never seen again, Garison was officially declared KIA a year later.

Jim Cupp and his wingman, Ted Brown, converged on a single Zero, and shared a victory as it plunged into the sea. Brown downed another one, while Cupp got two more confirmed, plus three probables on the way home. When it was over, all three of the future double-digit aces had now achieved ace status. Shaw claimed a Pete, a Zero, and a Rufe "floatplane Zero" to become an ace and bring his total to six. Cupp also became an ace, bringing his total to 5.5.

The bombers had also wrought a great deal of damage to the Imperial Japanese Navy that day, including the sinking of one of its largest destroyers, the *Hatsuyuki*.

After the successes of July 17, AirSols did not hesitate to put another bomber mission over Kahili and southern Bougainville the next day. On July 18, the single-engine SBDs and TBFs were accompanied by 27 USAAF B-24 four-engine heavy bombers. VMF-213 was tasked with escorting the last nine of the heavies.

As the bombers were intercepted, VMF-213 shot down four Zeros, with both Cupp and Shaw each claiming one. However, the squadron lost two Corsairs in the battle. Red Hall was rescued by local islanders and repatriated a month later, but Charles Winnia was captured by the Japanese. He later died in captivity, possibly one of the many Allied pilots who were executed. His body was never recovered.

The next operation for VMF-213 came a few days later on July 21 during the vicious land Battle of Bairoko Harbor. Located on the northwestern side of New Georgia, Bairoko had long been used by the Japanese to support their large air base at Munda. On July 20, the 1st and 4th Marine Raider Battalions had landed there under fire with the objective of capturing the harbor. The Marines met stiff resistance and ultimately failed in their objective, but in the meantime, the role of VMF-213 had been to maintain top cover against intercepting Zeros for the bombers supporting the Raiders.

As the VMF-213 after-action report for July 21 notes, "the Zeros did not come all the way in but stayed off in hopes of luring the patrol out to them. The sky was very cloudy and the Zeros played in and out of the clouds making contact with them difficult … Cupp started two of them smoking, but could not see the ultimate result."

Four days of further bomber escort missions with no contact with IJNAF aircraft brought the second six-week tour of duty for VMF-213 to a close. July 28 was spent packing their gear and waiting for transportation, and the following day, the tired aviators began making their way to Australia for a month of R&R.

They had by now scored a total of 57 aerial victories, including 38 Zeros. They had lost 14 Corsairs, half of them shot down, and six pilots, three of them shot down and still missing.

Of the squadron's aces, Bud Shaw was in the lead with nine—three Zeros, two Bettys, and four floatplanes. In second place was Gus Thomas with seven, followed by John Morgan with six, and Jim Cupp with 5.5. Major Weissenberger had just scored his fifth to become an ace, but it would be his last, as he was transferred out of the squadron after this tour. For Shaw, Thomas, and Cupp, the double-digit scores awaited.

17

The Ace and the Albatross

June into July

After spending all of May and most of June in Australia, the men of VMF-221 began filtering back into the Henderson Field complex on June 24, 1943, flying up from Espiritu Santo as space in SCAT transports became available.

Now commanded by Major Monfurd Peyton, who had taken over from Robert Burns on the first of June, VMF-221 was populated by a number of new faces, but had retained two veteran aviators destined to become double-digit aces.

There was Jim Swett, who had famously downed seven Japanese aircraft (or *eight* according to his Medal of Honor citation) in one day on April 7, 1943, and for whom the last day of June would be his next big day. Also returning was William Nugent Snider of Memphis, Tennessee, who had scored his first three aerial victories on April Fool's Day.

The man who would become VMF-221's third double-digit ace—excepting those who were with the squadron in its pre-Midway incarnation—was one of the new faces who first appeared on Guadalcanal in June 1943. He was also one of the few city boys in the ranks of the Marine aces. Born in Chicago, Harold Edward "Manny" Segal was the 22-year-old son of Christina "Ruth" Robb and Manuel "Manny" Segal. He had borrowed his father's nickname, and he would name his Corsair "Ruthie" after his mother.

VMF-221 began flying routine air patrols on June 26, even before all of its aircraft and aviators had arrived from Espiritu Santo. The first few days were uneventful, but June 30 would be different.

The first patrol, including Snider, was launched at 0530 and took up an orbit over Rendova. For the aviators, it proved uneventful. The second, launched at 1010hrs, was led by Major Peyton. Jim Swett was part of the foursome, with Manny Segal flying as his wingman. While orbiting in empty skies over Rendova, they learned that VMF-121 had made contact with a substantial IJNAF force, but they saw nothing.

At 1440hrs, after refueling, Captain J.S. Payne led 16 Corsairs back to the skies over Rendova. This time the airspace was no longer devoid of Japanese antagonists. Below, they counted 27 G4M Bettys in a vee formation, escorted by Zeros, heading toward Allied ships offshore.

Payne led the fighters into a dive and picked out a Betty, which he shot down. As he pulled out, he saw another bomber, with its left engine trailing smoke that appeared as though on a suicide course for an American ship. He attacked, shooting up its right engine. "I pulled up and looked back," he wrote in the VMF-221 after-action report, "there was no bomber."

Jim Swett observed casually that he "knocked off two Bettys which broke up in the water." As he closed in on a nearby Zero, he saw that it was in the sights of an F4F Wildcat from another squadron, so the two aviators shared the victory.

Manny Segal, Swett's wingman, accompanied him down and attacked another Betty as Swett set his sights on his first. He followed the bomber, pouring lead into one engine, until the G4M sliced into the water.

Pulling up, Segal saw a Wildcat break off from its attack on a Zero and picked up where this aviator had left off. He chased the Japanese fighter almost to Kula Gulf, staying on its six and firing as the two aircraft raced across the sky. At last, as Segal fired a long and final burst, it exploded.

It was a remarkable first day back in combat for VMF-221. Jim Swett led the pack with 2.5 victories to bring his total to 9.5, but a dozen of the squadron's pilots scored, erasing 3.5 Zeros and 13.5 G4M Betty medium bombers from the IJNAF roster in one day. Payne and Segal were each credited with a pair, with Segal claiming one of the several probables. There were no Marine losses.

While the IJNAF made itself scarce over the central Solomons during the first week of July, the Imperial Japanese surface fleet was on the move in the form of destroyers running a Tokyo Express resupply mission. The US Navy intervened with three cruisers to intercept them in the Battle of Kula Gulf on July 6. Two Japanese destroyers were sunk and two damaged, but they launched a torpedo attack that sunk the USS *Helena* (CL-50). Overhead, VMF-221 was pressed into service flying top cover as other American ships picked up survivors.

Sunday, July 11 dawned bright and clear on Guadalcanal. It was almost 1000hrs when Walter Schocker and Jim Swett departed, each leading a four-ship flight up toward Kula Gulf. Without notifying him, two of the aviators flying with Schocker aborted early because of mechanical issues, leaving just Swett and Manny Segal.

Schocker's flight encountered a formation of Japanese aircraft and downed two. When they got back, they learned that neither Swett nor Segal had turned up, and were now officially missing. When the after-action was typed up for the day, it read "they have no gas by now so we are anxiously awaiting news of them."

Both of the men had become aerial victory scores for the IJNAF, but while their aircraft went down, the men themselves had cheated death.

Around 1155hrs, they had been over Kula Gulf off Visuvisu Point at the north tip of New Georgia when Segal had reported engine trouble. Swett scissored back and forth to try to stay with his wingman. Though he was having a hard time keeping up with

Swett, Segal was determined to remain on his wing as long as possible.

When they were alerted to bogeys in the area, Swett told Segal to return to base, and said that he would remain over Kula Gulf, off Kolombangara, for a short while to see what turned up. About two minutes later, they saw the enemy below at nine o'clock.

Segal later recalled that there were around 40 aircraft, including 21 G4M Betty bombers. Swett more conservatively put the number at 12 to 15, noting that they were flying in a "vee of vees," at 20,000 feet, escorted by about a dozen Zeros flying 2,000 feet above.

Swett picked the trailing bomber on the right echelon and descended in a 20 to 30 degree dive. He directed his fire into its engines, and saw that he was getting hits, but he was frustrated that "it did not burn."

Having nearly collided with the bomber, Swett rolled out, rolled over and dived into a cloud about 5,000 feet below.

As he followed Swett, Segal saw Zeros starting to close in on his leader's tail. In turn, Segal tucked himself in behind one of the Zeros. He later wrote, "I caught the top Zero first. He blew up like matchwood. The second Zero never knew what hit him. My dive practically carried me into his cockpit."

Now finding himself below the bomber formation, Segal climbed to attack the "tail-end Charlie," the last one in the formation. As had been the case for Swett moments earlier, he scored numerous hits on the bomber, but it did not catch fire. As he passed through the formation, he found himself in a hail of fire from gunners aboard the bombers. At first, they seemed to miss, but at last he started to feel his Corsair taking hits.

Out of the corner of his eye, he saw two Zeros heading for him, so he executed a split-S maneuver and headed down to escape. From about 25,000 feet, he descended to 6,000 off the southeastern tip of Kolombangara. Seeing that the Zeros had not followed him, he then climbed back to his previous altitude. By then, he had lost track of Swett, and had tried unsuccessfully to raise him on the radio.

Segal could see no friendly aircraft anywhere, but he did see two widely separated Zeros about 4,000 feet below. Despite the damage to his Corsair, he attacked. He dived on one, which exploded almost immediately, and, giving his aircraft a slight kick of left rudder, he tore after the other.

When it began smoking and burst into flames, Segal did not have time to contemplate that he was now an ace. He felt rounds hitting his own aircraft. He saw oil streaming from his engine and watched as a bullet ripped into his cockpit, smashing his radio.

He looked around to see three Zeros closing in for the kill. As he later wrote, one of them "had me perfectly boresighted and was shooting hell out of me."

As he executed another split-S, he saw "about 20 Zeros making runs on me from all sides. I almost rammed one."

Finally, at about 6,000 feet, he was able to duck into a cloud. He passed through it and leveled out just over the water near Visuvisu Point, where the whole battle had begun. He saw four Zeros in the distance, and they saw him. Carefully applying power to his compromised engine, he slowly pulled away from his pursuers, and two of them banked away.

Still being chased by a pair of Zeros, Segal wanted to head for the newly opened American airfield at Seghe on the southern end of New Georgia, but he was afraid to turn because he knew that the Zeros could outturn a Corsair, so he maintained a straight course in the general direction of Seghe.

Segal felt himself losing speed, watched his oil pressure drop to nothing and his cylinder head temperature skyrocket. He was not going to make it.

Meanwhile, as he came out of his dive after making his initial and unsuccessful pass at the A6M, Jim Swett had emerged over Ramada Island off the east coast of New Georgia, and had seen a Corsair in the distance, with three Zeros chasing him by about two miles. Swett later reported that he thought the Corsair was trailing smoke, and tried in vain to tell the pilot to "get out of that thing."

Though in his after-action report, Swett said he did not recognize the Corsair as being Segal's, it almost certainly was.

Swett lost sight of the Corsair in the clouds, but went after one of the three Zeros, firing a short burst into it. As the Zero pulled up, the outboard half of its right wing ripped off and "he fluttered into the water."

When the other two Zeros fled, Swett looked unsuccessfully for the Corsair, but sighted a Betty low to the water and "going like hell," with a Zero about 2,000 feet above "doing wing-overs and rolling all around."

Waiting for the Zero to get out of the way, Swett attacked the bomber, firing at its engines. At a range of about 50 yards, the Betty suddenly nosed over and sliced into the water.

Swett passed through the spray kicked up by the crash and turned, only to find another Zero on his tail. He was about 1,000 feet above the wave tops when he saw a line of bullet holes appear across his cowling. As he ducked into a cloud to escape, he noted that both fuel pressure and oil pressure were reading as zero, and his engine conked out.

Deciding to ditch, Swett pointed the Corsair's nose toward Seghe, and made his water landing about five miles out to sea. The Corsair remained afloat, providing a good target for a pair of Japanese pilots who were bent on killing him. Swett dived overboard and spent around ten minutes dodging behind the aircraft as the Zeros began making strafing passes, each one coming at him from an opposite direction. He deliberately did not inflate his life jacket so that he could duck underwater to hide himself.

Finally, the enemy pilots gave up, and Swett was able to inflate both his Mae West and his life raft, and to retrieve his parachute from the cockpit of his still-floating aircraft. He spent all afternoon paddling toward shore, and it was afternoon when he finally made it to the coral reef on New Georgia's west coast. Staggering ashore, he wrapped himself in his parachute and went to sleep.

At around the same time that Jim Swett was ditching in the waters of the Slot off New Georgia, Manny Segal was doing the same. His aircraft was leaking oil at a tremendous rate, and his radio had been shot out. As Segal throttled down and pulled back on the stick, he could feel Japanese slugs slamming into the armor plate behind his seat.

The impact of ditching at around 100mph slammed his head forward into the control panel, which lacerated his face and smashed out two teeth. He had not tightened his seat belt. Fortunately, he was not knocked unconscious.

His face drenched in blood, Segal climbed out of his cockpit and quickly inflated his rubber raft. The two Zeros that had downed him turned back without making a strafing pass, probably low on fuel.

Unable to find the paddles, he was now adrift in his raft at the mercy of the currents, but glad to be alive. How close he was to the place where Jim Swett came down is not known, but it was probably within a radius of 20 miles or so, and possibly closer.

Segal spent the afternoon hoping to see passing aircraft that would see him; what did see him was a curious albatross. The huge bird landed nearby and sized up the human in the yellow boat. Finally, he lumbered into the air and landed again on Segal's leg. Apparently unperturbed, it walked down his leg to his foot and seemed otherwise to ignore him.

Carefully, he put his other ankle over the bird's feet, and trapped it. For about five minutes, the enormous albatross, with a wingspan greater than Segal's height, struggled to get free. "At first, I was going to let it go," Segal recalled. "But I figured I might not make land and might need [to eat] the bird, so I killed it. While I was choking it, it spit up about three fish into the bottom of the boat, which I also kept."

Apparently, Segal gave no thought to the fate of the Ancient Mariner in Samuel Taylor Coleridge's poem, upon whom disastrous bad luck descended when he slew an albatross.

Putting aside any further thought of eating the bird, Segal refocused his attention on getting to shore. He tried using his two survival knives in lieu of the missing oars, but found them "more than useless."

He had the idea of stripping off his clothes and trying to pull the raft while swimming. For the remainder of the day, he alternated between swimming and resting in the raft, but at nightfall, he returned to the raft and tried without success to use the small sail in the raft. He finally dozed off as rain began to fall.

It now began to look as though Segal's fate, like that of the Ancient Mariner, had taken a turn for the worse.

Segal awoke, cold and wet, after hearing the motors of several boats passing in the darkness, and tried to get their attention. He tried firing his pistol, but it was inoperable. This was probably a good thing, because anyone in the boats who heard shots would be likely to return fire.

Awakening around daybreak, he discovered that his raft was growing "pretty soft" as air leaked from it. He was trying to reinflate it by blowing into the valve when he spotted four destroyers about four miles away. As the nearest one approached within 1,000 yards, he tried to signal to it by waving the sail. When it seemed to pass without slowing, he slumped into dejection. However, when it finally slowed and came about, "my relief was intense."

As it neared him, Segal began waving his dead albatross to get their attention. The men on the still-moving destroyer tossed him a line, which he grabbed and held tight, even as he was dragged out of his raft and through the water.

Finally, he was hoisted aboard and taken to the sick bay, where a doctor put five stitches into his lacerated lip. This done, the ship's captain gave him a cigar, "which really tasted good, though the mechanics of smoking it with half a mouth all sewed up were somewhat involved."

It was nearly 1700hrs on Monday, July 12, when Segal walked back into the bivouac of VMF-221 to a hero's welcome. Now with five victories, he was heralded as "our newest ace." In reporting his adventure, the after-action report noted "his bag for this trip: 3 Zeros and 1 Albatross." He was now honored with the nickname "Murderous Manny" Segal.

At about the same time on Monday that Segal was lunching in the destroyer's wardroom, Jim Swett was ashore on New Georgia and looking for something to eat.

After a fitful night wrapped in parachute cloth on the beach, waking to the slightest noise, Swett arose at first light and rowed his raft to a nearby lagoon. He landed near a deserted village around 1100hrs, where he found a ripe melon still on the vine and ate it. He gathered some limes and papayas, and proceeded to continue his exploration of the lagoon.

Around 1500hrs on Monday afternoon, two islanders in a dugout canoe caught up with him and threatened him with axes until he was able to convince them that he was an American. They then took him to the jungle hideout of the well-known coastwatcher Donald Kennedy, a New Zealander who had lived in the Solomons since 1921. After dining with Kennedy, Swett was taken to Seghe, where he spent Monday night. He embarked the following afternoon aboard a coastal transport ship, probably USS *APC-25*, and finally reached Guadalcanal on Wednesday morning, two days after Segal's return.

Both Swett and Segal were back in the air on July 22, and they flew several routine, but uneventful, combat air patrols and a couple of strafing missions through the final two weeks of a very memorable month.

Winding down after the turn of the month, they made the "last hop" of the tour on August 17, then began transiting through Espiritu Santo on their way to Australia. Swett was in double digits with 12.5, while Segal had five—not counting the albatross.

The careers of Manny Segal, Jim Swett and Bill Snider would continue in the Solomons later in 1943. For Swett and Snider, they would reach their climactic moments in the skies over Okinawa in 1945.

────────

Another future double-digit ace whose career began in 1943 and reached into double digits over Okinawa was Herbert Harvey "Trigger" Long.

Originally assigned to VMF-122, Long had transferred to VMF-121 in December 1942 and scored his first three aerial victories in January 1943. In March, Long was back "home" with VMF-122, which was commanded for two months by Major Greg Boyington in an often-overlooked moment of his colorful career.

In June 1943, having just converted from Wildcats to Corsairs, VMF-122 was in the Solomons under Major Herman "Hap" Hansen. In July, the squadron started to see significant action during the campaign that had begun with the Allied landings on New Georgia on the last day of June.

On the afternoon of July 7, Herb Long, now a captain, was leading one of the two VMF-122 divisions on a combat air patrol over Rendova. At 1430hrs, while flying at 23,000 feet, they made contact with nine IJNAF Betty bombers escorted by around 30 Zeros.

When Long went after one of the Bettys, a running gun battle worthy of cinematic interpretation ensued. He got on the bomber's tail, which, had it been a fighter, would have been its most vulnerable point. However, the Betty had a tail gunner who was more than capable of returning fire, which he did.

Dodging and weaving, Long tried to put a stream of fire into his quarry while dodging the fire coming back at him. At last, there was a lucky split second of opportunity and Long's tracers ripped into the gunner's position.

Long turned to the Betty's right engine, but just as he seemed to be getting some hits, the bomber disappeared into a cloud.

Searching urgently for his quarry to finish the job, Long passed through the cloud himself. As he came out the bottom he saw the Betty below him, close to the water and training smoke. He watched as the enemy aircraft slid into the sea in a mountain of foaming spray.

VMF-122 claimed four additional Bettys and three Zeros that day.

It was while leading another patrol over Rendova, on the early morning of July 12, that Trigger Long made ace, downing a Zero in a much shorter aerial battle than the one five days earlier. His sixth victory came on July 17 as VMF-122 was escorting SBDs against Japanese shipping in the area of Kahili and Buin on the southern tip of Bougainville. Again, as ten days earlier, the squadron ran up an impressive score. Among the two Rufes and a dozen Zeros that went down that day was Trigger Long's last victory of 1943. After three in January and three in July, Long would not add to his score again for nearly two years.

18

Finding Their Momentum

August into September

On August 12, 1943, after lying low for several weeks, testing the AirSols pilots only timidly if at all, the IJNAF intervened in force to attack a formation of B-24s from the USAAF Thirteenth Air Force that had just bombed the Kahili airfield on the southern end of Bougainville. Similar strikes over the previous days and weeks—one had occurred just the day before—had gone unchallenged by the Japanese, but today would be different. It was a day with ample cloud cover, which provided camouflage for the bombers, as well as for the Zero pilots, who used it to screen their hit and run strikes at the bombers.

En route back to Guadalcanal, the Americans could still see flames from the burning airfields below as they passed over Balalae Island, 20 miles to the south. Escorting the bombers were Corsairs from VMF-124 and VMF-215, squadrons that had been escorting the bombers on previous days when the Japanese had not attacked.

One of these squadrons was a veteran unit that was just returned from leave in Australia, and working on getting its momentum back. VMF-124 had been the first squadron to take the Corsair into combat six months earlier, but had only just returned to the Solomons at the end of July, and had seen little action.

Returning with the squadron was Kenneth Ambrose Walsh, who had become the first-ever Corsair ace back in May. Walsh was leading VMF-124 on August 12 because Major Bill Millington, the squadron commander, had engine trouble and had to divert to an auxiliary field.

VMF-215 was the fresh outfit. Under the command of Major James Neefus, the squadron's aviators had forward deployed to Guadalcanal from Espiritu Santo on July 24, and had flown their first mission the next day before their ground echelon had even arrived. The squadron had gone overseas and had spent six weeks at MCAS Ewa and two months flying patrols out of Midway before going to the South Pacific.

Though still untested, VMF-215 would eventually be home to three double-digit aces. One of them, Donald Nathan Aldrich, would score his first aerial victory on August 12. It would also be the first for VMF-215.

When the B-24s descended to 14,000 feet near Choiscul Bay, more than 30 Zeros emerged from the clouds to attack. Major Robert (Bob) Owens, the VMF-215 executive officer and its future commander, attacked the two Zeros nearest to the bomber formation. One of these turned to make a head-on pass, but Owens returned fire and noticed that he was trailing smoke as he disappeared into the clouds, although his fate would not be confirmed.

Aldrich went on the attack, hitting another Zero which also proceeded to escape into the clouds. Just as this was happening, yet another Zero emerged from a cloud and passed through Aldrich's sights. The Marine aviator cut loose with a stream of .50-caliber fire, watching as the Japanese fighter flew straight though it and burst into flames almost immediately.

Ken Walsh recalled that the Zeros attacked "from below, head-on, then from the rear and side ... they would roll over on their backs after firing their guns."

About five minutes into the battle, as the dogfight descended into a deep valley between cloud banks, the American fighters became separated. Walsh was surrounded by the three other members of his division, and still able to see the bombers, but the rest of VMF-124 could not be seen.

Don Aldrich, meanwhile, had lost his whole squadron, so he joined up with Walsh, as did eight USAAF P-40s.

"The fight got pretty rugged," Walsh remembered, adding that the battle raged across 100 miles of sky. "Especially for the bombers in the rear of the formation since the Zeros were paying particular attention to them."

The Zeros would line up about 500 yards behind the bombers and aim for the tail gunners, trying to kill them before pulling in close. Seeing this, Walsh and his wingman, Bill Johnston, countered the tactic by waiting about 5,000 feet above the rear of the bomber formation, then pouncing when Zeros moved into position.

On his first pass, one unlucky Japanese pilot never saw Walsh coming. Walsh fired his guns until he was so close to the Zero that he felt he had to duck. As the enemy aircraft rolled over, flames poured from its belly.

Over the course of at least four such maneuvers, Walsh destroyed two Zeros for certain, and sent another one into the clouds trailing smoke.

Don Aldrich got his own first aerial victory in a diving attack. He spotted a Zero to his right and about a thousand feet below. Running in from behind and above, Aldrich opened fire. As pieces began flying off the Zero, the Japanese pilot nosed over into a cloud.

Finally, a Zero pilot tried to turn the tables on Walsh and managed to get on his tail without being seen. Smoke filled the cockpit and the impact of machine gun and cannon rounds shook the Corsair. Walsh later said that it sounded like "rocks on a tin roof."

The Zero pilot came so close that when Johnston moved in to take him out, he had to be careful not to hit Walsh as well. In his after-action report, Walsh expressed his thankfulness for Johnston, adding that "another second later I surely would [have] 'got it.'"

By the time the formation came over New Georgia, the surviving Zeros had vanished. Most of the Corsairs, which were low on fuel after the great dogfight, dropped in to Seghe airfield to refuel. Walsh's landing, with his hydraulic system shot out, was the clumsiest. He had neither flaps nor brakes and had to lower the landing gear manually. His Corsair rolled most of the length of the runway, then careened off and hit another aircraft, but Walsh lived to fight another day.

After refueling at Seghe, Don Aldrich returned to Guadalcanal as VMF-215 was celebrating his confirmed victory and probables attributed to him and to Owens.

Along with Aldrich, future double-digit ace Harold Leman Spears was already part of VMF-215. The squadron's third such ace, Robert Murray Hanson, scored his first two aerial victories with VMF-214 before transferring to VMF-215 at the end of October.

On August 14, 1943, two days after the great shootout south of Bougainville, Robert Owens of VMF-215 had the distinction of being the first AirSols pilot to land at the newly captured airfield at Munda. VMF-124 arrived hot on their heels and Ken Walsh had the distinction of leading the first Marine patrol out of Munda that afternoon.

Within a couple of days, the Munda airfield was in service, first as a forward staging base for fighters and later hosting more permanent operations.

On the following day, August 15, American forces landed on the island of Vella Lavella, 50 miles northwest of Munda. On the island, the airfield at Barakoma would be reworked by the SeaBees and begin operations on September 24; it was soon to become one of the most important AirSols bases in the Solomons.

Ken Walsh led five Corsairs from VMF-124 that afternoon, providing top cover for the landings. They arrived over the beachhead at 1645hrs, and things were momentarily quiet.

About a half-hour later, "Cracker Base," the Fighter Direction Officer who was at his radar scope aboard a destroyer below, alerted the Marine aviators to an enemy formation approaching from the southwest.

Walsh sent three of the Corsairs up to take a high cover position, while he and Addison Raber went down to 10,000 feet. Here, they were jumped by five Zeros that made a fast, but ineffective, diving pass.

As Walsh turned, he spotted another Zero that was not part of the first five, and got on his tail. A single burst and this Zero crashed into the sea about five miles from Cracker Base.

Raber, meanwhile, was nowhere to be seen. Later he reported that he had seen eight Zeros above and was evading them. His radio had failed when he tried to alert Walsh.

Now flying alone, Walsh began patrolling the north shore of Vella Lavella at low level. Here, he saw a formation of nine Aichi D3A Val dive bombers. Alerting Cracker Base, he attacked the Vals from below and behind and sent two down in flames.

When he moved toward a third, he discovered that a Zero had closed in on his tail and was putting 20mm cannon shells into his right wing, severing the hydraulic line and aileron control. Another cannon shell damaged his tail as 7.7mm machine gun rounds peppered the whole Corsair. Somehow, he managed to hold the aircraft together long enough to make his second perilous emergency landing in four days.

Of VMF-124's count of 13 victories that day, three belonged to Ken Walsh.

Hal Spears of VMF-215 scored his first two aerial victories on August 19 during a strafing mission to the IJNAF floatplane base at Rekata Bay on the northeast side of Santa Isabel Island, about 170 miles north of Guadalcanal.

Spears and George Sanders broke off from a larger formation as it passed through a rain squall and investigated several nearby inlets before coming back over Rekata Bay. Flying through a hail of Japanese antiaircraft fire, Spears targeted a taxiing A6M2-N "Floatplane Zero" and blew it up. Nearby, two other A6M2-Ns had just taken off, so he came in behind them and opened fire. In quick succession, they both exploded.

Turning to strafe some others that were still on the surface of the bay, Spears noticed that Sanders was in trouble. His engine had taken some antiaircraft fire and he was trailing smoke.

Spears recalled that he "coached him on a water landing outside the two islands off Rekata Bay [and] saw him climb out into the water just before his plane sank."

Sanders was now listed as missing in action.

After several days of routine patrols, VMF-124 next made contact with the IJNAF on August 21. That afternoon, Ken Walsh was over Vella Lavella at 23,000 feet at 1515hrs when he heard that "Sirius Base," the main control tower at Barakoma airfield, was under attack.

He spiraled down, looking for Japanese bombers, but saw about 15 Zeros at 18,000 feet. He slashed through the formation scattering the Zeros and lined up behind one that was headed north trailing smoke, possibly from an earlier attack by another American pilot. He made a firing pass from behind and watched the Zero hit the water.

Walsh was on a roll. He flew an hour-long patrol on the morning of August 23, and took off a second time just before noon. As he was touching down from his first patrol, a call came in from Barakoma that enemy aircraft were in their area.

Walsh taxied to the fuel depot, took on 100 gallons, and was airborne ten minutes later. Flying the short 50 miles to Vella Lavella, Walsh had begun to circle at 30,000 feet when he spotted 15 Zeros below. He radioed some other VMF-124 aviators whom he knew to be in the area and invited them to join him.

While waiting, he got word of an ongoing dogfight northwest of Vella Lavella, and decided to make himself part of it. He saw three Corsairs exiting the scene in opposite directions and a larger number of Zeros, which were flying in pairs.

Walsh dived on the leader of one such cell, pouring fire into it, but seeing no results other than a thin smoke trail. When he passed the aircraft later, it was still trailing smoke, but he did not see it go down.

Walsh next found himself under attack from above by three Zeros, but he got away and ducked into a cloud. He waited at least ten minutes before venturing out, then climbed up to 35,000 feet. He lingered just for a short time, because his oxygen pressure was down, but he did see some Japanese activity over Mundimundi, about 20 miles north of Barakoma.

Descending, he saw several clusters of Zeros at 25,000 feet, and proceeded to pick off two stragglers by making quick diving passes. He rendezvoused with James English from VMF-124 over Kundurumbangara Point, but English broke off because his oxygen was practically used up. Walsh remained in the area until his own oxygen was spent, then returned to Munda at 1305hrs.

Including Walsh's pair, VMF-124 downed five Zeros in the various air battles of August 23.

During the last week of the month, the temporary duty at Munda ended for the aviators of VMF-124, and they began making their way back to Guadalcanal in small groups as transportation became available. Many of them were transported by Skytrain, but some, such as Ken Walsh on August 25, made the hop in their Corsairs.

Don Aldrich of VMF-215 scored his own second and third aerial victories on August 25 and 26, while flying bomber escort missions against Kahili from the base at Munda. The first day's mission began badly with the six USAAF B-24s missing the target because of cloud cover, and the Corsairs losing track of the bombers because of the same mountains of cumulus.

Robert Owens, who was leading the nine Corsairs, recalled coming out into clear sky at 16,000 feet and seeing the bombers behind, at the same level, and about ten miles away. Four P-40s, nearer to the bombers, were engaged in a fight with about 50 Zeros.

Owens led the Corsairs to attack, picked the Zero nearest the formation and gave it a short burst. He found another and sent him trailing smoke into the clouds below. As Owens later recalled, "targets were by now so numerous that it was impossible to turn without encountering Zeros."

He tailed another, fired a five-second blast, and followed as the Zero rolled to the left and went down. When it had rolled onto its back, trailing smoke, both wing roots exploded.

Owens also encountered several inline-engined fighters that he identified as Kawasaki Ki-61s, the Japanese Army Air Force aircraft codenamed "Tony" by the Allies. He fired on one and left it smoking, though he did not see what happened afterward. The Tony was faster than the Zero, quite maneuverable, and equipped with self-sealing fuel tanks, so that it did not burst into flames as easily. It was a worthy opponent for the Corsair, but not yet present in the Solomons in significant numbers.

Generally speaking, enemy aircraft that were attacked and last seen trailing smoke, but not on fire, were considered to be probable aerial victories, but not confirmed, and therefore were not counted in the ongoing tally of an aviator's total score.

Don Aldrich, meanwhile, made his first pass at a Zero around the same time as Owens, but lost him after he made a tight split-S turn. A second Zero then presented itself at about 7,000 feet and Aldrich dived from behind. He fired a long burst and watched the Zero plummet straight into the water below.

He next saw three Zeros approaching, two together and one alone. He opened fire on the latter and watched him "smoking in huge clouds of black smoke," but did not stay to see him crash, so he was listed in Aldrich's log as a probable.

The next day saw VMF-215 taking on two bomber escort missions to Kahili, with Aldrich flying on the first, which consisted of four Corsairs. Having attacked at 20,000 feet, the bombers began their decent over Balalae Island. It was here that Aldrich spotted a Zero approach one of the B-24s from behind. He quickly got onto the Zero's six, opened fire and watched the enemy aircraft explode into a plummeting ball of flame.

When Aldrich maneuvered to attack another, he found himself on the receiving end of a 20mm pounding. His tail was badly damaged and he took a hit in the cockpit that injured his arm and put shrapnel in his face. Luckily, the enemy pilot chose not to finish him off and Aldrich made a safe landing at Munda.

On August 30, for the fifth time that month, B-24s of the USAAF Thirteenth Air Force headed north to blast the IJNAF base at Kahili. Tasked as part of the escort force, VMF-124 launched its Corsairs from Guadalcanal at 1115hrs, rendezvoused with the bombers and headed north.

As the formation was passing over New Georgia, Ken Walsh felt his supercharger conk out and he started falling behind. Thinking quickly, he dropped out and down, making a fast landing on the advanced field at Munda. Major Jim Neefus, VMF-215's squadron commander, greeted him as he taxied in from his landing. When Walsh quickly explained the situation and asked to borrow a VMF-215 Corsair, Neefus pointed to several that were fully fueled and armed, and told him to take his pick. Ten minutes later, by Walsh's reckoning, he was back in the air.

By the time that Walsh caught up with the bomber formation over Bougainville, they were in the midst of their bomb run at Kahili and already under attack by 50 Zeros. The Japanese had caught the two dozen B-24s over the target, and had forced them to disperse to an extent that the handful of American fighters could not protect them all.

The battle, which Walsh later described as "the worst I've ever been in," reached a ferocious melee as it tumbled across the sky south of the Shortland Islands 30 miles from Kahili. Walsh watched as a USAAF P-39 went down in flames, as did a USAAF P-40 with three Zeros on its tail. Over the radio, he heard a call from a fellow Corsair aviator that he was going down over Fauro Island, one of the Shortlands. Nearing Vella Lavella moments later, Walsh saw a B-24 trailing smoke.

Walsh tore into a cluster of Zeros, scoring hits on at least four, and perhaps five. Of these, two went down blazing, one of them disintegrating in an explosion.

Just as Walsh spotted Bill Millington and joined up with him, a desperate call came in over the radio that "lots of Zeros [were] raising hell with B-24s off the water." As Walsh and Millington quickly responded, Walsh got behind two Zeros "that never knew what hit them." One Zero crashed just off the beach at Vella Lavella, and the other sliced into the water trailing black smoke.

However, Walsh came out of this engagement with the tables turned and four other Zeros on his six, pounding away with 20mm cannon shells. Despite at least one shell exploding inside the engine of the borrowed Corsair, Walsh wrung as much power as he could out of that R-2800 and got away. His oil pressure was heading south just as the cylinder head temperature was at the top limit.

Moments before, he had seen Walt Mayberry of VMF-123 bail out of his Corsair over Ganongga (Ranongga) Island, 20 miles south of Vella Lavella. Luck was not with Mayberry that day, however. He was captured by the Japanese three days later, taken to Rabaul and executed in March 1944.

Conversely, luck rode the Corsair down with Ken Walsh, though it was a bumpy ride. Bracing himself for a water landing, he hit the water just off Barakoma Point, within sight of the airfield. He was in a US Navy Higgins boat a few minutes later and was soon ashore on Vella Lavella.

Walsh was turned over to a pair of Navy doctors, D.A. Anderson and J.H. Morten, who gave him dry clothes and "couldn't do enough for me." As Walsh wrote in his after-action report, "since they didn't have any bones to set, they took it out on me by giving me lots of Brandy, but in spite of this I couldn't sleep that night."

During August 1943, VMF-124 scored a total of 38 aerial victories, of which Ken Walsh was responsible for more than half. The man who had earned his wings as a private only to become the first Corsair ace had now brought his own total to 20, eclipsing that of any Marine aviator still in the South Pacific. Walsh had exceeded the scores of the great first-generation aces such as John L. Smith and Marion Carl, and among Marines, he was now second only to Joe Foss. There was already discussion of a Medal of Honor.

After having found its momentum, VMF-215 scored 22 aerial victories during August. Among the aviators, Hal Spears had his two A6M2-N floatplanes, while Aldrich and Owens had each claimed three Zeros. Leading the squadron though was Major Raynold George Tomes, who also had three Zeros to his credit, as well as an Aichi D3A Val dive bomber.

As September began, everyone at VMF-124 and VMF-215 was counting down toward the end of the first week of the new month, when the tours of duty for both squadrons would come to a close and they would all be winging their way westward for a month of R&R in Australia.

However, there were still battles to be fought, and an ace to be made.

Both squadrons were part of an escort of USAAF B-24s on a mission to Kahili on September 2. Over Kahili, the Corsairs came in at 28,000 feet, and the bombers at 20,000. Bomb hits on the runway and adjacent area were noted, and as they passed over Balalae Island, the formation descended for the run back to Guadalcanal.

Don Aldrich, leading one of VMF-215's two four-ship flights, was behind and slightly to the left of the B-24s when he spotted a lone Zero at a higher altitude, possibly scanning the bombers for interceptors. At the same time, Aldrich saw some radial-engined aircraft below, but upon investigation these turned out to be US Navy fighters.

When he banked away, Aldrich saw six Zeros about 2,000 feet below, with one apart from the others. Picking this one, he closed in on it and opened fire, but missed.

This Zero then turned his attention to Hal Spears, but made only a quick, half-hearted pass.

Pulling up after his own attack, Aldrich found that he had a clear shot at another Zero that was inverted in the midst of a roll. He took the shot and both he and Spears watched the Zero go down.

The Marines then came under attack. Spears later recalled that "Zeros were popping at me from behind, so I dove and pulled up in a steep left wingover and got away."

Meanwhile, after the Japanese made their pass, Aldrich followed one Zero into a steep dive, opened fire and chased him down from 22,000 feet to around 13,000, where the Japanese fighter burst into flames and fell into the sea.

As Spears came out of his dive at 18,000 feet, he saw a Zero circling below him and dived into his circle, came up on his six and opened fire. As this Zero tumbled out of the sky, Spears found another Zero on his own six. Taking evasive action, he was descending below 16,000 feet as the Zero overshot him. Spears took a full deflection shot and saw the Zero engulfed by smoke and flame.

Aldrich and Spears had become separated during their dogfights, and found their way to Munda independently. Comparing notes and bullet holes in their Corsairs—including one in the prop of Spears' aircraft—they were able to congratulate one another on two aerial victories each. These gave Spears a total of four, while Aldrich now had five to become VMF-215's first ace.

Major Ray Tomes, who had led VMF-215 in aerial victories at the end of August, did not come home on September 2. He had led one of the flights that took off at 0555hrs for a strafing mission to Balalae Island and Kahili. Tomes had led a low-level pass on a barge offshore from Balalae, but came under small-caliber and 20mm antiaircraft fire as his Corsair passed over the island at about 50 feet. Two members of his flight saw his aircraft crash in a fireball on the island.

VMF-124 didn't score any aerial victories on the September 2 Kahili bombing mission, but the squadron's Bill Cannon shot down an IJNAF G4M Betty bomber that day while on a "test hop" over distant Rennell Island, 360 miles southeast of Bougainville and 150 miles due south of Guadalcanal.

At VMF-215, as one aviator, Tomes, was lost, another returned from the dead. George Sanders, who had been shot down on August 19 while strafing A6M2-Ns with Hal Spears at Rekata Bay, suddenly reappeared on Guadalcanal on September 4.

Sanders had inflated his life raft and made it ashore on a nearby island. The following day, he saw the Corsairs that came to search for him, but they were too high to see him. After dodging the Japanese for five days, he made contact with some islanders who got word to a coastwatcher, Michael Forster, who had been the prewar British district officer for the area. Sanders met Forster on August 26, and spent several days with him before being picked up by a PBY on September 4 and taken back to Guadalcanal.

Sanders was reunited with most of his VMF-215 mates the following day when they returned to Guadalcanal from Munda on their way to their month-long break in Australia. For most, including Aldrich, Spears, and Sanders, there would be another tour of duty and more aerial combat to come in October.

Ken Walsh would head the other way in October, to the United States, where he would be awarded the Medal of Honor personally by President Roosevelt on February 8, 1944—the first Corsair aviator to be so honored. He would come back to fly in combat over the Pacific once again, but not until the final months of World War II in 1945, and not with VMF-124. He would score a single victory, his last and his only after August 1943, with the "Triple Deuces" of VMF-222.

VMF-222 had first reached SOPAC just as Walsh was leaving, coming in to formally relieve VMF-215 in September 1943. With them was Major Donald Hooten Sapp of Miami, who would be the squadron's only double-digit ace—excepting Walsh.

After nearly a month of familiarization flights out of Espiritu Santo, the VMF-222 aviators began arriving on Guadalcanal aboard SCAT Skytrains on September 2, the same day that the aviators of VMF-215 scored the final aerial victories of their first tour.

As it was for many squadrons, VMF-222's first taste of aerial combat on September 9 was rather inauspicious. Flying a fighter sweep after a bombing raid on Kahili, they tangled with at least eight Zeros. The squadron claimed one probable, but lost four Corsairs—although the pilots were rescued.

September 14 was a much better day over Kahili for VMF-222. Don Sapp was leading the squadron's second division that day as they took off at 0730hrs to rendezvous with the bombers headed for Bougainville. They were flying at 25,000 feet above Balalae Island when Sapp's wingman, Charles D. "Mother" Jones, first saw the Zeros below at 18,000 feet.

Sapp let Jones take the lead as they plunged downward out of the sun. As Jones slashed through the enemy formation, two Zeros were on his tail about 1,000 feet apart—and Don Sapp was on their tails. Sapp opened fire, picking them off neatly. As the right wing of the second Zero disintegrated, Sapp could see the engine engulfed in flames.

Sapp scored two of VMF-222's five victories that day. It was a good first day, but it would be five months before he finally made ace.

19

A Wanderer in the Wings

August into September

For most of 1943, Major Gregory Boyington had been like a nomad. He was one of many staff officers from all the American services who drifted through SOPAC from New Caledonia to Espiritu Santo to Guadalcanal, never seeing combat, but envying those who did. He had been in the South Pacific longer without flying in combat than most Marine aviators with previous experience elsewhere—but it had been more than a year and several lifetimes since his days with the Flying Tigers in China.

That he was in SOPAC at all was good luck for an aspiring fighter pilot, but the circumstances in which he found himself once he got there were an allegory for bad luck. Boyington was one of those people whose lives consist of the deepest of lows, which seem to alternate with amazingly fortuitous peaks and troughs. The horror of alcoholism continuously stalked his days and haunted his nights.

A year earlier, he had been parking cars in Seattle with co-workers who were still in high school. He was broke, with alimony and child support only part of the indebtedness hanging over him.

Had it not been for the personal intercession of Brigadier General Ralph Johnson Mitchell, the director of aviation at Marine Corps headquarters, Boyington might have spent the war in that garage. Boyington's request for reinstatement as a Marine aviator had been mired in red tape, buried in the pile, and sidetracked every which way, until Mitchell took an interest and fast-tracked Boyington's request. More than that, he had brought garage-attendant Boyington back as a Marine Corps major in September 1942.

Unfortunately, when Boyington went overseas in January 1943 he was without a squadron assignment, a homeless wannabe fighter pilot. Arriving at the Turtle Bay airfield on Espiritu Santo, he was given the job of assistant operations officer at the headquarters of Marine Air Group 11 (MAG-11), an administrative parent of operational squadrons including VMF-121, VMF-213, and VMF-214.

In this post, he ran afoul of Lieutenant Colonel Joe Smoak, the MAG-11 operations officer. He was an old nemesis from Pensacola years earlier when Smoak was an instructor and Boyington a cadet. Smoak apparently harbored a deep animosity for Boyington, and the feeling was mutual. In his memoirs, Boyington referred to him only as "Colonel Lard," a name that many people later assumed was his actual name.

In his memoirs, Boyington described the job given to him by Smoak as being "as next to nothing as I had ever hoped to be in charge of in my life. I had the say of nothing. All I did was count the planes when they went out for training flights, and count them again when they returned."

Marine aviators and Marine fighting squadrons destined for combat passed through Turtle Bay heading north, but what made Boyington's life especially frustrating were the Marine aviators who passed through Turtle Bay heading south. These included people whom he knew, men who had become aces that people talked about. The likes of Joe Foss, Bob Galer, Ken Walsh, and others each passed through with stories of adventures that Boyington feared he would never experience.

There were breaks in the monotony that included occasional opportunities to ferry replacement aircraft up to Guadalcanal. In April, he even filled in briefly as commander of VMF-122, but they flew only routine patrols over the Slot and made no contact with Japanese aircraft during a short 16-day tour of duty.

After this came a couple of weeks in Sydney, Australia, where the abundance of nightlife and female companionship certainly suited Boyington, but where the demons of his alcoholism courted him at every turn. When he returned to Turtle Bay in May, Boyington's proclivity toward drunkenness and brawling gave Smoak an easy opportunity to justify disciplinary measures. Boyington had been looking forward to going back to Guadalcanal with VMF-122, this time flying Corsairs, but Smoak refused to approve this assignment.

Furious, Boyington took the matter up the chain of command to Brigadier General James Tillinghast Moore of the 1st Marine Air Wing, whom Boyington had known at Quantico back in the late 1930s when Moore was a lieutenant colonel and Boyington a lieutenant.

Boyington and "Nuts" Moore were kindred spirits, both eccentrics who enjoyed the occasional libation. Moore had not gotten his nickname for naught. A one-time aerobatic pilot, he carried a cane—not to aid walking, but for twirling. In the Sherwood Forest of SOPAC, Nuts Moore was the King Richard figure to Smoak's Sheriff of Nottingham. Moore promptly overruled Smoak's grounding of Boyington.

Unfortunately, the good luck that had impossibly superseded the bad was itself quickly replaced. In typical Boyington style, a drunken celebration ensued that led to Boyington suffering a broken leg. This sidelined him to a medical facility in New Zealand for two months.

When he was passing through Noumea on his way back to Espiritu Santo at the end of July, Boyington dropped into the Army Officer's Club, which he described as "the only place to eat," and discovered that he was broke—literally penniless. It was neither the first nor last time in his life that he was in such straits, but this may have been the only time that it was completely *accidental*.

In Auckland, he convalesced for a while at a boarding house run by a "truly fine" young woman named Carrie with whom he became friendly. When he was on his way to board his SCAT flight out of New Zealand, he had made the kindly gesture of giving her his roll of New Zealand bank notes, which he rightly assumed would have no value elsewhere. Unfortunately for him, he had forgotten that his sizable roll of American dollars was at the center of the New Zealand currency he gave her.

Upon his return to Turtle Bay, the continuing plague of bad luck cascaded over Boyington like a tropical waterfall. He developed an ear infection, which gave Smoak an excuse to ground him medically. Not only did this take away his ability to fly, it denied Boyington his flight pay.

To add insult to his misery, Smoak gave Boyington a new job. He made him the commander of VMF-112. At one time, earlier in the year when aces such as Jefferson DeBlanc and Archie Donahue were making names for themselves, an assignment to lead VMF-112 would have been a prize post. In July 1943, the assignment was a cruel joke. VMF-112 was now being used as an administrative agency to which men arriving or departing SOPAC were assigned for the time that it took to process them in or out.

A glance at the squadron's war diary for July shows little other than the occasional patrol by VMF-112's forward echelon, mixed with long lists of men passing through the squadron's rear echelon heading this way or that. On July 27, it is noted that "Boyington, Gregory" had assumed command, effective July 23. The last page of July's war diary bears Boyington's signature. He was in this job for less than three weeks.

The momentum at Turtle Bay was like that of ocean waves upon the shore. Waves come in and recede, each one with its own character. It was a melting pot of varied stories and aviators at different stages of their careers. There were old-timers anxious for a well-earned furlough in Australia, or a return to the States. There were those who had gone to war in Wildcats, who were coming back from Australia and transitioning to Corsairs. And there were fresh-faced aviators who had yet to see combat.

Within this constant state of flux, it was hard for Smoak, with his thumb on Boyington's career, to control all the variables. At last, it came time for VMF-112 as an entity, to pack up its tent and go back to the States to be rebuilt for redeployment. Effective on August 12, 1943, Boyington handed the reins to Major Herman

"Hap" Hansen, who would take the squadron home to develop it into a fresh, combat-ready organization.

This left Boyington on Espiritu Santo as a free agent. With all of the pilots, old and new, who were washing through Turtle Bay, he was not alone. There were a lot of free agents. At the same time, up in the Solomons, there was a need for more Corsair squadrons.

By the first week of September, there was another squadron at Turtle Bay, which like VMF-112, had once been an active fighting organization, but was now just an administrative shell. Unlike VMF-112 which was rotating Stateside, though, it would remain in SOPAC, an empty slate, just waiting for Boyington to fill it.

VMF-214, originally given the name "Swashbucklers," was formed at MCAS Ewa in Hawaii in July 1942. Equipped with F4F Wildcats, the squadron had passed through Espiritu Santo in February 1943 en route to Guadalcanal. Ten aerial victories had been scored by the Swashbucklers in the great air battle over the Slot on April 7, but its record was overshadowed by those of other squadrons. The only Swashbucklers to become aces did so with aerial victories carried over from their service with other squadrons.

During August 1943, VMF-214 had been based at Munda under the command of John "Smiley" Burnett, who got his nickname because of his genial disposition, but it was also a nod to well-known western singer (and Gene Autry sidekick) Lester "Smiley" Burnette. Having seen little combat in their final month, the Swashbucklers returned to Espiritu Santo on September 3.

Most of VMF-214's aviators were anxious for their Australian furloughs. Meanwhile, there were rumors that the MAG-11 bureaucracy had new ideas for their squadron, or at least for their squadron number. VMF-214, as with VMF-112, had become a replacement pool, more of an administrative shell, and it was about to have its designation attached to an all-new entity.

The "new" VMF-214 came into being on September 7 with Greg Boyington as its commander. The core of the new squadron was probably a group of aviators whom Boyington brought over from VMF-112, such as Major Stan Bailey, who became the VMF-214 executive officer. Others included John Begert, Henry "Hank"

Bourgeois, William "Bill" Case, and Paul "Moon" Mullen—who took his nickname from Frank Willard's famous "Moon Mullens" comic strip. All in this group had combat experience, though none had achieved ace status yet.

Also joining VMF-214 was the eccentric Christopher Lyman McGee, who had been in SOPAC since late July and who had flown with Ken Walsh in VMF-124. Born in 1917 in Omaha, McGee had grown up on the South Side of Chicago, and was a cousin of fighter pilot John Gillespie McGee who penned the famous and widely quoted 1941 poem "High Flight," that begins: "Oh! I have slipped the surly bonds of Earth / And danced the skies on laughter-silvered wings; / Sunward I've climbed, and joined the tumbling mirth / Of sun-split clouds—/ ... I've chased the shouting wind along, and flung / My eager craft through footless halls of air . . ."

Like his cousin, Chris McGee was a gifted writer, and like John, he was so anxious to fly against the Axis before the United States entered World War II that he went to Canada to join the Royal Canadian Air Force (RCAF). John was killed in action in 1941 while flying a Spitfire over England, and Chris left the RCAF in 1942 to join the Marines. Before becoming part of VMF-214, Chris had spent most of his time familiarizing himself with the Corsair, but not in combat.

Not all the prominent personalities in the squadron were pilots on their way to becoming aces. Perhaps just as important was Lieutenant Frank Walton, the VMF-214 intelligence officer and air combat information officer. He was a former Los Angeles cop with a natural flair for Hollywood-style public relations, whose after-action reports and exciting tales shared with war correspondents would help shape the VMF-214 legend that was just beginning to take root.

Most of the new VMF-214 aviators, unlike Boyington, McGee, and a few others, had no experience either with combat or Corsairs. They were strangers thrown together as part of a family with no familial traditions. In the Sherwood Forest of SOPAC, they would become Boyington's "Merrie Men."

The rudderless, parentless, ad hoc nature of their squadron led to the men to calling themselves "Boyington's Bastards." One of the best-known stories about the squadron is that this name, as an "official" title, did not pass muster with the MAG-11 hierarchy, so the name had to be changed. Thus, the squadron adopted the softer, though equally applicable, appellation: the "Black Sheep."

Greg Boyington had at last found a home.

20

The Black Sheep Go to War

September

It was in the second week of September 1943 that everything started to go well for Greg Boyington. After half a year of the faded glory symbolized by his stint in the parking garage, and another eight months as an administrator wandering through SOPAC, he had landed a job as the chief of a tribe of fellow nomads. And thanks to Boyington's old benefactor, Major General Ralph Mitchell, this tribe was on its way to war.

Mitchell, who had been director of aviation at Marine Corps headquarters when he saved Boyington from oblivion in 1942, was now in the South Pacific as the commander of the 1st Marine Air Wing, essentially the top Marine Corps aviator in SOPAC. On September 11, he told Boyington to have his men pack their bags for the Solomons.

In this new role, Boyington was tailor-made for the media. As a bureaucrat, his rumpled shirt, self-promotion, and salty language made him boorish. But as the commander of a newly patched-together band of aviators, he was the perfect archetype for a feature story. He was not yet what one might call a heroic warrior, though his heavily embellished tales of being a Flying Tiger gave him a superb backstory. His personality was certainly the definition of colorful.

He even had a nickname that played well in print. Because of his advanced age—he was three months shy of 31—the mostly much younger men of VMF-214 called him "Gramps" or "Grandpappy," names which were not uncommonly assigned to senior officers of advanced years on the cusp of 30. Much later, the nickname was shortened to "Pappy." It rolled easily off the tongue, or the portable Smith Corona of a war correspondent, but, in fact, the men of VMF-214 did not call him that. When it was not "Major Boyington," it was the familiar "Greg," or "Gramps," but not "Pappy."

For his part, Boyington would often refer to the aviators of VMF-214s as "my clowns," which he qualified in his memoirs, saying that the term was used "with the same sort of affection" with which they had called him "Gramps." He added that "because of my age and longer experience I was able to save them from a lot of mistakes that young pilots make and thereby lose their lives."

On September 12, Boyington climbed into an F4U to lead 19 other Black Sheep Corsairs up to the airfield on Banika in the Russell Islands, which would be their first operating base. True to the vagabond image of the Black Sheep, they would operate out of several bases, including Munda and Barakoma on Vella Lavella, during their first six-week tour.

Two days later, Boyington and the new VMF-214 flew their first combat mission. They were one of several squadrons escorting SBD Dauntlesses, TBF Avengers, and USAAF B-24 Liberator heavy bombers against the big Japanese base at Kahili on Bougainville. It was on the same day and on the same mission that Don Sapp's first two aerial victories were part of VMF-222's first five, but the Black Sheep did not connect with the enemy that day.

"The clouds being what they were, no [Japanese] planes could find us," Boyington complained in his memoirs. "Damn the luck."

The next day found the Black Sheep escorting a photoreconnaissance mission that the Japanese chose not to challenge; but everything changed on September 16. Boyington took off at 1300hrs, leading two dozen VMF-214 Corsairs in six divisions of four each. While most of the aviators were new to combat, Boyington installed veterans to lead each division. The after-action report boasted that all 24 Corsairs got off the ground in the space of seven minutes. To say that they were eager was an understatement.

At 1350hrs, they rendezvoused with Dauntlesses and Avengers heading north against the antiaircraft gun nests on the fortified island of Balalae, a short distance southeast of Bougainville.

With VMF-214 flying high cover at 21,500 feet, and P-40s and US Navy Hellcats farther below, the strike force came over the target out of the west at 13,000 feet one hour after the rendezvous. Here, they were greeted by as many as 40 dark, brownish-green Zeros and Hamps, which, according to John Begert in the after-action report, "spilled out of the clouds."

As the Black Sheep dived to attack, a Zero slow-rolled past Begert, who opened fire and watched the enemy aircraft burst into flames from the underside of its engine. It was just 30 seconds later that another Zero passed through Begert's view, slow-rolling to escape another Corsair. Begert rolled with the enemy fighter, opened fire and watched him go into the sea.

Stan Bailey went after another Zero, chasing it downward as his wingman, Bob Alexander, dutifully disrupted a pack of three that tried to get on Bailey's tail. While Bailey watched his Zero, which was starting to spew smoke, disappear into a cloud, Alexander turned toward a pair of Zeros and made a rear approach on the leader's wingman.

At 200 yards, Alexander watched his bullets stitching their way along the Zero's tail, mid-fuselage, and cockpit. Small pieces flaked off and smoke belched from the engine. As he passed over the Zero's right wing, he looked down into the cockpit. Here he saw, as VMF-214 air combat information officer Frank Walton colorfully described in the after-action report, "flames come up from under the instrument panel and immediately fill the whole cockpit, making it look like a *movie kill.*"

Meanwhile, Bill Case, leading another division, had dived on seven Zeros flying at 16,000 feet. Seeing the Corsairs coming, two Zeros climbed to meet them. All four members of Case's division took short bursts at the Zeros, which banked to the right, rolled over and made overhead passes on the Corsairs as they passed by.

Case corkscrewed down, attacked several Zeros and chased one until it was trailing smoke, but like Bailey's it disappeared into a cloud. Case's wingman, Rolland "Rollie" Rinabarger, reported nine Zeros at nine o'clock high, but they made "only short, ducking, ineffectual passes."

When the Zeros and Hamps had spilled out of the clouds, Boyington circled left with his wingman, Don "Mo" Fisher, about 200 yards behind him. When a Zero rolled in between them and lined up to make a starboard pass on Boyington, Fisher opened fire. The Zero rolled left, and when it was inverted, Fisher put a short burst into it. The Zero exploded into a fireball.

A second Zero then appeared behind Boyington. Fisher fired but missed. As the Zero rolled, Fisher took another shot, then followed the now-smoking Zero until it caught fire and spiraled down.

Boyington, meanwhile, was watching a Hamp that overtook and passed him. According to Walton's after-action report, Boyington merely "flicked his gun switch and gave him a long burst."

In his memoir, however, Boyington admitted that it had not been so simple, writing that "it seemed like an eternity before I could get everything turned on and the guns charged."

After that interval, which was closer to seconds than to eternity, he fired a long burst at about 50 yards, watching the enemy's cockpit burst into flame as the Hamp rolled to the left and went straight down.

When this aircraft hit the water, Boyington was watching Fisher out of the corner of his eye as he scored his second.

Boyington passed a pair of Corsairs and continued a left turn under a layer of clouds. Seeing Japanese aircraft all around him, Boyington circled back up through the clouds to gain altitude and headed southeasterly toward Vella Lavella in parallel with the bombers coming out of their bomb runs.

He picked out another Hamp that was attacking the bombers and made a diving pass from above and behind. Opening fire at 300 yards, Boyington bore down, firing on the Japanese fighter, which exploded into a cloud of debris as Boyington closed to just 50 feet. The explosion was so close that Boyington instinctively "threw up [his] hand in front of [his] face in a feeble attempt to ward off these pieces."

Climbing to the right into the sun, Boyington saw Hamps diving on a pair of US Navy Hellcats. He dived to 10,000 feet to hit them just as they climbed out after overrunning the Hellcats.

Boyington opened fire on a Hamp at 300 yards and stayed with him as he looped up and over. At the top of the loop, the Hamp started to burn and dived uncontrollably as Boyington raced past.

Gaining altitude once more, Boyington could see the enemy fighters at around 6,000 feet as they began to break off from their attacks on the bombers and head north toward Bougainville. Picking out a lone Zero, Boyington "decided to make a run on this baby."

The Japanese pilot began making what Boyington later described as "an ever-so-gentle turn."

"As long as he is turning, he knows he isn't safe," Boyington thought to himself. "It looks too easy."

He was right. Boyington had taken the bait.

"Sure enough, there was his little pal coming along behind," Boyington recalled. "He was just waiting for the sucker, me, to commence my pass on his mate."

Turning into a storm of 20mm and 7.7mm gunfire, Boyington dived to make a head-on pass against the wingman. Fortunately, the streams of tracers fell low, while Boyington's own gunfire found its mark, ripping up the underside of the Mitsubishi fuselage. Trailing smoke, it plunged into the sea below.

Boyington climbed back to 10,000 feet, but just as he turned for home, he saw a lone aircraft below at about 3,000 feet, flying westward toward Vella Lavella. Then he saw two others, headed the opposite way, toward Balalae. As he watched, the latter, which proved to be Zeros, attacked the former, which was a Corsair.

Telling the story in the VMF-214 after-action report, Frank Walton wrote "low on gas from his long runs at high speed and his dives and climbs during his engagements, nevertheless, [Boyington] made a run on the two Zeros, opening fire at extremely long range to drive them off the friendly plane."

As one Zero climbed straight up, Boyington followed him "holding the trigger down all the way."

When the Zero slow-rolled and burst into flames, Boyington was also on his back, and he found himself in a spin. Boyington recovered from the spin and, as mentioned in his memoirs, he took a shot at the other Zero. This is not mentioned in the after-action report.

Walton did remark in the report that Boyington landed with only 10 gallons of fuel and 30 rounds of ammunition left. Boyington said that he was so low on fuel that he had had to land at Munda to refuel before returning the Banika. Walton noted that Boyington returned to Banika at 1755hrs, more than an hour later than any of the others.

———

The following day, VMF-214 forward deployed to Munda, which was to be their home for the rest of their first tour.

The baptism of fire for the Black Sheep on September 16, 1943 was the stuff from which legends are made. This legend, already percolating because of the quirky character of the aviators and their leader, now had a firm foundation forged in battle.

VMF-214 had downed 11 Japanese fighters, with an additional eight listed as probables. However, the Black Sheep had suffered their own first loss. Robert Thomas "Bob" Ewing of Lafayette, Indiana, one of the division leaders that day, did not return. No trace of him was ever found.

Both John Begert and Mo Fisher had downed a pair, but Boyington himself was the high-scorer of the day with five. They were reckoned in Walton's report to include four Hamps and a Zeke.

Had he had no previous aerial victories, Boyington would have been an "ace-in-a-day" with five scored entirely with the Marine Corps. However, in his overall tally, these five were added to the aerial victories he had scored with the Flying Tigers. These numbered two, according to AVG records, or six by Boyington's own unsubstantiated, but widely accepted, claim.

In either case, an aviator who shot down Japanese aircraft while flying with the Flying Tigers, and who was now an ace-in-a-day with the Black Sheep of the Marines, was headline gold for the media. Fortuitously, one of America's greatest war correspondents just happened to be at Munda that week.

George Anthony Weller of the *Chicago Daily News* would become famous for filing stories from every major theater of the war, and he earned the 1943 Pulitzer Prize for reporting a story about a US Navy pharmacist's mate performing an appendectomy aboard a submarine in enemy waters. He was one of the last journalists to escape Singapore in 1942, and he reported from defeated Japan in 1945. His book *First into Nagasaki* was finally published in 2006.

In September 1943, though, Weller was in the Solomons writing stories for the *Daily News* about fighting men with a Chicago connection. He learned that several, including Chris McGee, were in VMF-214, then he discovered that nearly everything about the Black Sheep and their colorful skipper made excellent copy. Between Frank Walton, the squadron's tireless promoter, and the reporting from George Weller, VMF-214 had found its niche as a media icon.

Four days after Boyington's five victories, the Associated Press wire service carried a story about the new American ace from Okanogan, Washington who had "emerged," and this was being picked up by newspapers all over the United States.

By that time, the Black Sheep had already been in battle again. On September 18, they flew both morning and afternoon combat air patrol missions in support of the US Navy task force that would land troops on the northern part of Vella Lavella. The Allies already controlled Barakoma on the southern tip of the island and it was now time to push the Japanese out of the rest.

Boyington suffered engine and radio trouble, and did not tangle with enemy aircraft in the September 18 battles, but two other Black Sheep scored aerial victories. Shortly before noon, Bill Case downed a Zero, while Chris McGee, flying in another division, destroyed two Aichi D3A Val dive bombers in rapid succession.

Boyington's next aerial victory came on September 27. The plan that day was for a dozen VMF-214 Corsairs to rendezvous with 27 USAAF B-24 Liberators off the south coast of Choiseul at 1135hrs and escort them in a raid against Kahili. However, only eight Corsairs took off, and they arrived at the meeting point late, so they had to hustle to catch up with the bombers.

Meanwhile, though, Boyington had been briefed that should the Corsairs be running late on an escort mission, they should conduct a fighter sweep of the fighter fields at Kahili to preempt the Japanese interceptors from taking off. They would have space in their schedule for this because in the time it took the bombers to fly north of Kahili, turn, and make their bomb runs southbound, the Corsairs could easily strike from the south.

When the division reached Kahili at 25,000 feet at 1205hrs, ahead of the bomber strike, planned for 1230hrs, Boyington saw a Japanese aircraft high above at 35,000 feet that was emitting smoke in such a way that it looked like a signal. Taking this to be an alert for interceptors to launch, Boyington took his division down to 10,000 feet to engage the enemy.

Finding the field empty and seeing no black puffs of antiaircraft fire, Boyington took his men back up. This time, they saw 20 Zeros in flight, so they continued climbing above the Zeros, then attacked.

Boyington came in from behind one, firing at 200 yards and watched its tail start to disintegrate. As it went into a 30-degree dive, Boyington followed it down as it passed through a low cloud. Emerging from the cloud, Boyington saw the Japanese aircraft hit the water almost immediately, and had to pull back hard to avoid going in himself. Mo Fisher, on Boyington's wing, had also chased a Zero down through a cloud and had watched it splash into the sea.

When it was all over, Fisher, Case, and Boyington had all scored one, while Don Moore, flying in the other division, had also claimed a single.

An enthusiastic Frank Walton was now turning to journalism, crafting tabloid-style headlines for his action reports after the daily missions. Referencing a series of disruptive diving maneuvers that Bill Case had made through the formation of Vals, Walton's headline for September 18 was "One Corsair Scatters 15 Jap Dive Bombers."

The one that Walton penned five days later, "I Got that Old Feelin'!," was a quote from the squadron's Denmark "Quill" Groover, a "Georgia boy," who was in turn quoting his grandfather's rheumatism-inspired weather prognostications. The Japanese lost four aircraft to the Black Sheep on October 23, and Groover was injured extinguishing a cockpit fire with his hands.

As September came to a close, VMF-214 had been in combat for just two weeks and had claimed 23 enemy aircraft, all of them fighters except for the two dive bombers that Chris McGee had downed. October would see them reaching the heights for which the Black Sheep became legendary.

21

Three Aces Reach Double-Digits

September into October

On September 11, 1943, as Lieutenant Stirling Harrison, the intelligence officer for VMF-213, stepped out of a SCAT Skytrain at the Munda airfield, two dogs pushed past him, eager to run and stretch their legs after the flight up from Guadalcanal. Black Sun and Doc, the squadron mascots, had arrived with human members of the squadron for a forward deployment that Harrison estimated in the squadron's war diary would last from ten days to two weeks.

"Munda, very clearly, shows the effects of our six months of pounding by bombs and shells," Harrison wrote of his first impressions. "Only stumps or overturned roots show where many coconut trees once stood. Craters, wrecked planes and other vehicles and other debris of all kind cover the landscape."

When they explored, Black Sun and Doc did not seem to care.

Overhead, VMF-213 Corsairs circled to land. Leading them was Major James Anderson, who had just assumed command of the squadron from Major Gregory Weissenberger, who had become an ace on VMF-213's previous tour.

"The remainder of the squadron arrived today from Espiritu Santo," Harrison wrote on September 7. "We are all together and ready to go."

In many ways, VMF-213 was a new squadron. There were 15 new men on their first tours of duty, although there were still familiar faces. Among them were the squadron's four top-scoring aces, three of them on their way to double-digits. As operations had ended in July, and as they began again, Bud Shaw was in the lead with nine, followed by Gus Thomas with seven, John Morgan with six, and Jim Cupp with 5.5. It would be on this very afternoon of September 11 that their story would resume.

All except Morgan were among eight VMF-213 aviators who took off from Guadalcanal at 1015hrs that morning as part of an escort mission. They would be joining with some US Navy F6Fs in riding herd on two dozen USAAF Thirteenth Air Force B-24s headed north to continue giving the Japanese airfield at Kahili a pounding.

At about 1230hrs, as the bombers were coming in for their target run at 20,000 feet, Jim Cupp noticed an IJAAF Ki-61 Tony below at about 15,000 feet, which seemed to be doing aerobatics. Cupp and his wingman, Jim Walley, dived on the Tony, which then nosed over into a dive itself. Following it down, Cupp opened fire. The enemy fighter exploded and fell. As this was happening, Walley also found a target and shot it down.

As he was climbing back to 20,000 feet, Cupp watched another Japanese fighter passing though his view, opened fire, and watched it fall.

At the same time, in another patch of the Bougainville skies, Bud Shaw's division was being attacked from all angles by 15 to 20 Japanese fighters, including IJAAF Tonys as well as IJNAF Zeros. The fight was on. A Zero lined itself up on the tail of the Corsair piloted by Shaw's wingman, Robert "Bob" Roberts. Shaw inserted himself on the six of the Zero pilot and promptly shot him down.

Meanwhile, Lloyd Handschy, flying as wingman to Gus Thomas, became separated from the others while trying to shoot a Zero off Thomas's tail. With this, Thomas fell in with Shaw and Roberts. As another Zero dived on them, Thomas pulled up into it. As Thomas opened fire, the Zero's left wing exploded.

While this was happening, Handschy reappeared with a Zero on his tail, and Thomas attacked. As this Zero exploded, Thomas checked his six and saw a Zero targeting him. He nosed over, dived at high speed and escaped.

As Thomas was in his dive, a Zero passed through his view and he took the shot. The Zero tried in vain to escape the stream of fire from Thomas's guns. Bursting into flames, it tumbled out of the sky.

When they landed, Thomas and Handschy each counted more than a dozen 7.7mm bullet holes in his Corsair. Gus Thomas led the VMF-213 scoring for the day with three aerial victories. Cupp scored two, while Walley and Shaw claimed one each.

During September 1943, the land battle on Vella Lavella still raged, as American and New Zealand forces fought the Japanese for control of the island. Overhead, Japanese dive bombers were still on the attack, and AirSols fighters were still swatting them back.

On September 18, two divisions of VMF-213 Corsairs took off from Munda at 1120hrs to do just this.

Jim Cupp's division arrived on station over Vella Lavella by 1215hrs, and began receiving periodic updates about an incoming Japanese formation from the Sirius Base radar at the AirSols base at Barakoma on the south end of Vella Lavella. The enemy was over Vella Gulf at 20,000 feet and on a heading to attack Barakoma. They were 36 miles out and approaching fast.

When the Corsairs climbed to meet the enemy, the layers of stratocumulus clouds compromised visibility, but at last they rounded a corner and got a visual on the Japanese. At a distance of five miles, and closing, Cupp noted two formations, each with nine Aichi D3A Val dive bombers. They were about 2,000 feet higher than the Corsairs.

A moment later, a flight of six IJAAF Ki-61 Tony fighters passed about 50 feet above, flying in single file on the same heading as the bombers. This certainly got Cupp's attention, but the Japanese fighter pilots apparently did not see the Corsairs, because they kept going and disappeared into the clouds.

Cupp then led his division higher and onto a course parallel to that of the Vals, of which they had lost sight. About five miles out from Barakoma, the Marines popped through a hole in the clouds at 17,500 feet and saw the 18 dive bombers spread before them. They had dispersed into six sections of three and were beginning to descend into their bombing run. Cupp could see some of the Ki-61s about 1,000 feet above.

The Corsairs rolled into a steep dive to go below the Vals and attack upward so that the rear gunners could not get a clear shot.

Cupp and his wingman, W.E. Stewart, picked one of the threesomes of Vals in the center of the formation and climbed into them. Cupp picked the one on the left, and Stewart the one on the right. Both Vals went down in flames.

The Marines then accelerated to catch up with the Vals at the head of the formation. As Cupp chased one Val out of the clouds, he found himself over the Barakoma airfield in the midst of friendly antiaircraft fire, so he banked into a turn and headed out to sea.

Cupp now found himself over Vella Gulf looking at the main dive bomber formation. They had dropped down so low that they were practically skimming the waves at an altitude of just 50 feet. He and Stewart both picked a Val from the crowded pack and gave chase.

"We scissored across an area of about five miles, shooting dive bombers as we traveled," Cupp wrote in his after-action report. "Two of the bombers I fired on here, caught fire and crashed in the water."

He chased another dive bomber about ten miles eastward toward Kolombangara before putting it in the sea, then banked back toward Vella Lavella.

By now, Stewart had claimed three Vals, and the battle climaxed with Cupp and him both firing on yet another Val, which burst into flames and fell helplessly into Vella Gulf.

Preparing to break off and head back to Munda, Cupp checked his six and discovered that a Japanese fighter was shadowing him. A hail of machine gun and 20mm rounds began pounding Cupp's Corsair. When he looked back, Cupp saw other Ki-61s that were about to add their firepower to that of the fighter that had hit him.

Skimming the water at 50 feet, Cupp decided to use the Corsair's superior power and make a run for it. He "put on the steam," banked right and headed east, then south along the west coast of Kolombangara.

Stewart was at about 1,000 feet and headed south when he was attacked by two Zeros. They were diving on him and closing fast. A bullet shattered his canopy, and he was taking some serious hits, but he still had the power to pull away, and finally he was in the clear.

Cupp made it back to Munda, but Stewart's aircraft was too badly damaged to get home. Deciding to abandon ship south of Vella Lavella, he considered a water landing, but changed his mind and climbed to 1,500 feet to hit the silk.

Stewart managed to make landfall on a small island before dark. He was planning to spend the night on the beach, but an islander passing by in a canoe picked him up and took him to a place where other islanders were camped. They treated him very well, sharing food and cigarettes. A boy at the camp, who turned out to be an excellent ukulele player, shared a number of songs, including some American pop songs, which Stewart enjoyed. By 1500hrs the next afternoon, thanks to his friends and their canoe, he was back at Munda.

In the big aerial battle over Vella Lavella, Stewart emerged with 3.5 aerial victories, while Cupp could claim 4.5. Combined with his score from June and July, and two Zeros earlier in the month, Cupp had now edged into double digits with a dozen, as one of the highest-scoring American aces in SOPAC.

This was to be the end of Cupp's career. On September 20, he and two others were about ten miles west of Kolombangara in pursuit of a G4M Betty bomber.

As was standard operating procedure when attacking a bomber with a rearward-firing gun position, Cupp attacked from below, but things went wrong. In the after-action report it is said that he was hit by fire from the tail gun, though later reports suggested a makeshift 20mm gun position located in the bomb bay that had been installed in response to Marine tactics.

In any case, Cupp took hits in the vicinity of his cockpit and wing root, starting a fire in the cockpit. He turned and attempted to bail out, but the speed of the Corsair complicated this, and cost him time when making a successful escape.

The after-action report said that he was evacuated to the US Navy MOB-8 Mobile Hospital on Guadalcanal with "severe 2nd and 3rd degree burns to both his legs, from his thighs to his ankles, his right arm and hand, and his head and face."

On September 23, Bud Shaw and Gus Thomas, along with Lloyd Handschy and Bob Roberts, comprised a VMF-213 division tasked with escorting a strike force of bombers as they hit the antiaircraft concentrations at Jakohina, about three miles west of Kahili airfield. These guns had been taking a toll on the USAAF heavy bombers that were targeting Kahili every few days and they needed some sorting out.

The patrol launched from Munda airfield at 0800hrs, and promptly rendezvoused with the bombers. They were joined by 28 other Corsairs from various other squadrons, as well as USAAF P-38s and RNZAF Curtiss Kittyhawks (listed in Marine Corps reports as "P-40s"). They rendezvoused with two dozen SBDs and a dozen TBFs, which were scheduled to be on target at 0930hrs just as two dozen USAAF B-24s passed over after having blasted Kahili. Compared to the small strike packages that the venerable Cactus Air Force had been able to put into a mission a year earlier, this armada was borderline unimaginable.

Thinking back to the fall of 1942, there was a time when the IJNAF had been able to launch sorties with this number of G4M medium bombers, but those days were so far back that almost nobody still in SOPAC had any direct memory of it.

For its part, though, the IJNAF had managed to cloud the skies over southern Bougainville with fighters that morning.

Climbing as they went, Shaw's patrol passed south of Vella Lavella, then circled west of the Shortland Islands to approach

Kahili from the west, keeping the bombers in sight as they went. As they approached Kahili, they saw the B-24s coming toward them at 22,000 feet.

While this was unfolding, Shaw watched fighters below them over Balalae Island, which turned out to be Zeros slipping beneath a thin layer of clouds to pounce on the bombers. In the clouds, Shaw had lost track of the others in his division, so he radioed that he was diving to attack.

When he emerged from the clouds at 15,000 feet, Shaw could see the Zeros below sparring with P-40s. Shaw dived 4,000 feet on a Zero that was chasing a P-40, opened fire, and watched it hit the water. He attacked several other Zeros, but did not wait long enough to watch them go down.

Gus Thomas, with Lloyd Handschy on his wing, recalled that the Zeros had turned to attack them head on. One of the Zeros that Shaw had attacked was trailing smoke when it went head on at Thomas. As it pulled up, exposing its belly, Thomas fired and watched it burst into flames. The two Marines shared this kill.

Seeing that two Zeros were closing on Roberts, Thomas attacked and the two Japanese fighters slipped away, but a few moments later, another Zero got on Roberts's tail. As he recalled in his after-action report, Thomas "was able to sneak in behind it, fired into it and it burst into flames."

When another Zero then dived at Thomas head on, he "pulled into it, fired at it and it began to burn around the wing roots and cowling. It passed under me and as I looked down, I saw the Jap pilot jettison his hood and bail out."

By this time, Thomas had lost sight of Handschy and the others from his own division, but as he leveled out after downing the third enemy aircraft, a Corsair from another squadron appeared beneath him with a Zero on its tail. As this Zero passed before him, Thomas took a 45-degree deflection shot and the Zero became a plunging fireball.

Yet another Zero presented itself at 45 degrees and Thomas took the shot. He watched pieces of aileron flying off as the Zero went into a spin, but he lost sign of it as he began to take fire from behind.

Thomas dived away from whoever was shooting at him and managed to get away. However, oil spewing from his engine told him that he had suffered some serious damage to his oil line. His Corsair was in trouble.

He made contact with Shaw on the radio, explained the situation, and said he would try to make it home. Even as he did this, though, Thomas could see by his oil pressure gauge that it was not going to happen, so he started looking for piece of ocean nearby where the odds of rescue were good.

His engine finally froze when he was northwest of Vella Lavella and still a long way from Munda. Using the forward momentum that he had, Thomas looped the Corsair and dropped out of the cockpit at the top of the loop. As he drifted down beneath his parachute, he watched his aircraft falling, and just before it hit the water, he heard a loud roar as though the engine had started again.

When he splashed down, he saw Corsairs from VMF-214 circling, watching to be sure that he had survived before they flew away. Thomas inflated his raft, dragging his parachute aboard. He began paddling in the direction of Vella Lavella, as much in an effort to get there as to beat the prevailing wind and put distance between himself and the south coast of Bougainville, where capture by the Japanese was the probable outcome.

Exhausted by rowing for about five hours in the excruciating heat, he finally decided to take a rest. He could not really tell whether he had made any progress at all, but he told himself that he had.

As he was starting to fall asleep, he heard the sound of something above him. When he opened his eyes, an albatross was landing on his foot, just as another had landed on the foot of Manny Segal of VMF-221 back on July 11.

Thomas may have recalled the fate of Coleridge's Ancient Mariner, or he may have decided from the start that he was not ready to eat raw albatross. Instead of killing the bird, as Segal and the Mariner had done, Thomas reached out to pet its head.

The bird took exception to this, but instead of flying away, it grabbed the aviator's finger in its beak and began shaking it. Thomas recalled that this did not hurt—at least not as bad as the cuts on his leg from the parachute straps that he had received because of he hadn't tightened them before he bailed out.

About a half-hour after the bird landed, Thomas saw a PBY and several P-40s passing at a distance of about five miles. He was elated at the prospect of rescue, and tried to get their attention. He waved and shouted, which were pointless gestures, but ones that came from an urge that could not be suppressed. He fired three tracer rounds from his pistol, but the aircraft turned away and soon disappeared.

Through all of this, the albatross remained, watching the behavior of this man with great curiosity. Growing tired of the big bird using his raft as a toilet, Thomas tried to chase it way. Finally, he had to push it out into the water.

Dejected, Thomas accepted the idea that he would have to spend the night in the middle of the dark ocean drifting ever closer to the Japanese on Bougainville.

At around 1730hrs, though, he heard the sound of engines and looked up to see a PBY circling overhead. The rescue crew dropped a smoke canister to check wind direction, then touched down, motored over, and pulled Thomas aboard. He asked them to also take in his raft because it had his gear, including his jungle pack and pistol. They said they would, but instead they sank it with machine gun fire. They were in a hurry to get out of there because Zeros were overhead chasing the SBDs and TBFs that had just attacked Kahili.

The PBY dropped Thomas at a PT-Boat base on Rendova, about 20 miles south of Munda, and he was back with VMF-213 the next day.

Bob Roberts, who the other members of the division had glimpsed a couple of times during their big dogfight south of Kahili on that fateful September 23, was never seen again. No trace of him or his Corsair was ever found and he was declared missing in action.

During this battle, Gus Thomas had single-handedly shot down three Zeros and had shared one with Bud Shaw, who got another on his own.

On October 11, after two weeks of uneventful patrols, things got lively once again. Bud Shaw's division took off from Munda at 0800hrs, bound for Kahili. Jim Walley flew as Shaw's wingman, while Gus Thomas led the second section with Lloyd Handschy on his wing. They rendezvoused with TBFs over Rendova and headed north.

Walley turned back because of engine trouble, but the other three continued, climbing to 22,000 feet over the target. As the TBFs released their ordnance at around 0940hrs, the Corsair aviators could see 15 Zeros approaching below, so they dived to attack.

Shaw later reported in his after-action report that the Zeros were "not in any formation, but scattered all around." Thomas wrote that "we made a number of passes at the Zeros, chasing them off each other's tails." In the VMF-213 war diary, intelligence officer Stirling Harrison reported that "a running fight ensued which covered the area from the target to southwest of the Shortlands."

Thomas watched Shaw "scissor to the right, pass under me and shoot a Zero that had just sneaked in on my tail. This Zero dove down about 1,000 feet, smoking, and then burst into flames."

The Corsair pilots then observed a P-40 below with a Zero on its tail and went to help.

Shaw opened fire at close range, but found that only one of his six guns was operable. "I was so close to him that I couldn't have missed," Shaw recalled. "But he pulled away to the right. I was traveling at such great speed that I over ran the Zero and was barely able to pull up over the P-40."

Thomas, following close after Shaw, caught the Zero as he also pulled right and opened fire. The Zero pilot did a wingover to the left and went into the water just north of Shortland Island.

Just as Thomas rejoined Shaw and Handschy at 8,000 feet, he saw more P-40s battling about eight Zeros below and "turned to lend a hand." He made a high side-firing pass on one Zero, watched it go down on the southwestern end of Shortland Island, and looked for more.

Thomas did not have long to look. Moments later, he was on the tail of a Zero that was separated from the others and opening fire. As he raced past it, the Zero was rolling over, diving straight down and trailing smoke, though Thomas did not actually see it hit the ground.

Having once again climbed to 8,000 feet and found Shaw and Handschy, Thomas looked down to see a Zero stalking a P-40. Once more, he intervened, descending 3,000 feet, firing as he went. As this Zero exploded, another turned to attack Thomas. Despite the Zero's legendary tight turning radius, Thomas turned his Corsair tighter and came out on its six.

"The Zero turned and rolled in violent evasive maneuvers, but I was able to stay on its tail," Thomas wrote. "On closing on this Zero, I gave it three or four shorts, and when in close range, I pressed the button for a good long burst, but only one of my guns would fire. Smoke poured from beneath the cowling around the forward area of the fuselage."

When their second tour of duty came to a close on October 13, three VMF-213 aces had entered into double-digit territory. Gus Thomas and Bud Shaw had 16.5 and 14.5, respectively, the totals reflecting their shared victory on September. Jim Cupp had brought his score to 12 before the debilitating incident of September 20. Burned over most of his body, he had been evacuated Stateside.

While the totals for Cupp and Shaw were final, Thomas's story was not yet finished. In February 1945, after a stint in the States, he would add a pair to his total—flying from aboard the USS *Essex* (CV-9) off Okinawa.

Shaw took command of VMF-213 in December 1943 and took it back to the States, where it was assigned to MCAS Mojave in the California desert to be rebuilt for redeployment. On July 31, 1944, while taking a Corsair through a dive test at Mojave, Bud Shaw crashed and was killed.

22

The Major Leagues

October

After weather scrubbed the VMF-214 mission for October 3, 1943, the same mission was on for the next day. The antiaircraft guns on a place called Malabeta Hill were delivering a beating to the bombers attacking Kahili, and the mission saw a strike force of 20 Dauntlesses headed out to hit the hill.

With Boyington in the lead, eight Black Sheep took off at 1115hrs on October 4 to fly as escorts, but two aborted, and then there were six. In his after-action reports, Frank Walton had been complaining that the squadron's Corsairs were overdue for their major overhauls.

Nevertheless, Boyington and company arrived at the rendezvous point at 1155hrs ahead of the bombers and began flying lazy circles through the clouds at 10,000 feet as they waited. They bided their time, listening on their radios to voices in English which they knew to be Japanese radio operators spoofing them and pretending to be other American aircraft.

More than half an hour passed, and Boyington grew impatient with waiting and feeding false locations and altitudes to the eavesdropping Japanese. Finally, he decided to lead his troops in search of the Dauntlesses—or some Zeros with which to tangle. As Boyington recalled in his memoirs:

The next thing I saw, about the most beautiful sight a fighter pilot can dream of, climbing in an easterly direction coming from beneath a white cloud, was a formation of thirty Nippon Zeros ... We were fortunate in having the midday sun coming over our shoulders, pointing down in front of us upon the backs of our climbing enemy ... I recall placing my finger to my lips to caution silence [knowing the enemy was listening to their radio chatter], while throttling back to lose altitude as I tried to keep in line with the rays of the sun. Whether my signal was passed on visually made no difference, for my boys were as silent as the little lambs I knew they were.

The Corsairs descended 3,000 feet, moving lower and closer to the Zeros. Boyington felt as though he'd had the leader in his sights for "at least an hour," but it was a few minutes at most.

At 300 yards, Boyington throttled back, situated himself on the Zero's six and opened fire. The enemy aircraft "practically disintegrated in front of my eyes."

Because he was surrounded by tracers from Corsairs firing at the Japanese in parallel to his direction of flight, Boyington knew he dare not turn so he plunged "straight ahead completely across the top of the Japanese formation."

With debris flying everywhere, the formation "started into a deep left spiral, which reminded me of watching soapy water whirl out of a bathtub." As soon as he was clear of friendly fire, Boyington joined this "mad whirlpool."

When he spiraled downward, Boyington made a high port quarter pass on another Zero. In what seemed like just one second, he was watching the pilot leaping from the cockpit with his parachute. Continuing his 360-degree corkscrew dive, Boyington was on the tail of a third Zero, and flame was pouring from its wing root.

The phrase "three Zeros in 60 seconds" rolled off the tongue as smoothly after the October 4 battle as "five-in-a-day" had for Boyington back on September 16. Boyington's brand, duly noted by George Weller and a growing fan base among Stateside feature writers, was in its ascendancy. He had become a star.

It was around this time that someone had an idea. As public relations schemes go, it was hard to beat. The suggestion, which probably originated with Frank Walton, VMF-214's publicity-savvy intelligence officer, but branded with the imprimatur of Greg Boyington, was, in retrospect, as obvious as it was brilliant. As any advertising professional will agree, the best ones are the obvious ones.

It was pure in its simplicity and precision. It had nothing to sell but good will. It brought together two of the most sympathetic icons that were most on the minds of the American public in October 1943—war heroes and the golden moment of the National Pastime, the World Series baseball.

The Series that year, a rematch of the 1942 pairing, brought together the champion St. Louis Cardinals and the American League's perennial pennant holders, the New York Yankees. But things were not the same as they had been in past World Series. Because of the war, the respective hall-of-famers, such as Enos Slaughter of the Cards, and Phil Rizzuto and Joe DiMaggio of the Yankees, were not in the line-up. They were in different uniforms, playing on armed forces exhibition teams.

The Yankees, who seemed naked without DiMaggio, nevertheless won Game One of the 1943 Series at Yankee Stadium on October 5, but dropped the October 6 game to the Cardinals. All eyes were on Game Three.

Enter Greg Boyington.

On October 7, the Associated Press carried the story that his VMF-214 "has an offer to make."

The offer was that his Black Sheep would trade downed enemy aircraft for baseball caps from the Series winning team. He was, according to the Associated Press, "willing to shoot down a Japanese Zero in trade for each cap of the winning team."

Baseball caps, which are ubiquitous today, were less common in daily life in the 1940s, but were highly sought after by the aviators in the South Pacific because the bills provided excellent shade for their eyes in the bright sun.

Today in a similar situation, the squadron would have been immediately deluged with crates of caps from every team in the major leagues, but in 1943, it was the Cardinals who responded. Though they lost Game Five—and the Series—at home on October 11, they did ship 20 baseball caps to Boyington and his boys. Publicity photos were taken of Chris McGee standing on the wing of Boyington's Corsair with a stack of caps and Boyington handing back a Japanese flag decal from the cockpit.

With Joe DiMaggio out of the game, eyes that eyed the tabloids— and even the sports pages—now eyed Boyington.

For eleven days running, though, Boyington's own eyes were denied that "most beautiful sight a fighter pilot can dream of" as the Black Sheep were flying top cover for convoys coming through the Slot, operations for which the enemy did not show. On October 10, the squadron did see some action, but Boyington missed these sorties for several days in a row.

Boyington was not flying that week. He was at Munda enjoying the company of his old friend and drinking companion, Brigadier General James "Nuts" Moore, who was now the Commander of Allied Air Forces in the Northern Solomons (ComAirNorSols).

When they learned that Moore had invited Boyington to a dinner that included many of the top brass in the Solomons, the Black Sheep asked, "see if you can bring us back anything."

As if on cue, Moore later casually asked Boyington "by the way, how are you lads fixed for whiskey?"

"The whiskey situation is rough," Boyington lied. "We have been completely out of it for some time."

"This must be a coincidence," Moore said with a smile, nodding to a wooden box. "Here's a case with no name on it. I don't know who [this whiskey] belongs to, but take it with you."

Boyington left that night, with the crate on his shoulder, but not without noticing that it was actually addressed to "another major general whose judgment in fine whiskey had been respected for a good number of years."

Boyington was back in the air on October 11, leading VMF-214 in a bomber escort mission to Kahili, but Bill Case was the only Black Sheep to score on this mission.

October 15 at last brought Boyington's return to combat. Again, the mission was a B-24 strike on Bougainville, scheduled for noon, for which a dozen VMF-214 Corsairs were providing escort. Boyington led the third of three Black Sheep divisions that took off between 1045hrs and 1120hrs.

When the 21 heavy bombers came over Kahili at 22,500 feet at 1215hrs, two of the VMF-214 divisions flew top cover, while Boyington's foursome went low for a strafing run. They circled wide and behind to attack from the west, a direction from which they would be least expected.

"When I figured I was west of the Kahili clearing, I pulled our flight up to four abreast [to] enable a perfect line-up on the runways," Boyington recalled. "This gave the maximum amount of target over the full length of the field as we strafed eastward with guns and throttles wide open."

It was a lot like Boyington's raid against Chiang Mai back in March 1942 with the Flying Tigers.

In the after-action report, Frank Walton mentioned that VMF-214 was challenged by at least ten Zeros between Kahili and Balalae Island, engaging them at 4,000 feet before they had managed to climb to reach the bombers.

In the ensuing fight, Bill Case and Warren Emmerich each scored a pair of aerial victories, while Burney Tucker got one. Boyington came home with one confirmed victory and three probables. This was his tenth victory as a Marine.

Walton, who readily accepted—and promoted—Boyington's claim of six while with the AVG, wrote in the squadron after-action report that this was Boyington's sixteenth aerial victory. Eager for the prestige of a Flying Tiger ace in his squadron, Walton never questioned nor sought third-party confirmation of the earlier claim from Boyington's China days.

23

Two Squadrons Over Kahili

October

There were three days in October 1943 that were especially costly for the Japanese in the skies over Kahili, that great thorn in the side of AirSols aviators. The story of how this happened, from October 16 through 18, weaves together the actions of Greg Boyington's VMF-214 and VMF-221, now under the command of Major Monfurd Peyton.

VMF-214 had been making a name for itself in SOPAC and the American media since mid-September, but VMF-221 had been back from Australia for less than a week. After nearly two months out of the action, the VMF-221 aviators had begun arriving at Munda on SCAT flights on October 13.

Shortly thereafter, they forward deployed 50 miles northwest across Vela Gulf to become the first of an eventual half-dozen Marine fighting squadrons to operate out of the Barakoma airfield on Vella Lavella. US Navy SeaBees had constructed a 4,000-foot runway and a sprawling campus of support facilities at Barakoma, and it had been in operation since September 24.

With 12.5 aerial victories, Jim Swett was VMF-221's leading ace, while newly minted ace "Murderous Manny" Segal was still a local legend for his hand-to-hand combat that had unofficially added an albatross to his score of five back on July 11. That date had proven infamous for both Swett and Segal, as on that day they had helped to add two victories to the overall score of the IJNAF when both of them were shot down. Fortunately, both of them lived to tell the tale.

Naturally, the VMF-221 aviators were anxious for a piece of the air-to-air combat which they had missed for two months, and about which they were hearing from the squadrons who had been in the fight. After several days of writing "no enemy contact" in the VMF-221 war diary, James Tyler, the squadron intelligence officer, was seen to type the phrase "in hopes," when describing Corsairs going out on patrol on October 16.

They did not have long to wait.

The "hopes" came true by way of Bill Snider. Having scored his first three back on April Fool's Day, Snider had scored none on his entire second tour over the summer, and he was eager for action.

At 0815hrs, Snider was leading a VMF-221 division in a fighter sweep over Kahili in conjunction with four divisions from Boyington's VMF-214.

"We circled Kahili and spotted Zeros taking off. I counted eight," Snider wrote in his after-action report. As the VMF-221 aviators dived through the clouds from 20,000 feet, this pack of Zeros had made a turn and were gone, so the Marines began climbing, taunting the Japanese pilots on the radio and inviting them to "come up to fight."

When VMF-221 reached 18,000 feet, they saw a very loose formation of as many as 40 Zeros coming toward them from the south. As both the Japanese and the Americans began jockeying for the altitude advantage, Boyington and VMF-214 plunged into them. Snider and VMF-221 followed.

Three Zeros broke off from the pack and headed toward Snider and his division.

"The first one got in front of me, rolled on his back and pulled through while still out of range," Snider wrote. "The second made a determined head-on, rolling as he came in and pulled down through in front of us. I gave him a long burst and could see my tracers going into him. He trailed smoke, but I did not see him go in."

Pulling out of his initial pass, Snider and his wingman climbed back to their original altitude, where three Zeros on a parallel course "seemed reluctant to attack."

Deciding to initiate the fight, Snider and his wingman turned into them, and two of the Zeros banked away. Snider went for one, taking a 30-degree deflection shot from about 200 yards, "holding fire until very close."

Knowing that his bullets had found their mark, Snider nosed over suddenly to get away from a second Zero, while his wingman watched Snider's first hit spiral into the water below.

When Snider made a quick right turn and climbed 1,000 feet, he saw the second Zero off to his left. He dived at it, taking a 60-degree deflection shot into its belly.

"I could see rather large pieces flying from his plane," Snider recalled. "He seemed to float aimlessly for a short period, smoking badly—then went into a spiral dive. I then looked around for friendly planes to form up on. As I circled I kept glancing down at him and finally saw him hit the water between Balalae, offshore from Bougainville, and Kahili. No parachute was seen. I saw no planes after that so I put my nose down—full gas and headed for home."

Bill Snider became the first VMF-221 aviator to score aerial victories on this tour. His two confirmed kills had made him the newest ace in the squadron—and put him on his way to becoming the squadron's eventual number two ace.

Boyington fought hard, moving like the skilful maneuverer he was, against the Zeros, but did not score on October 16. The *next* day, October 17, *would* belong to him—and to the Black Sheep of VMF-214.

At 0615hrs that morning, they were off. There were 16 Corsairs of VMF-214 and seven of VMF-221, all intertwined in a fighter sweep against Kahili. Two aborted—Begert and Bourgeois of VMF-214—but the others pushed north, up the Slot to Bougainville. Antiaircraft fire of "medium intensity ... big black puffs of smoke ... with long red steamers" was noted as originating from the island of Balalae.

One division of VMF-221 came in low, at about 6,000 feet—the after-action report called them "bait to draw the enemy fighters off

Form ACA-1
Sheet 1 of 5

AIRCRAFT ACTION REPORT

RESTRICTED
(Reclassify when filled out)

I. GENERAL

(a) Unit Reporting **VMF-214**   (b) Based on or at **Munda**   (c) Report No. **6**

(d) Date of Action **17 October 1943** (e) Take off: Time **0815L**   **XXXX** Lat   Long

(f) Mission **Fighter Sweep over Kahili Airfield**   ~SECRET~   Return **1215L**   (XXX)

II. OWN AIRCRAFT OFFICIALLY COVERED BY THIS REPORT.

(a) TYPE	(b) SQUADRON	(c) NO. OF SORTIES	(d) NO. ENGAGING ENEMY A/C	(e) NO. ATTACKING TARGET	(f) BOMBS AND TORPEDOES CARRIED (PER PLANE)	(g) FUZE SETTING
F4U-1	VMF-214	16	12			
F4U-1	VMF-221	8	?			

III. OTHER U. S. OR ALLIED AIRCRAFT EMPLOYED IN THIS OPERATION.

TYPE	SQUADRON	NUMBER	BASE	TYPE	SQUADRON	NUMBER	BASE

IV. ENEMY AIRCRAFT ENCOUNTERED (By Own Aircraft Listed in II Only).

(a) TYPE	(b) NO. OBSERVED	(c) NO. ENGAGING OWN A/C	(d) TIME ENCOUNTERED	(e) LOCATION OF ENCOUNTER	(f) BOMBS, TORPEDOES CARRIED; GUNS OBSERVED	(g) CAMOUFLAGE AND MARKING
OOSSF Zero (Zeke)	30	30	0915L (GCT)	east of Ballale	normal	Normal brown; some with red stripes around fuselage.
OOSSF Zero (Zeke)	10	10	0915L (GCT)	east of Ballale	normal	Glistening black.

(h) Apparent Enemy Mission(s) **Interception of fighter sweep.**

(i) Weather and Clouds at Location of Encounter(s) **Clear, scattered clouds.**

(j) Sun or Moon **sunshine.**   (k) Visibility **unlimited.**

V. ENEMY AIRCRAFT DESTROYED OR DAMAGED IN AIR (By Own Aircraft Listed in II Only).

(a) TYPE ENEMY A/C	(b) DESTROYED OR DAMAGED BY: TYPE A/C	SQUADRON	PILOT OR GUNNER	(c) GUNS USED	WHERE HIT, ANGLE	(d) DAMAGE CLAIMED
OOSSF Hap	F4U-1	VMF-214	Lt. B.J. Matheson	fixed	7 o'clock, level	destroyed
OOSSF Zeke	F4U-1	VMF-214	Lt. E.L. Olander	fixed	High, 12 o'clock	destroyed
OOSSF Zeke	F4U-1	VMF-214	Lt. J.F. Bolt	fixed	Level, 6 o'clock	destroyed
OOSSF Zeke	F4U-1	VMF-214	Lt. C.L. Magee	fixed	Level, 10 o'clock	destroyed
OOSSF Zeke	F4U-1	VMF-214	Lt. C.L. Magee	fixed	High, 8 o'clock	destroyed
OOSSF Zeke	F4U-1	VMF-214	Lt. B.L. Tucker	fixed	Level, 6 o'clock	destroyed
OOSSF Zeke	F4U-1	VMF-214	Lt. B.L. Tucker	fixed	Level, 6 o'clock	destroyed
OOSSF Zeke	F4U-1	VMF-214	Maj. G. Boyington	fixed	High, 6 o'clock	destroyed
OOSSF Zeke	F4U-1	VMF-214	Maj. G. Boyington	fixed	Level, 9 o'clock	destroyed
OOSSF Zeke	F4U-1	VMF-214	Maj. G. Boyington	fixed	Level, 9 o'clock	destroyed
OOSSF Zeke	F4U-1	VMF-214	Lt. W.D. Heier	fixed	High, 3 o'clock	destroyed
OOSSF Zeke	F4U-1	VMF-214	Lt. W.D. Heier	fixed	Level, 6 o'clock	destroyed
OOSSF Hap	F4U-1	VMF-214	Lt. W.D. Heier	fixed	Level, 12 o'clock	prob.dest.
OOSSF Zeke	F4U-1	VMF-214	Lt. R.W. McClurg	fixed	... o'clock	prob.dest.

~SECRET~

60

FIGURE 2   As seen on this page from a VMF-214 Aircraft Action Report, October 17, 1943 was a remarkable day for the Black Sheep. The dozen enemy aircraft downed by them in 40 minutes included three by Boyington. (USMC)

the strip." VMF-214 went high. Climbing to 22,000, they came over Kahili, its grass surface green as a meadow, at 0910hrs.

The Japanese fighters began to take off as Boyington led two Black Sheep divisions down into what Frank Walton called "broad sweeping 'S' turns." At 10,000 feet, Boyington ran into between 15 and 20 Zeros, while the higher flight met 15 Zeros at 18,000 feet over Balalae.

As Walton summarized, 21 VMF-214 Corsairs fought as many as 50 Zeros for 40 minutes across an area south of Bougainville that comprised roughly 375 square miles. In that piece of Solomons sky, the Black Sheep downed a dozen Zeros, all seen crashing and or burning. VMF-214 suffered bullet and cannon shell damage to several Corsairs, but returned with no losses.

Among the dozen victories, Burney Tucker and Chris McGee each got a pair, while William "Junior" Heier got two plus a probable. Greg Boyington scored three, one while diving head on into it, and two with level, nine o'clock deflection shots. This gave him a total of 13 in the space of 31 days since his five in one mission back on September 16.

On October 18, the mission was to cover SBD Dauntlesses in a strike against Balalae that was coordinated with attacks by TBF Avengers and USAAF B-24 Liberators. VMF-214 launched a dozen Corsairs in three divisions, while VMF-221, who had not flown the day before, launched two. One was led by Jim Swett and the other by Nathan Post. According to Post's account, the Japanese did not seem to be expecting the Marines, which is a wonder, if true.

The squadron came in at 18,000 feet and had circled the field before the Zeros took off. In his after-action report, Swett noted that there was a great deal of antiaircraft fire that was "quite accurate in altitude, but inaccurate in deflection." In other words, the effort was there, but the effectiveness was absent.

After taking off, the roughly 45 Zeros flew out over the ocean to form up before starting to climb to meet the Corsairs.

"At this point we jumped them," Post wrote in his after-action report. "We made a pass down through them. I got one from overhead going straight down. As I pulled up, I saw I had one on my tail; somebody, I don't know who it was, shot him off."

"I followed Major Post's division," Swett recalled. "I got a smoker in the first run, coming in on him from overhead. Then I made one 360-degree turn and got a flamer, coming in on him from almost dead ahead."

In Marine aviator parlance, a "smoker" was a probable, unless or until it burst into flame. A "flamer" was a confirmed kill.

Post and Swett had scored their victories in the first moments of the battle. There were two confirmed to have been destroyed by Post, while Swett had one confirmed and another that was probable. For VMF-221, Jack Pittman was the real star of the October 18 engagement, accounting for three Zeros confirmed plus two probables.

VMF-214, meanwhile, had an unlikely scenario play out early in the battle. The Corsairs were orbiting Balalae between 20,000 and 25,000 feet, watching the bombers and a pack of about 15 Zeros. The enemy aircraft were far below and at first seemed to show no interest in engaging VMF-214.

Suddenly, Bill McClurg's engine cut out, and he nosed over into a dive to try to get it restarted. This worked, but the engine was running rough, so he aborted the mission and headed for an emergency landing on Choiseul. As he came over Fauro Island, he saw two aircraft below and ahead of him. A pair of slate gray Zeros was on the same heading as he was, and climbing.

Noting that they were oblivious to him, he gently descended and slipped in behind them. Picking the wingman first, McClurg thumbed his trigger at 800 yards and closed in, watching his tracers pierce the fuselage.

When the first Zero lurched to the right, nosed over and crashed into the water below, McClurg turned his attention to the second Zero. Again, bullets pierced the fuselage and the Japanese aircraft went down.

Harold Edward "Murderous Manny" Segal downed a dozen Japanese aircraft, but he is best remembered in the lore of VMF-221 for an albatross. On July 11, 1943, he was shot down off New Georgia and wound up adrift in his rubber raft. Here, he was visited by a curious albatross that he bagged, intending to eat it if necessary. (USMC)

F4U-1 Corsairs of VMF-222 on the flightline at Barakoma airfield on Vella Lavella. (USMC)

The aviators of VMF-214, the "Black Sheep" squadron, pose with a Corsair for this group photo taken at the Turtle Bay airfield on Espiritu Santo. They departed from here for the Solomons on September 12, 1943. Major Greg Boyington, wearing a cap, is in the center of the front row, directly below the prop spinner. (USN)

Donald Hooten Sapp of VMF-222 is seen here at Barakoma airfield on September 15, 1943, one day after he had scored the first two of his ten aerial victories. (USMC)

Greg Boyington (center) briefs members of his squadron ahead of a mission. Many have identified this as VMF-214, but the lettering on the life vest worn by the man to Boyington's left seems to indicate that this might be VMF-122, which Boyington commanded earlier in 1943. (USN)

A later variant Corsair (note blown-Plexiglas bubble canopy) belonging to VMF-214 touches down on the Marston Matting runway at Torokina airfield on Bougainville. In a typical VMF-214 mission over Rabaul, the aviators took off from Barakoma and touched down at Torokina to top off their fuel tanks. (USMC)

Major Greg Boyington, the storied leader of the Black Sheep of VMF-214, poses for a photographer on the flightline. (USMC)

A well-worn Vought F4U-1 Corsair belonging to VMF-214 is seen here parked between missions on the flightline at either Barakoma or Torokina. (USMC)

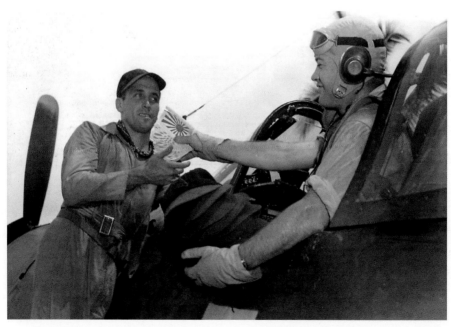

A favorite story from VMF-214 lore involves Boyington offering to shoot down a Japanese aircraft for each ball cap delivered from a team participating in the October 1943 World Series. In this photo, Chris McGee of VMF-214 "trades" a St. Louis Cardinals cap to Boyington for a decal indicating an aerial victory. (USMC)

The men of the Black Sheep pose for an October 1943 publicity photo on and around a Corsair in a Barakoma revetment, wielding baseball bats and wearing the caps that were sent to them by the St. Louis Cardinals. Boyington is fourth from left in the front row. (USMC)

Corsairs on the flightline at Vella Lavella's Barakoma airfield. With a 4,000-foot, coral-surfaced runway and a 6,000-gallon avgas tank farm, Barakoma hosted the Corsairs of VMF-214, VMF-215, VMF-221 and VMF-321. (USMC)

Major Greg Boyington enjoys a light moment beneath the swaying palms with four of his aviators. (USMC)

A Vought F4U-1 Corsair aircraft from Boyington's VMF-214 lifts off a packed coral runway, possibly for a fighter sweep over Rabaul. (USMC)

An F4U Corsair being prepared for flight, possibly at Torokina airfield on the western coast of Bougainville. The 3rd Marine Division captured the area in November 1943 and Boyington's Black Sheep were operating there soon after. (USN)

Harold Edward "Murderous Manny" Segal was a ten-victory "double ace" with VMF-221 when he went back to the States in November 1943, but he decided to return to combat. (USMC)

Robert Murray "Butcher Bob" Hanson of VMF-215 scored 20 of his 25 aerial victories in the space of two weeks in January 1944. He was lost the following month, one day short of his twenty-fourth birthday. (USMC)

When Manny Segal came back to the Pacific, he was assigned to VMF-211, with whom he scored the two victories indicated by these Japanese flags, in January 1944.
He finished his combat career with an even dozen. (USMC)

Donald Nathan Aldrich of VMF-215 was a 20-victory "quadruple" ace, scoring eight of them in just two missions. He took home a Navy Cross for his actions in January 1944. (USMC)

Ken Walsh was awarded the Medal of Honor on February 8, 1944 for his actions of the previous August. Here he shakes the hand of President Franklin D. Roosevelt while Beulah Walsh smiles broadly. In the background (left to right) are Chief of Naval Operations Admiral Ernest King, Marine Commandant Lieutenant General Alexander Vandegrift, and Assistant Secretary of the Navy Ralph Bard. (USMC)

Archie Glenn Donahue scored nine aerial victories with VMF-112 in the Solomons through June 1943. He returned to the Pacific in 1945 with VMF-451 aboard the USS *Bunker Hill*. On April 12, 1945, he downed five enemy aircraft in a single mission. (USMC)

William Nugent Snider scored his first aerial victories with VMF-221 in April 1943, but did not become an ace until October. In the spring of 1945, he came back to the Pacific with VMF-221 aboard the USS *Bunker Hill*. Snider then scored 6.5 victories in less than three weeks. (USMC)

After being a prisoner of the Japanese since January 1944, Greg Boyington was freed from the prison at Omori near Tokyo in August 1945. On the right is Commander Harold Stassen, the former governor of Minnesota, who was then on the staff of Admiral William "Bull" Halsey. (USN)

An F4U-1D of VMF-124 aboard the USS *Essex*, December 28, 1944. Flying with VMF-124, Ken Walsh scored his twenty-first and final aerial victory off Okinawa on June 22, 1945. (USMC)

Test pilot Major Marion Carl (left) and USN Commander Turner Caldwell with a Douglas D-558-1 Skystreak at Muroc Army Airfield (later Edwards AFB) in California. Carl set a world speed record of 712mph in a Skystreak in August 1947. (USN)

In the years after he left the Marine Corps in 1945, Joe Foss served as a brigadier general in the Air National Guard, as the two-term Governor of South Dakota, and as the Commissioner of the American Football League, where his ideas for a national pro football championship game led to the creation of the Super Bowl. (Arlington National Cemetery)

Brigadier General Robert Galer began his Marine Corps combat career commanding VMF-224 in the Solomons in 1942, and retired from the service in 1957 having served as director of the Guided Missiles Division of the Navy Department's Bureau of Aeronautics. In the meantime he flew combat missions in Korea in 1952. (USMC)

Lieutenant Kenneth Walsh, the fourth highest-scoring Marine Corps ace, began his flying career in April 1937 as a private, and retired as a lieutenant colonel in February 1962. (USMC)

Major General Marion Carl as seen in August 1967 after commanding the 1st Marine Brigade at Danang in Vietnam. There, he flew combat missions in armed Huey helicopters and F-8 Crusader jet fighters. He later served as Inspector General of the Marine Corps until his retirement in 1973. (USMC)

As this one hit the water, McClurg's engine stopped again. He began gliding toward Choiseul resigned to a water landing, but he was able to reach the emergency field for a dead stick landing instead. It was not typical that a pilot headed toward an emergency landing with a crippled aircraft would shoot down *two* enemy Zeros on the way.

As McClurg was in the midst of his adventure, Boyington and the rest of the Black Sheep had gone north toward Bougainville for a fighter sweep over Kahili. Meeting medium-intensity antiaircraft fire, as they came in at 15,000 feet, they observed about 60 Zeros on the ground that appeared reluctant to engage. Knowing that the Japanese had English-speaking radio operators who tuned into American radio traffic, Boyington teased them, cajoling them to come up.

"Major Boyington, what is your position," the Japanese radioman asked in clear English.

"Right over your airport," Boyington replied. "Why don't you yellow bastards come up and fight?"

"Major Boyington, why don't you come down if you are so brave?"

Seeing no movement among the Japanese aircraft, Boyington and Bill Case accepted the invitation and went down for a fast strafing pass against the antiaircraft guns.

Finally, at least 15 Zeros began their takeoff roll, and Boyington took VMF-214 down to 6,000 feet, where they intercepted them about halfway between Balalae and the south coast of Bougainville.

The Marine aviators used the power of the Corsairs, and the speed generated in a dive, to their full advantage. They slashed into the enemy aircraft, chasing many of them down to 2,000 feet before destroying them. Altogether, this brief battle on the afternoon of October 18 cost the Japanese eight Zeros. The one claimed by Boyington that day would be the last of his first tour with the Black Sheep, and his last until December 23, 1943.

Chris McGee was the star of the day among the aviators of VMF-214. He scored his fifth aerial victory to become an ace, then added two more to bring his total to seven. Bill Case got one, to bring his overall score to eight, but he almost paid the ultimate price. A 7.7mm machine gun slug passed through his leather helmet leaving a nasty cut on his scalp. A fraction of an inch lower—or a tracer round—would have marked his demise.

At VMF-221, there was no sigh of relief after the October 18 mission. "Reports of the fight helped our box score, but lowered our morale," wrote the VMF-221 intelligence man, James Tyler, of the October 18 battles. "We got six Zeros and four probables, but Lieutenant Schneider did not return. All planes except Milt landed by 1730."

Milton Edward "Milt" Schneider, who had filled in with Swett's division at the last minute that morning, was never seen again.

For the cost of this one aviator, though, the two Marine fighting squadrons had erased 31 Zeros from the roster of the Imperial Japanese Navy Air Force in those three October days. Most of these aircraft were the new and improved A6M5 Model 52 variant that had begun entering service from late summer.

For both VMF-214 and VMF-221, these were the last aerial combat actions of their current tours. Within days, after flying a few final strafing missions against ground targets, they were all aboard SCAT flights for Australia.

24

Cherry Blossom Over Bougainville

November into December

November 1, 1943 was to be a very busy day on the 3,598-square-mile island of Bougainville. It had long been a target of AirSols operations, but today it was to be the focus of Operation *Cherry Blossom*, the amphibious landing by the US 3rd Marine Division at Empress Augusta Bay on the west coast of Bougainville.

The objective of *Cherry Blossom* was to secure a foothold at Cape Torokina on the north side of the bay at which an airfield would be built to support air operations by Marine fighting squadrons and RNZAF units flying Curtiss Kittyhawks.

To provide air support for *Cherry Blossom*, the new Allied airfield at Barakoma on Vella Lavella put AirSols aircraft just 100 miles from Kahili and Buin on the south coast of Bougainville. Also within easier reach was the Japanese airfield at Buka at the north end of Bougainville, which was 220 miles away.

November 1, 1943 would be an important day in the history of VMF-215, which was flying top cover for *Cherry Blossom*.

After leave in Australia through the end of September 1943, and spending most of October flying familiarization flights out of Espiritu Santo, VMF-215 had taken up residence at their new duty station at Barakoma on October 20. Leading VMF-215 into its second tour of duty was Major Herbert Williamson, who had replaced Major James Neefus.

All three of the men who would later go on to be VMF-215's double-digit aces were aboard by then. Don Aldrich, who had scored the squadron's first aerial victory on August 12, had become their first ace on September 2. In second place was Hal Spears, with four. Rounding out the trio was Robert Murray Hanson, who had just transferred in from VMF-214, where he had scored his first two aerial victories.

Air-to-air combat would be rare for VMF-215 during October and November, though their strafing attacks were taking a toll. On October 22, for instance, as many at 30 Japanese aircraft were erased from the Japanese roster on the ground at Buin. However, aircraft destroyed on the ground did not, of course, count in the reckoning of air-to-air victory scores.

November 1 was to be an especially active day for Bob Hanson. Having taken off at dawn as part of Captain Art Warner's four-ship division, Hanson was over Empress Augusta Bay when he discovered both his radio and his oxygen system had failed. He got Warner's attention and motioned that he was low on oxygen, so Warner took the flight down to 13,000 feet.

When they were descending, Hanson spotted six IJNAF Zeros passing beneath them through a trough in the clouds, with at least 20 more following. Seeing the Japanese beginning to head downward toward where the Marines were securing the beachhead, Hanson picked one, tailed in behind him and opened fire.

When the Zero pulled away to the left, it appeared to Hanson that he was traveling too fast to maneuver, so Hanson gave him another burst. The Japanese aircraft was on fire as Hanson passed over him, but the pilot still managed to take a shot at the Marine aviator. He missed, and the blazing Zero fell out of the sky.

Hanson then maneuvered himself into the six of another Zero and fired. Trailing smoke for just a moment, this aircraft exploded as Hanson began climbing away.

When he passed through 8,000 feet, Hanson observed a half-dozen IJNAF Nakajima B5N "Kate" torpedo bombers heading to attack the American invasion fleet offshore. He fired on one of the bombers as it banked to the right, but scored no hits. As he came around for a second pass, the B5Ns were releasing their ordnance over the bay.

Hanson made a run at the Kate on the left of the attack formation and watched it slowly begin to lose altitude. Firing short bursts, Hanson followed the aircraft down until it sliced into the bay and disappeared.

When he pulled out of his dive, Hanson realized that he had no power. He guessed that the rear gunner in one of the Kates had managed to fatally damage his engine—though he did not recall having seen any tracers coming his way.

Knowing that he would have to ditch his Corsair in the bay, Hanson pointed it toward the nearest American ships, which were a half-dozen destroyers escorting some transport ships. He hoped to get as close as possible so that he could be rescued, but the aircraft was rapidly losing speed, and he came down at a distance of about five miles. Hoping that they had seen him, he scrambled out quickly, inflated his rubber raft and climbed in as the Corsair sank out of sight.

He began paddling as hard as he could, because he knew that the American ships would be pulling out soon so as not to be caught in a vulnerable place if Japanese surface ships arrived to attack the invasion fleet. As he rowed, he recalled singing the Cole Porter show tune "You'd be So Nice to Come Home To," which had been released earlier in 1943 with vocals by Dinah Shore.

After more than four hours in the water, Hanson was spotted by a lookout aboard the USS *Sigourney* (DD-643) and rescued. The ship was headed to Tulagi on the first leg in a round-trip resupply mission for the troops on the beachhead, so the ship and its Marine passenger missed the naval battle that raged in Empress Augusta Bay that night.

Admiral Sentaro Omori dashed in with four cruisers and six destroyers to crush the inferior American force, but wound up losing so badly that he was sacked and sent back to Japan in disgrace to eat crow.

Bob Hanson, on the other hand, found himself eating ice cream and real eggs for the first time in many months and reflecting on how much better Navy food was than the spam that the Marines were being served. He finally reached Tulagi on November 3, caught a ferry to Guadalcanal, and commandeered a Corsair that needed to be ferried up to Vella Lavella.

Arriving back on November 5, Hanson learned that he had accounted for three of the five aircraft claimed by VMF-215 on November 1. These three, added to his previous pair with VMF-214, made him an ace, although the VMF-215 tally would list him with just these three that he scored while flying with the squadron.

After the excitement of the first day of November, however, VMF-215 operations for the remainder of 1943 proved routine and largely uneventful. VMF-215 would score no more aerial victories during November and just three in December. Neither Don Aldrich nor Hal Spears scored any during their second tour of duty with the squadron. However, the new year would mark big changes for them and for VMF-215.

———

Having last seen aerial combat in the battles of October 18, 1943, VMF-221 was back in action during Operation *Cherry Blossom* on November 1, the same day that was so significant for Bob Hanson and VMF-215.

VMF-221 was part of a combat air patrol relay that day, working to keep Japanese dive bombers away from the US Navy landing force that was disgorging men and materiel on the shores of Empress Augusta Bay. Jim Swett, now VMF-221's leading ace, had begun his combat career by famously downing seven Japanese dive bombers on April 7, 1943. Today, the task was the same.

Swett and his division had taken off at 0515hrs on November 1, but two of these Corsairs aborted, and he lost track of the other. Indeed, the squadron after-action report lists him as the only member of the squadron to complete the mission.

Finding himself thus alone, Swett had just joined with eight USAAF P-38s at 30,000 feet when they observed a group of IJNAF Vals, escorted by IJAAF Ki-61 Tony fighters. These approached the American ships at 12,000 feet and began to dive.

"I didn't see any hits on any of our ships, but antiaircraft fire from the ships was deadly," Swett recalled in the after-action report. "I could see bombs going into the water all over the place ... I ran over two Vals and fired at them but they got away from me. The next two I went after—still coming down—burst into flame before I stopped shooting at them."

As these two bombers went down, Swett saw a RNZAF Kittyhawk being chased by Tonys and he attacked the attackers. He opened fire and saw smoke spewing from the Ki-61, but he broke off the attack to take evasive action when he himself was attacked. He managed to escape with just a couple of 7.7mm machine gun holes in his tail. The after-action report noted "easily repaired."

Listing the Tony as a probable, Swett claimed the two Vals, which brought his score to 14.5. His next and final victory would come 18 months later in May 1945.

For the next two weeks, VMF-221's activities consisted mainly of strafing Japanese barges, though they did claim a number of these to have been sunk. Air combat resumed again on November 17, with what was to include the next installment in the story of the colorful "Murderous Manny" Segal.

As had been the case through much of this tour of duty, Segal was flying as the wingman to VMF-221 commander Major Nathan Post. The squadron took off at 0600hrs on November 17 to fly top cover for Destroyer Squadron (Dearon) 23 off Cape Torokina. Almost immediately upon taking up their position at 15,000 feet, the VMF-221 Corsairs were vectored to intercept unidentified incoming aircraft. As Post later recalled in the aircraft action report, he saw three aircraft at his altitude that he initially thought were Navy F6F Hellcats—but when he saw the Japanese "meatball" insignia, he knew they were the enemy.

Post attacked as soon as he saw the Japanese markings and the first aircraft exploded into a fireball. He banked right, lined up a second and watched flames erupt from its wingroots. When the third enemy aircraft went into a dive, hoping to escape, Post followed him down, watching the aircraft burst into flames as it hit the water.

Manny Segal, who had followed Post throughout this adventure, "figured he was OK, so I dove on three [Japanese aircraft] that I saw." This trio was below 5,000 feet and flying toward Dearon 23 in a "V" formation.

Segal pulled in on the six of the one on the right of the "V" and opened fire. As this one fell away in flames, he took out the others in rapid succession. The third rolled upside down as it caught fire, and Segal later reported that a large object dropped away. He did not have time to ascertain whether this was the pilot bailing out.

A review of the records reveals an uncertainty as to the types of aircraft that were shot down. The VMF-221 war diary lists them merely as "dive bombers," which usually meant they were Aichi D3A Vals. However, the pilot's description in the aircraft action report said they were "low mid-wing monoplanes with an in-line engine and a pronounced scoop under the nose."

VMF-221 intelligence man James Tyler provisionally identified them as Nakajima Ki-43 Oscars, which were IJAAF fighters. This was clearly improbable, and Tyler later commented that they were "believed to be the new reconnaissance dive bomber often referred to in reports as being in use in this area and designated 'Aichi 2.'" By the description, it is more probable that they were Yokosuka D4Y Suisei (Comet) dive bombers of the type codenamed "Judy" by the Allies.

VMF-221's third tour of duty ended on November 18, the following day, as the squadron formally received their anticipated order to stand down and await transportation out of the combat zone. Segal's score now stood at ten, making him VMF-221's second-highest-scoring ace behind Jim Swett, who ended the tour with 14.5 plus five probables.

Bill Snider, who had been the first VMF-221 aviator to score during the previous tour, scored none on this round. Destined to eventually be part of the squadron's double-digit fraternity, Snider ended the year with five.

While both Swett and Snider were to have a "second act" with VMF-221 in 1945, Manny Segal's second act would come less than two months later with VMF-211.

As the aviators of VMF-221 prepared to bundle themselves into SCAT transports to Efate by way of Guadalcanal, those of VMF-222 were arriving in the aftermath of Operation *Cherry Blossom*. The first of the squadron's flight echelon stepped off the transports at Barakoma on November 18, 1943 and flew their first bomber escort mission the next day.

During their previous tour, none of the squadron's aviators had yet achieved ace status. The highest score to date was that of Major Don Sapp, now the squadron executive officer, who had three victories. He was destined to be VMF-222's only double-digit ace.

Sapp did not have long to wait for his next opportunity for aerial combat. On November 20, he was leading a VMF-222 division in a patrol over Torokina Bay. At 0725hrs, moments after the air controller had vectored them to a new location, an unidentified aircraft was seen on the radar and they turned back to investigate. Sapp got a visual on a twin-engine aircraft with Japanese "meatballs" on the wings that was flying north toward Rabaul at 7,000 feet.

Sapp initially thought it was a Mitsubishi G4M Betty, the medium bomber widely used by the IJNAF since the beginning of the war in the Solomons. However, on second glance, he decided that it was too small to be a G4M, though only the red meatballs on the wings colored his choice of action. His first pass left the aircraft in flames, and it had exploded before the pieces hit the water.

For record-keeping purposes, Major Max Volcansek, the squadron commander, noted in the squadron war diary that the aircraft "was arbitrarily called a Helen." This Allied designation identified the Nakajima Ki-49 Donryu (Storm Dragon), a twin-engine bomber used by the IJAAF. It was inferior to the Betty in terms of performance and capability, and thus less widely deployed.

A victory on his second day in action bode well for Don Sapp's prospects for the month, but he ended November still one victory shy of becoming an ace. Yet he was still the highest-scoring aviator in a squadron with no aces, a squadron that had endured a paucity of aerial combat that month.

This lack of combat continued through December, with VMF-222 being tasked with escorting bombers against enemy positions throughout Bougainville, which the Japanese chose not to defend with their Zeros. Bad weather also played a role in curtailing operations, and is mentioned frequently in the squadron war diary. Even on December 23, during a maximum effort mission against Rabaul in which numerous victories were scored by aviators of other squadrons, only one aerial victory was recorded by the squadron.

The following day, VMF-222's flight echelon boarded SCAT flights to Guadalcanal, where they enjoyed their Christmas dinner. They arrived in Sydney, Australia on December 30 for their R&R furlough, and greeted 1944 still as a squadron with no aces.

25

Two Aces Over Rabaul

December

Two household-name Marine Corps aces led their squadrons back into the Solomons on November 27–28, 1943, converging at Barakoma airfield on Vella Lavella.

One had been away for about a month, the other for about a year. Greg Boyington and the veteran Black Sheep of VMF-214 were back from their raucous furlough in the bars and brothels of Sydney, Australia.

While there were a number of new replacements in VMF-214 now, Marion Carl was bringing in an almost entirely new iteration of the legendary VMF-223—the squadron that had been the "home of the aces" a year earlier.

Whereas VMF-214 had the continuity of having been in action quite recently, VMF-223 was a veteran unit in name only. Carl had taken over the shell of his former squadron at MCAS El Toro in California early in 1943 and had rebuilt it with just a handful of veterans. Among these was 11.5-victory ace Ken Frazier, who had been the third highest-scoring ace in the squadron after Carl and John L. Smith.

Finally embarking for the Pacific aboard the escort carrier USS *Breton* (CVE-23), VMF-223 reached Espiritu Santo on November 10, and were filtering into Barakoma by the end of the month.

Boyington's life, meanwhile, remained a magnet for the dramatic. As VMF-214 returned from Australia on November

28, his nagging nemesis, Lieutenant Colonel Joe Smoak, known to Boyington as "Colonel Lard," had tried to remove Boyington from the command of his own Black Sheep and reassign the now legendary SOPAC ace to a desk job on Vella Lavella.

There had ensued a hailstorm of verbal brawling, threats of arrest, and a blizzard of memoranda that washed up through the chain of command to Brigadier General James "Nuts" Moore, commander of AirNorSols, who had just written a glowing commendation of Boyington dated November 15. Ultimately, the whole matter was settled by Boyington's old admirer, Major General Ralph Mitchell, who was now the commander of the 1st Marine Air Wing and of AirSols operations in the entire Solomons. Smoak was overruled and Boyington promptly reinstated as the leader of his merrie band of Black Sheep.

The return of Boyington, Carl and their squadrons to the Solomons took place within the larger context of the grand strategy of Operation *Cartwheel* and Operation *Cherry Blossom*, the smaller, focused tactical component of *Cartwheel* that took place at Bougainville on November 1.

Operationally, the return of VMF-214 and VMF-221 was also part of the story of a keystone and a stepping stone.

As discussed earlier, the keystone was the great Japanese fortress of Rabaul on New Britain. It was ringed by a half-dozen important air bases, while Simpson Harbor at Rabaul was the IJN's key naval base for the region. As the center of Japanese power in the region, Rabaul had been the objective of Operation *Cartwheel* since April 1943. For most of the year, it had been a focus of operations by the airpower of General MacArthur's SWPA, specifically the USAAF Fifth Air Force, led by MacArthur's astute airman, Lieutenant General George Kenney. Now, the air forces of Admiral Halsey's SOPAC command would be brought to bear on Rabaul—among them, the Marine aviators and their Corsairs.

The stepping stone was the airfield at Torokina, which would make it possible for the Corsairs to engage in sustained combat over Rabaul.

Located at Cape Torokina on Empress Augusta Bay on the west coast of Bougainville, the site had been the objective of Operation *Cherry Blossom*, discussed in the previous chapter. Over the course of a month, the SeaBees had carved a forward operating base out of the jungle and had constructed a 5,150-foot runway that was ready for use by December 10 as a staging base for Corsair operations against Rabaul. Torokina became a game-changer for AirSols operations.

Ironically, Torokina was 60 miles *north* of Kahili, the scene of so much AirSols attention through the fall of 1943. Therefore, Torokina was actually *behind enemy lines*. It is illustrative of how much the balance of power had shifted in the past year that the Allies had achieved the naval and air superiority to make such audacity possible.

The Japanese had reinforced Kahili and Buin on one end of Bougainville, and Buka on the other, but had largely ignored the heavily jungled interior of the island. Allied operations at Torokina were virtually unhindered by enemy interference.

On December 17, both VMF-214 and VMF-223 at last set their sights on Rabaul. Boyington and Carl each launched his squadron from Vella Lavella before dawn and landed at Torokina to refuel. The eight Corsairs contributed by each of Boyington's and Carl's squadrons were joined by similar numbers from two other Marine squadrons, as well as two dozen US Navy F6F Hellcats and two dozen New Zealand Kittyhawks (listed in Marine Corps reports as "P-40s"). VMF-223 arrived over the target at 1020hrs, and VMF-214 at 1045hrs.

As Frank Walton noted, they were opposed by both Kawasaki Ki-61 Tonys of the IJAAF, and Mitsubishi A6M2-N Rufe "float-plane Zero" fighters of the IJNAF. When VMF-214's Bill McClurg broke formation to attack and shoot down a Rufe, Boyington was annoyed that he had left the formation, but he was hardly one to complain about breaking the rules. Before it was over, Don Moore had downed a pair of Tonys.

Among the VMF-223 aviators, Edward Fitzgerald engaged one Japanese fighter only to discover that he had expended his ammunition while strafing. He was then chased for at least 30 miles by a half-dozen more enemy aircraft, but he lost them in cloud cover. Both VMF-214 and VMF-223 had emerged intact from some of the most heavily defended air space in the South Pacific.

The nature of Rabaul as a target was several orders of magnitude more challenging than Kahili. Because Rabaul was the seat of Japanese power throughout the region, its air defenses were much more robust. While the Japanese airfields on Bougainville were dirt and grass strips, the major fields around Rabaul, such as Lakunai, Rapopo, Tobera, and Vunakanau, included concrete runways and a sophisticated infrastructure with hardened shelters and repair facilities. Between them, they had revetments for more than 400 combat aircraft. These bases hosted not only IJNAF squadrons, but those of the IJAAF as well.

It was nearly a week before the Marine aviators returned to Rabaul. Again, it was part of a sizable AirSols effort that also involved USAAF Thirteenth Air Force heavy bombers.

December 23, 1943 is remembered as the beginning of a maximum effort against Rabaul that was to be carried on through March 1944. Frank Walton's enumeration of the planned strike package included two dozen B-24s escorted by four dozen Navy and Marine fighters, as well as 20 Corsairs and 28 USAAF P-38s flying coordinated strafing sorties.

When the heavy bombers began their runs over the target from west to east at 1300hrs, only about five Navy Hellcats were on hand to engage at least 15 Zeros that made a diving attack. As more American fighters appeared, a number of Zeros were observed dropping white phosphorous bombs—or firing white phosphorous projectiles—at the bombers.

The B-24s, however, did considerable damage. Numerous towering fires were seen ashore in Rabaul. In Simpson Harbor, a large transport ship had been blown in two and was ablaze.

Two VMF-214 divisions, led personally by Greg Boyington, were part of the fighter sweep that came 15 minutes after the bomber strike. This allowed the strafing fighters to engage Japanese fighters that would otherwise have had a free hand to pick off the bombers as they moved south.

Boyington was at 18,000 feet over St. George's Channel, east of Rabaul, when he saw a flight of Zeros. Bill McClurg recalled him saying, "This is it fellows," as he led his own division toward them. Boyington saw one Zero below him and flying westward, toward Rabaul, and he dived to attack.

He maneuvered into the six o'clock position behind the Zero and closed to just 50 feet before he opened fire. A short burst turned the enemy aircraft into a torch. As it went into the channel, the pilot's parachute could be seen alongside it.

McClurg chased one Zero down nearly to sea level and opened fire at 100 yards. It skipped twice after it hit the water, then quickly sank.

Climbing back to 10,000 feet, Boyington saw a pair of Zeros headed for Rabaul. One was trailing smoke from an earlier encounter with another American aircraft, and the other was maneuvering around him as though trying to protect him. As Boyington attacked, the first Zero dived. As the second maneuvered to get into a position to shoot, Boyington "let the smoker have it— one burst that set that plane afire—and again the pilot bailed out."

Boyington dived as the second Zero tried to get on his six, and got away.

When he pulled out of his dive, Boyington saw the second Zero circling the descending parachute of his comrade.

"I remember the whole picture with harsh distinction—and on Christmas," Boyington wrote in his memoirs. However, he mistook the date of the action, confirmed in the VMF-214 after-action report as happening two days *before* Christmas. "One Japanese pilot descending while his pal kept circling."

Boyington waited until the parachute hit the water before attacking the circling Zero, which he watched roll onto its back 100 feet above the channel and crash.

About 20 minutes later, Boyington was back over Rabaul's Simpson Harbor. The ship that had been blown in two had almost completely sunk, and there was still a flurry of action overhead.

Seeing a formation of three groups of three Ki-61 Tonys, he dived on the ninth and last in the pack. He blew it to bits, evaded the rest of the Tonys in a fight that lasted ten minutes, then headed for home.

On the way, he spotted and strafed a Japanese submarine, which quickly submerged. In his memoirs, he recalled that "my only thought at this time," he wrote, "was what a hell of a thing for one guy to do to another guy on Christmas," again getting the date wrong.

The Black Sheep also took losses on December 23. Three men, Jim Brubaker, Bruce Ffoulkes, and squadron executive officer Major Pierre Carnegey, never came back. No one had seen them go down, so they were carried on the books as missing until after the war when they were declared KIA.

Marion Carl had led a dozen VMF-223 Corsairs into the Rabaul strafing attack on December 23, 1943. Like that of Boyington's VMF-214, this came just as the B-24s completed their bomb runs. As such, both squadrons had been in a position to intercept the enemy fighters as they tried to intercept the bombers.

This was the first aerial combat action for VMF-223 in more than a year, and the first ever for most of the men in the squadron.

Over Cape St. George at 1405hrs, Marion Carl found himself above a Ki-61. In his first taste of air-to-air combat in 15 months, and his first ever in a Corsair, he took a 15-degree deflection shot at 400 yards, then slid in on the Tony's six o'clock and thumbed the trigger at 100 yards.

As pieces of the Ki-61 began to tumble off, it wrenched to the right, rolled over and went down. Carl found himself nearly stalling out as he slowed to watch the enemy aircraft splash into St. George's Channel.

Ken Frazier also scored his first aerial victory since 1942 that day. He found himself head on and slightly below an enemy fighter, which he identified as a square-winged Mitsubishi A6M3, the Model 32 variant of the Zero. After they passed one another, the Japanese pilot pulled up, rolled on his back and was trying to get behind Frazier. At a range of 50 yards, Frazier opened fire and watched pieces flying off the cowling between the engine and the wing. The Hamp continued to roll and plummeted straight down into St. George's Channel.

When it was all over on December 23, VMF-223 had scored four confirmed aerial victories on their first day back, plus three probables. VMF-214, meanwhile, had downed a dozen confirmed, plus three probables. Chris McGee scored one aerial victory, to bring his total to eight. The first of two that were downed by Bill McClurg made him an ace at last, and the second brought his total to six.

The ratio of Japanese aircraft downed to American losses was tilting more and more in favor of the Americans. Missions against Rabaul, once a feared and formidable patch of sky, would soon be thought of as a scoring opportunity. Some overconfident American aviators had started referring to missions over Rabaul as the "gravy train."

Of Greg Boyington, Frank Walton was able to write in his December 23 after-action report of "the Commanding Officer's getting 4 to bring his score to 24." That this total was still padded with the six that Boyington claimed from China did not diminish the pride that the squadron—and the whole Marine fighter establishment in the Solomons—had in this eccentric character who led the Black Sheep.

Boyington, who later recalled the incidents of December 23 as having taken place on Christmas Day, did not actually fly on December 25, though eight other Black Sheep did. So too did eight aviators from VMF-223. Escorting two dozen B-24s against Rabaul, VMF-214 scored four aerial victories, while VMF-223 claimed three.

Both Marion Carl and Greg Boyington were back in the air on December 27, as their respective squadrons each took part in what was planned as a 64-aircraft fighter sweep over Rabaul involving both Marine Corsairs and US Navy Hellcats.

VMF-223 reached Rabaul at 22,000 feet around 1000hrs. The skies were clear, though there was some cumulus in the distance, and Zeros were taking off to greet the Americans. Carl found that several of his cockpit instruments were not working—nor was his radio. As he later recalled, despite all this, his guns were in "fine fettle."

Seeing a Zero beneath him by about 3,000 feet, he nosed over to make a pass from five o'clock high. Thumbing the trigger at a distance of 150 yards, he watched as his stream of bullets ripped into the enemy cockpit. When Carl broke off at just 50 feet, the Zero burst into flames, rolled over and went down.

Quickly picking out a second Zero, Carl made a head-on pass. Though Carl saw his bullets hitting the fuselage, the Zero got away. As summarized succinctly in the squadron after-action report, "the plane did not crash or burn." This one went into the log as "damaged," not as a probable.

Boyington and VMF-214 reached Rabaul via St. George's Channel at 1130hrs. Frank Walton reported that Boyington led the squadron into "a huge tilted Lufberry circle," referencing the widely used tactic originally popularized by the World War I ace Raoul Lufbery, in which a formation circles in such a way as to permit aircraft within it to provide defensive fire to protect one another from attacking enemy aircraft.

On December 27, Boyington's tilted circle, centered over Simpson Harbor, had a diameter of nearly six miles, with its high side at 20,000 foot and its lower side at 14,000. As the Japanese fighters approached them, Corsairs would break off for a firing pass, then rejoin the circle. In so doing, the VMF-214 downed six enemy aircraft that day, including the one which by official reckoning brought Boyington's total score to 25.

The significance of this milestone number, which was just one shy of the total achieved by Eddie Rickenbacker in World War I and by Joe Foss nearly a year earlier, was not lost on the media.

Fred Hampton of the Associated Press, who was at Torokina and who had spoken with Boyington on the day after Christmas, filed a report that flooded into the newspapers across the United States and the world. The newspapers in Spokane, Washington, the largest city near Okanogan, where his mother lived, were carrying short items about Boyington's exploits almost every day.

An uncredited United Press correspondent penned words that resonated most lyrically across the newswires. He wrote that Boyington "handles his fast, deadly Corsair fighter as he would a toy. Shy and nonchalant on the ground, he is a holy terror to the Japs in the air."

In a piece datelined from Torokina on December 28, this UP reporter explained that Boyington "planned to exercise his privilege as squadron commander to go up every day in an attempt to break Foss's record established over Guadalcanal."

Indeed, Boyington did fly again on December 28, but while Bill McClurg, Chris McGee, and two others each added a single aerial victory, Boyington claimed only a probable.

When bad weather closed in on the northern Solomons and missions were scrubbed in the last days of 1943, Greg Boyington was tantalizingly close to his goal, but knowing the third tour of duty for VMF-214 had less than two weeks to run.

When Marion Carl, as commander of VMF-223, signed off on the squadron's monthly report on the last day of December 1943, the cumulative tally of the squadron's aerial victories stood at 123.5. The squadron would down two more enemy aircraft before standing down from their final Solomons tour on January 4, 1944.

Of the VMF-223 aces, Carl himself was in the lead among those still in the squadron, with 18.5. He had almost caught up with John L. Smith's 19, but his aerial victory of December 27 was to be his last. In next place was Ken Frazier, the only other double-digit VMF-223 ace. His victory four days earlier brought Frazier's total to 12.5, his final score. Like Smith and Carl, he would receive the Navy Cross.

26

Everything They Had Left

January

"Everybody, it seemed to me, clamored for me to break the two-way tie," Greg Boyington wrote in his memoirs of the excitement of going around the air base at Barakoma on the first day of 1944. The climax of Boyington's career as a fighter pilot was in sight, but no one could imagine what was in store for the man whom United Press had anointed as a "holy terror."

As noted in the previous chapter, the "two-way tie" of which he spoke was the score of 26 that was shared by America's World War I ace of aces, Eddie Rickenbacker and Marine ace Joe Foss of VMF-121.

By his own reckoning, made official by VMF-214's air combat information officer and Boyington promoter Frank Walton, Boyington had achieved 25 aerial victories as of December 27. One more and it would be a three-way tie at 26. Two or more, and Boyington would be America's top-scoring ace—to date.

As 1944 began, USAAF pilot Richard Ira Bong, who was destined to be America's highest-scoring ace ever, had scored only 21 of his eventual 40, and he was then on leave in the United States and not actively adding to his score. The top USAAF aces in Europe were then still below 25.

"Everyone was lending a hand, it seemed," Boyington recalled, speaking of the support he received from his fellow Black Sheep. "I showed my appreciation by putting everything I had left into my final efforts," he said. "The reason for all the anxiety was caused by my having only ten more days to accomplish it." The contest was the talk of fighter fields across SOPAC.

The anxiety was weighing heavily. By Boyington's own admission, the VMF-214 flight surgeon, Navy Lieutenant James "Doc" Reames, was worried about how the squadron commander was handling this anxiety. "He said there were plenty of medical reasons for calling all bets off," Boyington recalled. "But I knew I couldn't stop."

Though Boyington mentions Marion Carl only in passing in his memoirs, Carl devotes a couple sentences to Boyington in his. He recalls the talk going around at Barakoma of how Boyington was "closing in" on Joe Foss's record. Carl referred to the ongoing "South Pacific 'ace race'" and used the phrase "score-happy" when describing Boyington.

Within VMF-214, and in other squadrons as well, aviators encouraged the contest. The VMF-214 men were naturally delighted by the light of Boyington's celebrity that shone upon their squadron, but with wire service reporters poking around, Frank Walton was especially excited. He was savoring his role as a public relations man for Boyington. Plans were already in place for an acetate disc recording to be made of Boyington describing his triumphant victories, and for this to be broadcast as widely as possible. Walton had already written a script to use in introducing "America's new number one ace."

The booze flowed freely on New Year's Eve at Barakoma, and Boyington, being Boyington, consumed copious quantities. Perhaps in anticipation of his "putting everything he had" into the welcome party for 1944, he was not on the roster for a B-24 escort mission over Rabaul on New Year's Day. Those from VMF-214 who did fly the mission reported no contact with enemy fighters, so Boyington missed no opportunities for the combat he craved.

Early on January 2, Boyington was back in the air as tactical commander of a fighter sweep over Rabaul by 20 Hellcats and three dozen Corsairs. When Boyington and the VMF-214 contingent reached the great Japanese base at 1205hrs, the aerial battle was already in progress, with fewer than 15 Zeros struggling against the American armada.

It was here in this great swirling air battle in which most of the Marine aviators were predisposed toward "lending a hand" in Boyington's quixotic quest that the gremlins of irony seized the moment.

On the threshold of a perfect scenario for his twenty-sixth—and maybe also his twenty-seventh—aerial victory, Boyington's big Pratt & Whitney R-2700 engine rebelled against him and against his Corsair.

A massive oil leak sprung up from within it, hurling the blackish-brown crud up and across his windshield. Boyington popped his seatbelt, stood up and frantically began wiping it with his handkerchief. He never made it into the battle. Among the VMF-214 aviators, Fred "Rope Trick" Loesch was the only man to score an aerial victory. Four members of Marion Carl's VMF-223 took part in the fighter sweep, but saw no air-to-air action that day.

Two days of 1944 had ticked by, with the end of his tour of duty that much nearer, and without Boyington having been in combat. One is reminded of Ernest Lawrence Thayer's *Casey at the Bat*, in which the legendary hitter lets the first two pitches go by before he swings on the third. No one knew on January 2 that Greg Boyington would have just *one more* chance at bat.

In their respective memoirs, both Boyington and Marion Carl recall that VMF-223 had been picked for the January 3 fighter sweep over Rabaul, but they agreed on VMF-214 taking the mission in the interest of Boyington getting the crack at the enemy that he so desired. Each man recalled that the idea for the swap originated with the other.

At 1740hrs on January 2, Boyington flew up to Torokina to spend the night ahead of the mission to Rabaul. With him, he took Black Sheep aviators George Ashmun, J.J. Hill, and Alfred Johnson. These men had seen relatively little aerial combat, and Boyington wanted to give them a chance at the "gravy train," even as he was anxious for his own next victory—or two.

On New Year's Day, the United Press wire carried a story in which the term "gravy train" was in the headline, and an example was made of VMF-222, which had reported to have "bagged 17 Nipponese in one day without losing a plane." The same article reminded readers that "all eyes" were on Boyington as viewers on the ground waited for him to do a "victory roll" after a successful mission.

"I can never forget George Ashmun's thin, pale face when I mentioned where I was going," Boyington wrote in his memoirs. "He insisted that he go along as my wingman ... You go ahead and shoot all you want, Gramps. All I'll do is keep them off your tail."

Flying at 22,000 feet, four other VMF-214 rendezvoused with Boyington's division at 0815hrs on January 3 over St. George's Channel.

According to both Boyington and Carl, VMF-223 was not officially part of the Rabaul mission that day. Seven Corsairs from VMF-223 were nearby, but Marion Carl himself was not among them.

Enemy aircraft were first spotted at 19,000 feet over Rapopo airfield, about ten miles southeast of Simpson Harbor. The skies were generally clear, but a smoky haze partially obscured the ground far below.

"Go down and get to work," Boyington ordered.

With Ashmun trailing on his wing, Boyington dived. He came in, guns blazing, on the enemy aircraft's six o'clock. Members of both VMF-214 and VMF-223 watched the Zero explode into flames and fall out of the sky. Boyington was now at 26.

Boyington and Ashmun continued to dive deeper into the swirling mass of enemy fighters, assuming that the other Black Sheep were close behind. Ashmun found a Zero in his sights, opened fire and they watched it go down. A moment later, Boyington did the same, but as he glanced at his wingman, he saw smoke pouring from Ashmun's Corsair.

By now, there were several Zeros on the tails of Ashmun's aircraft and his own.

When he contemplated their being in a sky full of Zeros, it had begun to occur to Boyington—and probably to Ashmun as well—that today, the "gravy train" was running in the *opposite* direction.

Seeing that Ashmun was barely descending to evade his attackers, Boyington shouted over the radio for Ashmun to dive. In a dive, the Corsair could easily outrun a Zero.

Ashmun made no move to push his nose down. He was probably already dead.

Boyington maneuvered in behind the Zeros that were shooting at Ashmun, but as he opened fire, he could feel 7.7mm slugs fired by other Zeros impacting the armor plate in the back of his seat. He was in the crosshairs of multiple Zeros that were dishing out a withering fusillade. If not for his armor, he would have been dead several times over.

Boyington's cockpit turned into a bin of torn metal, shards of which ripped into his leg.

As he watched Ashmun's Corsair burst into flames and hit the water, Boyington did as he had tried to get Ashmun to do. He pushed his own Corsair into a dive.

He pulled out when his aircraft was practically at wavetop level and was intending to climb out when his forward fuel tank exploded into flames.

"Well, you finally got it, didn't you, wise guy?" Boyington told himself.

He unbuckled his seat belt, unfastened the canopy, and with great difficulty, he pushed his injured body up and out of the stricken Corsair. His parachute opened just above the waves. By various accounts, it was later estimated to have been within 15 minutes either way from 0835hrs that Boyington hit the water.

His troubles continued as four of the Zeros that had destroyed his aircraft now followed him down and began to make strafing runs. Instinctively, he tried to dive out of the way, but his strength was quickly ebbing away because of his wounds.

Finally the enemy departed, and Boyington found himself treading water for what seemed like two hours before he got his life raft inflated. He took stock of his injuries, both bullet and shrapnel wounds, cracked open his first aid kit and started to patch himself. Having done this, he contemplated his position. He was in St. George's Channel, halfway between New Britain and New Ireland.

He was surrounded by enemy-controlled territory, but the enemy came from below. It was late in the afternoon when a vast dark shape emerged from the sea like a sea monster. At first he breathed easier, thinking that this huge submarine was American. US Navy subs often picked up downed American flyers.

But then his heart sank when he saw the dark red meatball insignia of the Imperial Japanese Navy.

While Boyington was still afloat, alone, and in contemplation, the remaining Black Sheep were back at Barakoma and comparing notes. Many of them had seen Boyington down one Zero, but nobody had seen either he or George Ashmun after that moment. They had faded into the haze and disappeared.

The only radio call that was unaccounted for was an anonymous one in which someone reported that he was going to make a water landing. It was speculated that this might have been Boyington.

At 0550hrs on January 4, six-victory ace Jack Bolt led a VMF-214 search party up to St. George's Channel to look for their boss, but Boyington was nowhere to be seen. Unbeknownst to them, he was beneath the waves and gone.

The news quickly reached the States that "Pappy" Boyington had been lost on the mission in which he tied the record of Rickenbacker and Foss. The tragedy of it all made good copy. The headlines read:

"American Flyer Out After his 26th Victory"
"Boyington Dies Tying Rickenbacker Record"
"Air Ace Missing on Raid in Which He Tied Record"
"Boyington Missing; Downed 25 Planes"

The United Press sent a reporter racing to Okanogan to interview Grace Hallenbeck, the fallen hero's mother, who held the Navy Department telegram in a shaking hand.

Noting that his tour of duty was nearly over, she said that she had been expecting him home by early February. The telegram said he was "missing in action," but the headlines suggested that he may have died a hero's death.

Back on Vella Lavella, life went on for VMF-214. Major Henry Miller took command of the squadron for its last four days in combat. Denmark Groover and Moon Mullen each scored an aerial victory on the day after Boyington disappeared, and Harry Johnson got a Zero on January 6. This was the last one.

VMF-214 had achieved 126 aerial victories, the majority of these in its 1943–1944 incarnation as the Black Sheep Squadron. There were ten VMF-214 aces, with Boyington being the only one in double-digits. Chris McGee was in second place with nine, while Bill Case had eight, including one with VMF-112.

As noted previously in these pages, the number of victories scored by Boyington has been a subject of endless debate for decades. In 1944, the media and the VMF-214 record credited him with 26 as of January 3, which included his claim of six with the Flying Tigers, though only two of these were verified. To this, he would later add the two from January 3, 1944 that are described above, but they were not witnessed by anyone else at the time, bringing his total to 28. If the six unconfirmed claims were backed out of the total, it would be 22. The speculation will continue indefinitely.

At 0715hrs on January 8, 1944, the Black Sheep departed from Vella Lavella for the last time, aboard a SCAT flight to Espiritu Santo. By the end of the month, they had moved on, some returning to the United States and some on furlough to Sydney.

VMF-214 was reorganized Stateside, and it returned to combat off Okinawa on March 18 aboard the carrier USS *Franklin* (CV-18). However, the ship was devastated in a Japanese air attack the following day, abruptly ending the squadron's wartime career.

VMF-214 would be reconstituted several times through the coming decades as a ground attack squadron, flying F4U-4B Corsairs over Korea, and operating A-4M Skyhawks as VMA-214 in Vietnam. In the twenty-first century, VMA-214 flew AV-8B Harriers in Iraq and Afghanistan.

As of January 1944, though, the squadron's aerial combat days were over.

27

At the Top of Their Game

January

For the first few days of 1944, the focus of media attention on Marine Corps aviation in the South Pacific was on the Black Sheep of Greg Boyington's VMF-214, and on the still-colorful legacy of Marion Carl's VMF-223, which had been the original home of the aces in the decisive fall of 1942. However, two other squadrons, VMF-212 and VMF-215, were returning to action in January, and were about to make history.

Back in 1942, VMF-212 had been the squadron commanded by the legendary "Coach" Joe Bauer. In 1944, it was the home of Phillip Cunliffe DeLong, not then well known, but as he emerged from the shadows, he was definitely at the top of his game.

Phil DeLong had flown in combat since May 1943, but scored no aerial victories until January 9, 1944, when he flew over St. George's Channel at 18,000 feet and saw three IJNAF Zeros 10,000 feet below over Tamalili Bay.

Major Hugh Elwood, VMF-212's commander, was leading two divisions as part of the escort for SBDs and TBFs flying a strike mission against Tobera airfield. DeLong was leading the second element of the division led personally by Elwood. They had seen other Zeros as they entered the target area, and had taken ground fire, but these three Zeros marked the beginning of their air-to-air action that day.

Making a high side pass, Elwood took the second of the trio, DeLong the third. Neither Japanese pilot took evasive action as the Marines opened fire. The Zeros rolled on their backs, burst into flames and went into the sea.

Moments later, Elwood and DeLong spotted a pair of Corsairs beset by eight Zeros and, as the aircraft action report recalls, they "dove through, breaking up the fight." Elwood downed a Zero in this intervention, while DeLong got a probable.

Climbing to 10,000 feet, the two aviators saw and attacked a trio of Zeros. This time, Elwood missed on his first pass, but another Zero got on his tail and closed in for the kill. However, DeLong was in a position to put a stream of tracers into this Zero, which rolled over and plummeted into the water below.

When January 9 was over and the scores were counted, Elwood and DeLong each had two of VMF-212's score of nine for the day.

When unheralded VMF-215 reached Barakoma airfield on Vella Lavella on January 6, there was no way of knowing that it would end the month with three double-digit aces, including one man who would reside in the pantheon of the Marine Corps' top three of all time.

Donald Nathan Aldrich had become the squadron's first ace on September 2, 1943 and Harold Leman Spears had a total of four during his first tour of duty with the squadron, but neither man achieved any victories during their second tour in November. Robert Murray Hanson, who came to VMF-215 having scored a pair with VMF-214, became an ace on November 1, but had scored no aerial victories since. However, each of these three aviators was about to embark on an incredible four-week run.

Both Aldrich and Spears were now captains and division leaders, while Hanson was still a first lieutenant.

On January 11 according to the VMF-215 aircraft action report (or January 12 by the squadron war diary, which used local, west of the International Dateline, time), two dozen VMF-215 Corsairs took off from Barakoma at 0600hrs, touched down to refuel at Torokina and were airborne again at 0920hrs.

An hour later, they rendezvoused with two dozen USAAF B-24s headed to attack Vunakanau airfield at Rabaul.

Between 15 and 20 Zeros intercepted the bombers as they passed over New Ireland and made their westward turn over St. George's Channel. VMF-215 was flying high cover, above 28,000 feet, with the bombers at 20,000 feet, when Aldrich saw three Zeros approaching from the west at about 25,000 feet.

"I swung wide and dove on the Zeros, approaching them from astern," he recalled. "My first burst (a fairly long one) started flames along the wing root of the first Zero. I looked back and saw that my wingman had flamed the second one. The third one rolled and dove out ... Very shortly thereafter I saw a pair of strays (Zeros which seemed to have no plan of action but were first flying a course paralleling the bombers). I dove on them from dead astern and saw one of them go into flames on my first burst."

Don Aldrich had now brought his score to seven.

On January 14 (by local reckoning), the mission involved a massive strike against Rabaul with more than 70 fighters escorting Navy SBDs and TBFs. VMF-215 contributed 24 Corsairs to this force, their rendezvous with TBFs coming at 1115hrs.

The enemy intercept began over New Ireland as on the previous mission. At first, around a half-dozen Zeros were observed, but gradually others appeared until there were as many as 70 Zeros above and behind the Americans.

Their passes against the American force grew increasingly intense as the bombers crossed St. George's Channel. Because Lakunai airfield, the primary target, was socked in with cloud cover, the bombers diverted and braved intense antiaircraft fire to attack shipping in Simpson Harbor and nearby Blanche Bay. Large numbers of Japanese aircraft attacked as the bombers emerged from their strike.

Don Aldrich put a stream of tracers into each of two Zeros, which fell into the clouds and would be listed as probables. He struck a third Zero with a 45-degree deflection shot as the bombers were attacking, and saw this one hit the water. His single confirmed victory was part of 19 confirmed victories that marked VMF-215's most intense aerial combat action to date.

It was Bob Hanson, though, who was in the right place at *five* right times that day.

As the TBFs were attacking, Hanson saw a group of SBDs in the distance that was under attack by Zeros and went to help. He and his wingman, Richard Bowman, came in behind two of the Zeros, firing until both enemy aircraft burst into flames.

Losing track of Bowman, Hanson closed in on another pair of Zeros, which veered off in the opposite direction. Hanson chased the one that tried unsuccessfully to hide in some thin cloud cover, opened fire and watched this Zero explode.

Surveying the scene, Hanson saw the sky above him filled with about 30 Zeros. He saw two Corsairs, but they disappeared into a cloud. Using the edge of this cloud to screen himself, Hanson began climbing toward the Zeros.

"The clouds got higher and higher as they got out towards New Ireland," he later recalled in the aircraft action report. "I stayed with [the Zeros], playing hide and seek in and out of the clouds—all the time getting altitude. At about 3,000 feet I saw two Zeros at nine o'clock at about 2,500 feet crossing my course. I dove and they turned away from me into the clouds. I opened up on one when I had a 45-degree deflection shot and saw him burst immediately into flame."

Hanson continued to climb, weaving in and out of the clouds until he found himself behind and a little beneath another Zero.

"I ran right up to him and fired," Hanson remembered. "My tracers went right into his belly and he burst immediately into flame. I think that this is the best way to shoot them: from astern and below—the belly seems to be the most vulnerable point."

With this, Hanson turned back toward the place where the American fighters were to rally together to return home. However, he saw no Corsairs here, only Zeros "flying around apparently without a plan."

Form ACA-1
Sheet 1 of 5

RESTRICTED
(Reclassify when
filled out)

AIRCRAFT ACTION REPORT

I. GENERAL

(a) Unit Reporting VMF 215   (b) Based on or at VELLA LAVELLA   (c) Report No. 10

(d) Date of Action Jan. 13, 1944 (e) Take off: Time 1900   (GCT), Lat. 6° 14' S Long 155° 06' E

(f) Mission Strike Escort to Rabaul   (g) Time of Return 0630 Jan. 14, 1944 (GCT)

II. OWN AIRCRAFT OFFICIALLY COVERED BY THIS REPORT.

(a) TYPE	(b) SQUADRON	(c) NO. OF SORTIES	(d) NO. ENGAGING ENEMY A/C	(e) NO. ATTACKING TARGET	(f) BOMBS AND TORPEDOES CARRIED (PER PLANE)	(g) FUZE SETTING
F4U-1	VMF 215	22	22			

III. OTHER U. S. OR ALLIED AIRCRAFT EMPLOYED IN THIS OPERATION.

TYPE	SQUADRON	NUMBER	BASE	TYPE	SQUADRON	NUMBER	BASE
TBF		18	Munda				
P-40	RNZAF#17	8	Ondonga				

IV. ENEMY AIRCRAFT ENCOUNTERED (By Own Aircraft Listed in II Only).

(a) TYPE	(b) NO. OBSERVED	(c) NO. ENGAGING OWN A/C	(d) TIME ENCOUNTERED	(e) LOCATION OF ENCOUNTER	(f) BOMBS, TORPEDOES CARRIED; GUNS OBSERVED	(g) CAMOUFLAGE AND MARKING
Zeke	50-70	50-70	0130 to 0215 (GCT) (GCT) (GCT)	Over New Ireland and Rabaul area of New Britain	Phosphorous bombs	

(h) Apparent Enemy Mission(s) Interception

(i) Weather and Clouds at Location of Encounter(s) Hazy, cumulus, and scud

(j) Sun or Moon Sun   (k) Visibility Poor

V. ENEMY AIRCRAFT DESTROYED OR DAMAGED IN AIR (By Own Aircraft Listed in II Only).

(a) TYPE ENEMY A/C	(b) DESTROYED OR DAMAGED BY				(c) WHERE HIT, ANGLE	(d) DAMAGE CLAIMED
	TYPE A/C	SQUADRON	PILOT OR GUNNER	GUNS USED		
Zeke	F4U-1	VMF215	1st Lt. H.M. Hanson	Fixed	Astern	Destroyed
Zeke	F4U-1	VMF215	1st Lt. H.M. Hanson	Fixed	Astern & above	Destroyed
Zeke	F4U-1	VMF215	1st Lt. H.M. Hanson	Fixed	45° astern & above	Destroyed
Zeke	F4U-1	VMF215	1st Lt. H.M. Hanson	Fixed	Astern & below	Destroyed
Zeke	F4U-1	VMF215	1st Lt. H.M. Hanson	Fixed	25° astern & above	Destroyed
Zeke	F4U-1	VMF215	Capt. A.T. Warner	Fixed	Head on	Destroyed
Zeke	F4U-1	VMF215	Capt. A.T. Warner	Fixed	45° astern & below	Destroyed
Zeke	F4U-1	VMF215	Capt. A.T. Warner	Fixed	Dead astern & slightly above	Destroyed
Zeke	F4U-1	VMF215	Capt. A.T. Warner	Fixed	90° from below	Destroyed
Zeke	F4U-1	VMF215	Capt. R.E. Robinson	Fixed	45° ahead	Destroyed
Zeke	F4U-1	VMF215	Capt. R.E. Robinson	Fixed	20° ahead	Destroyed
Zeke	F4U-1	VMF215	Capt. R.E. Robinson	Fixed	50° to 45° from above and astern	Probable

SECRET

35

FIGURE 3 This Aircraft Action Report for January 13, 1944 (by Greenwich reckoning) records one of VMF-215's remarkable days, the one when "Butcher Bob" Hanson downed five enemy aircraft on a single mission to Rabaul. (USMC)

Hanson, on the other hand, promptly formulated a plan. He picked out a Zero and dived on him from 3,000 feet. Taking a 25-degree deflection shot, he watched "tongues of flame" erupt from the wing roots and engine as the enemy aircraft's fuel tanks caught fire.

Bob Hanson touched down at Torokina 20 minutes after the rest of VMF-215, and with 20 gallons of fuel. By the time that he had settled back into Barakoma that afternoon, he had caught the eye of the Associated Press stringer on Vella Lavella who was looking for a story to tell. Bob Hanson had one.

This wire service dispatch, which would not reach the papers at home for several days, reported succinctly that Hanson had "shot down five Japanese Zeros before, during and after a raid on Rabaul." The article added that only Joe Bauer and Greg Boyington had previously downed five in a single day, adding ominously that both Bauer and Boyington were now MIA.

In fact, Bauer's total on September 28, 1942 had included four confirmed and a probable. No mention was made of the five in a day scored by Joe Foss in October 1942, nor Jefferson DeBlanc in January 1943, nor of Jim Swett's *seven* in one day in April 1943.

The excitement of the remarkable 19 aerial victories—plus a half-dozen probables—scored by VMF-215 that day was tempered by the loss of four pilots, one injured by shrapnel, one killed in a crash on takeoff, and two who never returned.

For Phil DeLong and VMF-212, the next scores came on a TBF escort mission on January 17. As the bombers were withdrawing from the target near Rabaul, he saw two US Navy F6Fs, also part of the escort package, under attack at 1,500 feet. Diving 4,000 feet, DeLong got on the tail of one of the attacking Zeros. As he took his shot from behind, fire erupted from near the enemy's cockpit and the Zero spun into the water below.

Pulling out from this action, DeLong watched another Zero making an overhead pass against three TBFs. Seeing DeLong, the Zero pulled away into a right turn. DeLong followed him into the turn, but could not get the Zero into his sights.

When the Zero went into a "Split S" maneuver to evade his pursuer, DeLong caught him as he pulled out and fired three quick bursts from his machine guns. The Japanese pilot accelerated to get away, but flames erupted from both wing roots and the Zero went down. DeLong's two victories on January 17, part of three for VMF-212 that day, brought his score to four.

On January 18, it was the turn of Hal Spears to get on VMF-215's third-tour scoreboard. The bombers, in this case USAAF B-25s, had attacked Rabaul without waiting for fighter cover, but the Corsairs reached them at 1140hrs as they were exiting the target area across St. George's Channel.

When Spears was coming up the Channel, his division and the division ahead of them encountered a trio of IJAAF Kawasaki Ki-61 Tonys. As the four Corsairs in the first division attacked, the Japanese aircraft evaded, with two breaking right, and the other to the left.

While the other division chased the pair, Spears and his wingman, Creighton Chandler, went after the lone Tony and chased him down to just 200 feet off the water. Spears opened fire, but the Japanese Army pilot turned hard to the right. Unfortunately for him, this placed his Ki-61 directly ahead of Chandler's sights. A long burst sent the Tony tumbling into the Channel.

As this was happening, Spears saw an all-black Tony racing westward at wave-top level.

"I dove right down on his tail and followed him while he did a series of rolls and quick turns, always keeping on a generally westward course," Spears reported. "I fired at him every time I got him in my sights. He finally rolled on his back and plunged into the water and exploded." This victory made Spears an ace, but his day was not yet finished.

Turning to rejoin the squadron, Spears and Chandler encountered an IJNAF Zero that made a quick pass and disappeared, but they spotted a second Zero chasing a Navy Hellcat, so they intervened.

Spears opened fire with a long burst at a deflection of 25 degrees and watched this Zero catch fire and crash into St. George's Channel.

Spears and Chandler emerged from the engagement to see two Zeros headed south. Quickly attacking from behind, Spears saw his Zero burst into flames and fall, while Chandler's exploded as it struck the water.

January 20 found all three of VMF-215's eventual double-digit aces in the sky simultaneously. Don Aldrich and Hal Spears each led a division, while Bob Hanson was flying in the division led by Art Warner. The mission as briefed was like those that had become routine for the squadron—an early morning launch from Barakoma, followed by a refueling stop at Torokina and a rendezvous with Rabaul-bound bombers around noon.

Flying medium cover, which actually worked out to be quite low, Spears and his division went into the target area with the USAAF B-25s. They outran the bombers about 15 miles south of Rabaul, and had to make a 360-degree turn.

It was here, at an altitude of about 600 feet, that an A6M3 Hamp, the square-winged variant of the Zero, challenged Spears head on. They made a firing pass against one another and the Hamp went up and over into a loop, while Spears climbed into him. Spears opened fire on the inverted Hamp and it burst into flames before it hit the ground. Spears and his division then rejoined the bombers as they made their bomb run.

Next, Spears and his wingman, Creighton Chandler, came in low to strafe the enemy field at Tobera, and Chandler shot down a Zero that was on final approach. At the same time, Spears watched a Zero get onto the tail of a B-25. He took a 20-degree deflection shot from behind and watched the enemy fighter slice into the jungle in a ball of flame.

Meanwhile, Aldrich and his division had followed the bombers as they exited the target in a sweeping right turn. They then turned inside and dropped behind. As a Zero made a firing pass at the bombers, Aldrich pulled back on the stick and chased the enemy aircraft as it climbed to about 4,000 feet.

"I was firing straight up when I got him," Aldrich recalled. "He burned and fell off ... Then I kicked right rudder and fell off to the right and went down towards the bombers and zig zagged behind them."

Two Zeros then raced past him on the left.

When Aldrich banked right in anticipation of a third Zero coming on his left, the third Zero passed him on the *right*, coming in low. He chased this Zero down, pouring machine gun fire into him until he hit the ground.

Bob Hanson had stayed with the bombers, flying near the front of their formation as they left the target area. When they were about four miles out to sea, Hanson moved to the back of the pack, where he intercepted a Zero that was attacking a B-25 at about 3,500 feet. He chased this fighter up to about 4,000 feet, opened fire with a 20-degree deflection shot, and sent it tumbling into the sea.

January 20 was the first day of eleven days in which Aldrich, Hanson, and Spears would score the majority of their aerial victories. An "ace race" was under way. A historic—and personal—aerial campaign had begun.

Two days later, the mission brief was again an escort mission for 18 USAAF B-25s bound for the airfields that ringed Rabaul. VMF-215 supplied 27 Corsairs to fly medium, low, and bottom cover for the bombers, with which they rendezvoused east of New Ireland at 1315hrs. There was cloud cover over New Ireland, but the skies were clear over the target.

Hal Spears was 12,000 feet above one of the targets, Lakunai airfield, when he noticed a Zero circling below. It seemed that it had just barely taken off from the field. Its pilot was probably glad to have escaped the bombs, but he was about to have something else to grapple with—a diving Corsair on his six.

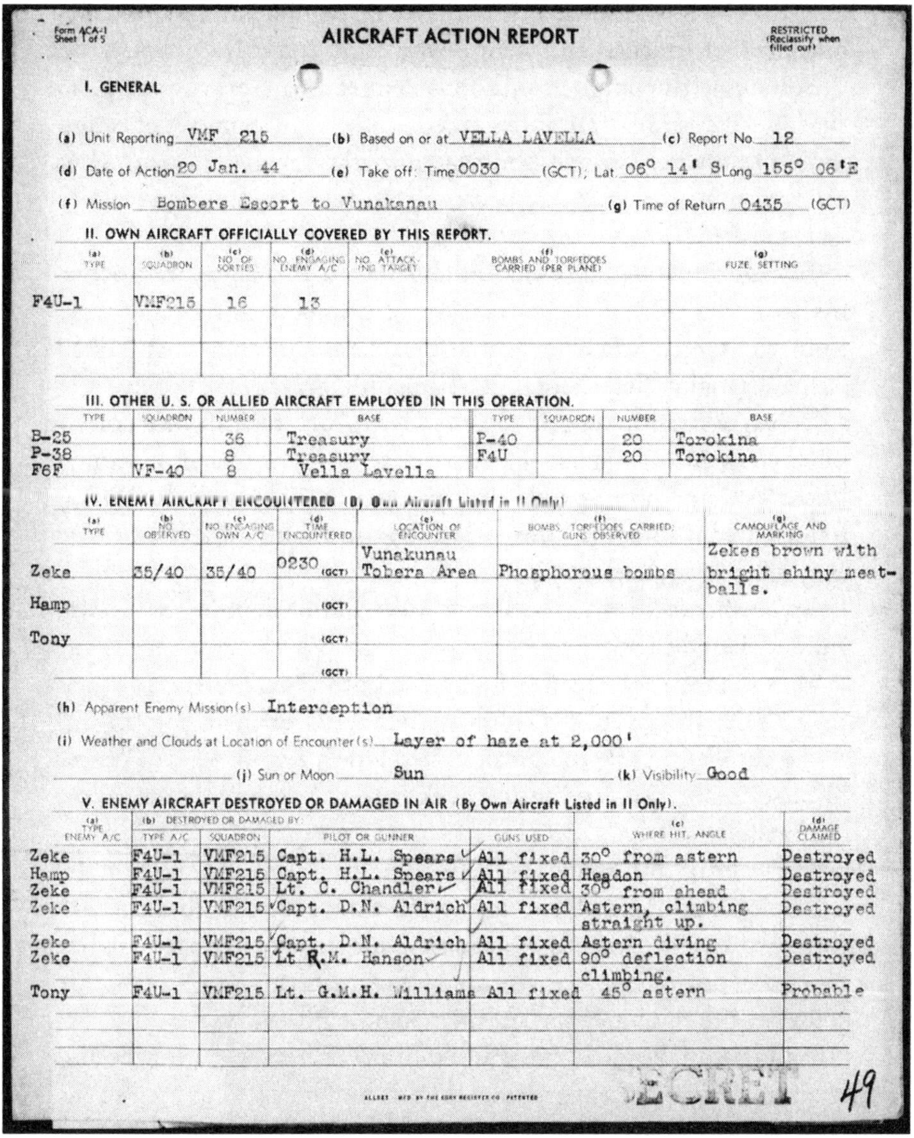

Form ACA-1
Sheet 1 of 5

AIRCRAFT ACTION REPORT

RESTRICTED
(Reclassify when filled out)

I. GENERAL

(a) Unit Reporting VMF 215 (b) Based on or at VELLA LAVELLA (c) Report No. 12

(d) Date of Action 20 Jan. 44 (e) Take off: Time 0030 (GCT); Lat. 06° 14' S Long 155° 06' E

(f) Mission Bombers Escort to Vunakanau (g) Time of Return 0435 (GCT)

II. OWN AIRCRAFT OFFICIALLY COVERED BY THIS REPORT.

(a) TYPE	(b) SQUADRON	(c) NO. OF SORTIES	(d) NO. ENGAGING ENEMY A/C	(e) NO. ATTACKING TARGET	(f) BOMBS AND TORPEDOES CARRIED (PER PLANE)	(g) FUZE SETTING
F4U-1	VMF215	16	13			

III. OTHER U. S. OR ALLIED AIRCRAFT EMPLOYED IN THIS OPERATION.

TYPE	SQUADRON	NUMBER	BASE	TYPE	SQUADRON	NUMBER	BASE
B-25		36	Treasury	P-40		20	Torokina
P-38		8	Treasury	F4U		20	Torokina
F6F	VF-40	8	Vella Lavella				

IV. ENEMY AIRCRAFT ENCOUNTERED (By Own Aircraft Listed in II Only)

(a) TYPE	(b) NO. OBSERVED	(c) NO. ENGAGING OWN A/C	(d) TIME ENCOUNTERED	(e) LOCATION OF ENCOUNTER	(f) BOMBS, TORPEDOES CARRIED; GUNS OBSERVED	(g) CAMOUFLAGE AND MARKING
Zeke	35/40	35/40	0230 (GCT)	Vunakunau Tobera Area	Phosphorous bombs	Zekes brown with bright shiny meat-balls.
Hamp			(GCT)			
Tony			(GCT)			
			(GCT)			

(h) Apparent Enemy Mission(s) Interception

(i) Weather and Clouds at Location of Encounter(s) Layer of haze at 2,000'

(j) Sun or Moon Sun (k) Visibility Good

V. ENEMY AIRCRAFT DESTROYED OR DAMAGED IN AIR (By Own Aircraft Listed in II Only).

(a) TYPE ENEMY A/C	(b) DESTROYED OR DAMAGED BY: TYPE A/C	SQUADRON	PILOT OR GUNNER	GUNS USED	(c) WHERE HIT, ANGLE	(d) DAMAGE CLAIMED
Zeke	F4U-1	VMF215	Capt. H.L. Spears	All fixed	30° from astern	Destroyed
Hamp	F4U-1	VMF215	Capt. H.L. Spears	All fixed	Headon	Destroyed
Zeke	F4U-1	VMF215	Lt. C. Chandler	All fixed	30° from ahead	Destroyed
Zeke	F4U-1	VMF215	Capt. D.N. Aldrich	All fixed	Astern, climbing straight up.	Destroyed
Zeke	F4U-1	VMF215	Capt. D.N. Aldrich	All fixed	Astern diving	Destroyed
Zeke	F4U-1	VMF215	Lt R.M. Hanson	All fixed	90° deflection climbing.	Destroyed
Tony	F4U-1	VMF215	Lt. G.M.H. Williams	All fixed	45° astern	Probable

SECRET

49

FIGURE 4 January 1944 was a month in which the skies over Rabaul were dominated by the three double-digit aces of VMF-215, Hal Spears, Don Aldrich, and Bob Hanson. As is seen in this Aircraft Action Report, all three of the men scored on the mission on January 20. (USMC)

Spears "spiraled down and ran right up his tail and fired directly into him. He burned and went down."

Following the bombers out of the target area, Spears saw a Zero chasing a Corsair and interrupted with a 30-degree deflection shot. He noticed smoke pouring from the Japanese aircraft, but claimed him as a probable because the Zero was not observed to have crashed.

Don Aldrich was about 20 miles southeast of Cape St. George, flying at the rear of the formation of bombers as they departed from the target, when he saw a lone Zero shooting at an Allied airman hanging helplessly in his parachute.

When Aldrich closed in on the Zero from behind, the enemy pilot went into a typical Japanese defensive maneuver, climbing into a loop and hoping to lose his pursuer. It did not work. Aldrich followed him into the loop, closed to as near as 50 feet and sent him flaming toward the sea.

Two other Zeros tried to attack Aldrich, but his wingman, John Burke, chased them away.

Bob Hanson was nearby, flying medium cover for the B-25s as they flew south over St. George's Channel after their bomb runs. As he recalled in the squadron's after-action report, he saw below him, several Zeros "trying to sneak in on the bombers from low altitudes."

He went on the attack, and after a pair of Zeros eluded him, he came down in a Split-S maneuver and took a 25-degree deflection shot into a third Zero. The Japanese pilot tried to wriggle free, but he could not escape the stream of fire from Hanson's guns. He rolled to the right and was on fire when he hit the water.

As Hanson climbed, he saw two more Zeros beneath him and went at them. One turned and carried on beneath him, while the other passed above. Hanson got on the six of the one above and opened fire. The enemy pilot pulled up, but could not get away. A moment later, this Zero was engulfed in flames.

Barely had he dispatched his second Zero of the day than Hanson spotted an IJAAF Ki-61 Tony diving toward him from his right. Hanson pulled left, maneuvered behind the Tony and opened fire.

The Japanese Army pilot tried to maneuver out of the Corsair's crosshairs, but he did so more sluggishly than the two Navy pilots had with whom Hanson had just tangled. Hanson kept firing until the Japanese aircraft did a wingover to the right and nosed into the water below.

January 22 was a remarkable day for VMF-215, as they racked up ten aerial victories among them. Hanson led the pack with three, while Aldrich and Spears got one each. With these three, five on January 14 and one in between, Bob Hanson was an ace on fire. He was also a man with a nickname. If he had not fully earned the moniker "Butcher Bob" on January 22, he certainly would two days later.

January 23 was a big day for VMF-212 and for Phil DeLong. The mission was to help escort TBFs in a strike against Rabaul's Lakunai airfield.

The first contact with the enemy came at 0925hrs, when a single Zero made a pass against Elwood, DeLong, and Allan Harrison. The Japanese pilot finished his fruitless attack dead ahead of the three Corsairs. In rapid succession each pilot took his turn, and each scored hits on the Zero. DeLong was first, with Harrison catching him as he turned, and Elwood finishing him off. Each man claimed one-third of this aerial victory.

Emerging into crowded skies, Elwood next downed an IJAAF Ki-61 Tony, and then found himself joined again with DeLong and Harrison. Together, they dived on a group of IJNAF A6M3 Hamps. Elwood scored on one with a deflection shot, while DeLong hit its cockpit and right wing and Harrison hit the left wing, finishing off this Hamp. Again, the trio would claim one third each.

After sharing these two victories, DeLong found himself headed north at low level—alone and in deep trouble with two Zeros on his six and firing on him. To make matters worse, two more then piled on from above. As DeLong accelerated to escape, he noted that the 7.7mm bullets from the first two "mostly missed" and that those from the second pair were hitting the water below.

Then, a fifth Zero dived on DeLong, scoring some hits on his Corsair. DeLong started into a 180-degree turn, pulled up into a chandelle to 3,000 feet, and reversed direction. He attacked the fifth Zero head on and watched him explode.

The squadron returned to the staging base at Torokina between 1040hrs and 1055hrs, but their day was not yet over. Elwood decided that they would join Corsairs from VMF-211 and VMF-321 in an afternoon fighter sweep over Rabaul. The 32 fighters made their rendezvous at 1540hrs and were 25,000 feet over Rabaul at 1705hrs.

While VMF-212 Corsairs circled down to 17,000 feet, Elwood and DeLong broke off and descended to 12,000 feet, where they saw a lone Zero below.

"He had three buddies sitting in the sun at 16–17,000," Elwood recalled. "We saw them but risked a high side pass."

Elwood's tracers hit the Zero aft of the cockpit, while DeLong hit the Japanese fighter from below. The Zero exploded into a fireball and crashed into the water below. This was the third aerial victory shared by the two men on January 23.

Phil DeLong was now an ace with 6.166 aerial victories.

The day ended with VMF-212 having downed a Tony, a Hamp, and 15 Zeros in the morning, plus four Zeros in the afternoon. However, Major Don Boyle was missing in action, having been last seen over St. George's Channel. He was captured and imprisoned in Japan, but he survived the war.

DeLong continued his scoring streak on both January 29 and 31. On the first of those dates, he was at 5,000 feet, southbound after a TBF strike on Tobera, when a Zero pilot diving on someone else came down on his right, presenting himself as a target.

"I caught him in the belly and he exploded and crashed into Keravia Bay," DeLong recalled succinctly.

On the last day of the month, VMF-212 was escorting SBDs to Tobera when it was an A6M3 Hamp that passed fatally through Phil DeLong's sights.

The man who began the month having not scored in over half a year ended January with 8.166, leading the squadron both in number of combat missions and in aerial victories.

On January 24, VMF-215 supplied 13 aircraft to fly a high cover mission for Navy TBFs attacking Japanese shipping in Rabaul's Simpson Harbor. The Corsairs were over the target at 1220hrs, ten minutes ahead of the bombers, and made two orbits above 25,000 feet over the area as IJAAF Tonys and IJNAF Zeros climbed up to greet them.

Bob Hanson later recalled in the after-action report that he found himself "straggling a little as my ship was not functioning properly at high altitude," but he did not have to worry long.

Seeing Japanese fighters engaging other Corsairs below him, Hanson dived to 22,000 feet to join the fight. As he did, he watched the Zeros looping in their typical defensive move and attacked one from above when it was on its back at the top of the loop.

Striking this Zero with a 30-degree deflection shot, Hanson saw flames pouring from its engine and wing roots as it began to disintegrate.

He next seized upon another Zero a half mile to the south and "ran right up his tail in a no-deflection shot when he was still in an inverted position." The Japanese aircraft exploded into flames and spun into the sea below.

Finding himself alone, separated from his squadron, Hanson ducked into a great mountain of cumulus that rose from 6,000 to 18,000 feet, and used this to obscure himself from the enemy as he flew north toward the Japanese airfields around Rabaul. Over Tobera, his eyes followed a lone Ki-61 Tony as it took off and climbed to 12,000 feet.

"I ran down on him and fired on him from a 25-degree deflection from astern and slightly above and continued to fire until I was dead astern of him," Hanson recalled. "He smoked and went into a turn and dive, trailing streamers of smoke that extended for a couple of hundred feet."

He claimed this one as a probable.

As Hanson continued waiting near his cumulus, he saw a pair of Zeros and turned in behind them. Knowing that they would break in opposite directions to evade him, he waited until this happened and followed the one that turned into the cloud. He gave it a long burst, watched it explode into flame, and then turned back into the cloud himself.

When he emerged from the clouds, Hanson could see the stream of American bombers over Rapopo, south of Rabaul. They were headed south and involved in a heavy air battle.

Then he saw at least five Zeros heading toward the bombers near Duke of York Island, and descended quickly to 14,000 feet to attack them. He came behind one, opened fire and watched him explode. He attacked another, but it got away. By then the Japanese attack on the bombers had broken off and the respective sides had begun to retire.

Hanson had scored four that day, and seven in his past two outings. From a score of just five when he took off ten days earlier, his sortie of January 24 brought Hanson to a confirmed total of 18.

As was being noted at Barakoma that week, and would be repeated in many postwar accounts, Butcher Bob was slicing the enemy from the South Pacific skies in clusters, as though with a sharp knife. The nickname was clearly appropriate.

Two days later, on January 26, VMF-215 dispatched six divisions of four Corsairs each, though two aviators had to abort. They flew low, medium, and top cover for a Rabaul strike by 18 TBFs and four dozen SBDs that turned into a running gun battle from the moment that the bombers made landfall.

Hal Spears was at 6,000 feet on the leading edge of the TBF force and next to the SBDs when they nosed over to make their dives. As he turned inside the bombers, he could see Zeros below at 5,000 feet and went after them.

He took a 30-degree deflection shot on one and watched him explode. He left a second Zero spilling smoke but did not see him go down.

Over Blanche Bay, Spears saw another Zero at 4,000 feet and got in a shot. The Japanese pilot rolled over, righted himself, took another fusillade from Spears and fell into the water.

Don Aldrich, meanwhile, passed through the target area with the TBFs. He and his wingman, George Gilman, encountered some Zeros five miles east of Rabaul that Aldrich thought to be making "half hearted passes" at the Americans.

There was nothing half hearted about the passes made by Gilman and Aldrich, though. They each picked a Zero that was isolated from the remainder of the pack and bored in. Aldrich watched the one he targeted as it burst into flames, and glanced over to see Gilman's Zero hit the water.

Climbing up to 9,000 feet, Aldrich saw a Tony beneath him. He later recalled that he "could see my tracers going right through him. As I pulled into him, I saw his left landing wheel drop and he started to spin right into the water without burning."

At 8,000 feet over Cape Gazelle, Aldrich opened fire on a Zero, watched pieces of its tail fall off, but did not see it go down, so it remained a probable on his scorecard.

Butcher Bob Hanson was continuing his deadly streak on January 26 (noted in Greenwich time as January 25 on the squadron aircraft action report). Flying at the trailing edge of the bomber force, he saw four Zeros headed for the TBFs. At 6,000 feet over Escape Bay, one of the enemy aircraft passed in front of him and Hanson pulled in behind. As this one exploded, Hanson went after the other three and pulled below the last in line, giving him a fatal burst in the belly.

Emerging from the target area, Hanson saw Zeros sparring with some Navy Hellcats and got into this fight. One Zero turned on him head on, but he left it smoking. Counting this one as a probable, he moved on to the point where the Corsairs were to rendezvous with the TBFs for the trip home.

Form ACA-1
Sheet 1 of 5   **AIRCRAFT ACTION REPORT**   RESTRICTED
                                                                                         (Reclassify when
                                                                                          filled out)

I. GENERAL

(a) Unit Reporting VMF 215   (b) Based on or at Vella Lavella   (c) Report No. 15

(d) Date of Action 25 Jan. 1944   (GCT)   (e) Take off: Time 0505 (GCT); Lat. 6° 14' S. Long. 155° 05' E.
                                                                                   26 Jan. 1944
(f) Mission TBF cover to Lakunai   (g) Time of Return 0500 (GCT)

II. OWN AIRCRAFT OFFICIALLY COVERED BY THIS REPORT.

(a) TYPE	(b) SQUADRON	(c) NO. OF SORTIES	(d) NO. ENGAGING ENEMY A/C	(e) NO. ATTACK ING TARGET	(f) BOMBS AND TORPEDOES CARRIED (PER PLANE)	(g) FUZE SETTING
F4U-1	VMF215	22	20			

III. OTHER U. S. OR ALLIED AIRCRAFT EMPLOYED IN THIS OPERATION.

TYPE	SQUADRON	NUMBER	BASE	TYPE	SQUADRON	NUMBER	BASE
TBF		18	Piva - Uncle	P-38		12	Treasury
SBD		48	Piva - Uncle	F4U-1	VF 10	8	Vella Lavella
P-40	RNZAF	12	Torokina	F4U-1	VF 17	36	Piva - Yoke

IV. ENEMY AIRCRAFT ENCOUNTERED (By Own Aircraft Listed in II Only).

(a) TYPE	(b) NO. OBSERVED	(c) NO. ENGAGING OWN A/C	(d) TIME ENCOUNTERED	(e) LOCATION OF ENCOUNTER	(f) BOMBS, TORPEDOES CARRIED, GUNS OBSERVED	(g) CAMOUFLAGE AND MARKING
Zeke	40/50		(GCT)	Lakunai area		
Tony	10/15		(GCT)			
			(GCT)			
			(GCT)			

(h) Apparent Enemy Mission(s) Interception

(i) Weather and Clouds at Location of Encounter(s) Clear

(j) Sun or Moon Sun   (k) Visibility Unlimited

V. ENEMY AIRCRAFT DESTROYED OR DAMAGED IN AIR (By Own Aircraft Listed in II Only).

(a) TYPE ENEMY A/C	(b) DESTROYED OR DAMAGED BY			(c) GUNS USED	(c) WHERE HIT, ANGLE	(d) DAMAGE CLAIMED
	TYPE A/C	SQUADRON	PILOT OR GUNNER			
Zeke	F4U-1	VMF215	Lt. R.M. Hanson ✓	6x.50	Astern	Destroyed
Zeke	F4U-1	VMF215	Lt. R.M. Hanson ✓	6x.50	Astern and below	Destroyed
Zeke	F4U-1	VMF215	Lt. R.M.Hanson ✓	6x.50	15° from headon	Destroyed
Zeke	F4U-1	VMF215	Lt. R.M. Hanson✓	6x.50	30° from astern	Probable
Zeke	F4U-1	VMF215	Capt. H.L. Spears✓	6x.50	30° deflection astern	Destroyed
Zeke	F4U-1	VMF215	Capt. H.L. Spears ✓	6x.50	Astern and below	Destroyed
Zeke	F4U-1	VMF215	Capt. H.L. Spears✓	6x.50	20° deflection from ahead	Probable
Zeke	F4U-1	VMF215	Capt. H.L. Spears✓	6x.50	Astern	Probable
Zeke	F4U-1	VMF215	Capt. A.T. Warner ✓	6x.50	Headon	Destroyed
Zeke	F4U-1	VMF215	Capt. A.T. Warner ✓	6x.50	90° deflection	Destroyed
Zeke	F4U-1	VMF215	Capt. A.T. Warner ✓	6x.50	30° astern	Probable
Zeke	F4U-1	VMF215	Capt. D.N. Aldrich	6x .50	Split S'd	Destroyed

ALL-621 — MFD BY THE CART REGISTER CO. PATENTED

SECRET 65

FIGURE 5 The space available for listing aerial victories on the Aircraft Action Report was not sufficient to record all of those from January 26, 1944 (January 25 by Greenwich reckoning). Bob Hanson claimed three, and Hal Spears had two plus a pair of probables, while the second of Don Aldrich's pair of confirmed kills spilled over onto the next page. (USMC)

Seeing a Zero chasing another Corsair at 4,500 feet, Hanson took a 35-degree deflection shot that sent the Japanese aircraft down in flames. Butcher Bob's third for the day brought his overall score to 21.

Neither Hanson nor Spears flew the January 28 mission, but for Aldrich, it was his best day ever. VMF-215 was flying low cover at 5,000 feet for 18 TBFs and 48 SBDs over Tobera airfield near Rabaul. The bombers had finished their run and were exiting southward when the Japanese interceptors hit them.

Flying near the end of the formation, Aldrich had a Zero make a nearly head-on pass at him. He returned fire and the Zero was in flame as he slid beneath Aldrich's Corsair.

Climbing to 6,000 feet, Aldrich saw another likely target below and dived. He took a 20-degree deflection shot from above and ahead and watched flames erupt from the Zero's wing roots and cowling as it went into the sea.

Climbing out after his second victory, Aldrich saw that he had a Zero on his tail. He maneuvered furiously, watching bullets ripping into his left wing and fuel tank before turning the tables. In the course of this, Aldrich dived to 2,000 feet where he came upon the tail of yet another Zero and opened fire.

When it was all over, Aldrich had downed four enemy aircraft to bring his score to 17, but he returned to Barakoma with shrapnel wounds to his right arm and leg.

Recuperating, Aldrich missed the last VMF-215 mission of the month on January 30, but both Bob Hanson and Hal Spears were among the 17 aviators from the squadron who took part.

Approaching Rabaul, Hanson saw a Corsair, possibly from the US Navy's VF-17, being chased by a Zero in a vertical dive. Because of the high speeds generated by the steepness of the dive, Hanson waited for the Zero to pull up before he attacked. Catching him with a 15-degree deflection shot at 3,000 feet, Hanson turned the Zero into a fireball.

He then climbed up and flew across the TBF formation as they began their attacks. Encountering a cloud layer at 10,000 feet,

Hanson climbed through it. As he emerged, he found himself on the tails of two IJAAF Ki-44 fighters. Known by the Japanese name "Shoki," meaning "Demon," the Ki-44 was codenamed "Tojo" by the Allies—after Japan's wartime prime minister.

The Tojo was Japan's fastest-climbing aircraft of that era, but Hanson did not need to challenge this capability. He opened fire on the first Tojo's six and watched a huge white flame gush from its belly. The second Tojo did not climb, but descended into the clouds below, with Butcher Bob on its tail. He took a 30-degree deflection shot from behind and watched flames erupt from the wing root.

When Hanson and his wingman met up with the bombers at the post-strike rendezvous point, there were numerous Zeros creating mischief in the area. One of them dived into a head-on attack against Hanson, but he opened fire first. Fire exploded from the belly of Butcher Bob's fourth victory for the day.

In the after-action report, Hanson recalled that "on the way home, we ducked down and strafed a large house on Cape St. George." Perhaps he said "lighthouse," and the word was mistranscribed in the after-action report. Four days later, he *did* strafe the lighthouse at Cape St. George on New Ireland.

Butcher Bob Hanson returned to Barakoma, flying into history as the third highest-scoring Marine ace of all time, and the third highest-scoring American ace in the Pacific—to date.

As with Greg Boyington just one month before on this same airfield, he had now reached a score of 25, the number that everyone noticed and discussed with great interest.

Hanson now felt the ominous excitement shared with only two other American Marine aviators. No other from either the USAAF or the US Navy had yet reached this number. Hanson was only one victory behind America's Ace of Aces, Eddie Rickenbacker. He now knew how Joe Foss and Boyington surely must have felt on the eve of the possibility of matching Rick's magic 26.

Would Bob Hanson match the record?

Would he break it?

The odds were certainly on his side. VMF-215's tour of duty had more than a week to run, and in the past week Butcher Bob had scored an incredible 11 aerial victories.

Few were willing to lay down good money against a sure thing.

28

The Ending of Eras

February

On Vella Lavella, February 1944 began with the attention of war correspondents and AirSols aviators from Barakoma to Torokina focused on Butcher Bob Hanson's next mission, the one in which he was expected to become America's new Ace of Aces.

Hanson was not on the schedule for VMF-215's B-25 escort mission for February 1, but in the event it was canceled, so nobody from the squadron was over Rabaul that day.

Thus it worked out that the next VMF-215 mission came on February 3, one day before Hanson's twenty-fourth birthday. It was also exactly one month to the day after Greg Boyington's last combat flight. This coincidence was duly noted both by those who were superstitious and by those who were not.

When two divisions took off at 0940hrs for a familiar TBF escort sortie, Hal Spears led one division, and Hanson the other. Don Aldrich, meanwhile, led a division in a mission later in the day that escorted USAAF B-24s to Rabaul.

Spears and Hanson took their divisions up the Warangoi River west of Rabaul, and accompanied the TBFs in a sweeping right turn that put them over the target, Tobera airfield, at 1115hrs.

The Zeros emerged, coming in groups of three to six, timidly probing the American formation as it exited the target and turned south through St. George's Channel. Aerial combat was sporadic.

Hanson scored none, but Creighton Chandler shot down one and Don Aldrich claimed a pair to bring his total to 14.

When the formation crossed the southern tip of New Ireland, Bob Hanson did as he had on his last mission four days earlier— he went down to shoot up the Japanese garrison at the Cape St. George lighthouse.

It did not go so well this time.

That night, Robert Owens, the squadron commander, briefed the Associated Press wire service reporter on Vella Lavella about what had happened to Butcher Bob Hanson at the lighthouse.

"He made a strafing run, and then his right wing was seen to hit the water twice," Owens explained, basing his comments on what he had gathered from eyewitness accounts, especially that of Don Aldrich who was with Hanson at the time. "The plane pulled up and the wing either exploded or caught fire. After a moment when it seemed he would make a normal landing, the plane twisted and rolled over into the water and disappeared."

The squadron made a number of passes over the area that day and the next, but no trace of Hanson or his Corsair could be seen. Next to Hanson's name, the after-action report simply carried the note "Did not return."

When the International News Service caught up with Owens, he told them wistfully that Hanson was "the greatest and most daring fighter pilot imaginable ... He did things no other pilot would dare attempt and always got away with them until he finally met death gallantly."

On February 4, Hanson's birthday, the squadron mustered at 1300hrs for a previously planned awards ceremony in which Colonel William McKittrick, the commander of Marine Air Group 24, decorated ten members of VMF-215. Don Aldrich received the Distinguished Flying Cross and the Navy Cross, while Hal Spears was awarded an Air Medal.

Bob Hanson had been written up for the Medal of Honor for his actions between November 1 and January 24, along with a Navy Cross for his actions between January 5 and the day he disappeared.

Two days after Bob went down, a United Press reporter was in Newtonville, Massachusetts to call on Hanson's parents. The 55-year-old Reverend Harry Albert Hanson, gripping the "regret to inform you" telegram from Marine Corps Commandant Lieutenant General Alexander Vandergrift, admitted "I had a premonition this would happen. Being the father of a war ace is nerve-wracking business."

Hanson's posthumous Medal of Honor was awarded to his mother on August 19, 1944. Named in his honor, the destroyer USS *Hanson* (DD-832) would be commissioned on May 11, 1945 and serve actively with the US Navy until 1973.

Combat missions continued unabated for VMF-215, and so too did the squadron's aerial victory count. When the squadron downed eight Japanese aircraft over Rabaul on February 7, Hal Spears chased a Zero from 20,000 to 7,000 feet and left him "burning brightly and spinning down."

At the same time, Don Aldrich had dived at a group of at least four Zeros and caused one to "fly apart in midair." He then chased another from 8,000 to 3,000 feet and pulled away when "a sheet of flame came from his belly."

This Zero was seen to hit the water.

On February 9, Aldrich was with the bomber formation over Tobera when he saw an IJAAF Ki-44 Tojo on the tail of a Corsair, and lined himself up on the tail of this Japanese fighter. The enemy aircraft "made a gradual right turn and dove right into the ground."

This was the final aerial victory by a member of that once-inauspicious trio of aviators who had returned to the South Pacific in January to become three of the Marine Corps' celebrated double-digit aces.

Hanson died with 25, just short of equaling Rickenbacker, Foss and the reported score of Boyington. Aldrich and Spears finished this tour, and their combat careers, with 20 and 15 respectively.

Art Warner and Alan Snyder scored the last two VMF-215 aerial victories on February 11. These were Warner's eighth, and Snyder's only one.

On February 14, the men of VMF-215 boarded a SCAT flight to Efate via Guadalcanal. The war diary noted that first and second tour aviators were headed on to Sydney, while third tour men were bound for "Uncle Sugar," the United States.

The squadron retired from the field of aerial combat with its aviators having achieved 135.5 aerial victories, nearly all of them in their final five weeks. Among VMF-215's aviators were ten aces. Aldrich, Hanson, and Spears represented the top tier, while Warner ended with eight. Gerard Williams and squadron commander Robert Owens each had seven.

During January and February 1944, the media's eyes had been fixed upon the unfolding stories of first, Greg Boyington and next, Butcher Bob Hanson—stories with the ingredients that grabbed the attention of editors who knew they'd resonate with readers. These narratives blazed with the excitement of a quest to match the score of the iconic Rickenbacker—America's Ace of Aces. Then came the unexpected heroic tragedy of both men lost in action— exactly one month apart—at the apogees of their careers.

In the background during that time, though, there were the stories of other men whose careers as aces had been interrupted at the end of 1943 when their tours ended.

First there was Murderous Manny Segal, late of VMF-221. He had gone back to the States in November 1943, but had decided that he was not finished as a Marine aviator. Now assigned to VMF-211, he was back in the air on January 2, 1944 flying the first combat mission of his third tour.

With his ten aerial victories scored in 1943 with VMF-221, "Murderous Manny" was the highest-scoring ace in his new squadron. The aviators of VMF-211 were to score more than 70 aerial victories in January 1944, and two of these belonged to Segal.

It was on January 24, one day after the squadron had downed 16 enemy aircraft in its most successful day in combat.

Segal was at 7,000 feet over Cape Gazelle, 20 miles southeast of Rabaul on a TBF escort mission, when he saw the enemy above his division. As seven A6M3 Hamps descended to intercept the Corsairs of VMF-211, Segal banked left and climbed to meet them. He made a head-on pass at one and watched as it exploded and plummeted downward.

His eyes then turned to another Hamp in pursuit of a pair of Corsairs. He came in behind, opened fire and watched as the enemy fighter that marked his twelfth and final aerial victory went down. As reported by journalist Avi Heligman in 2020, Segal said many years later that "I really didn't shoot them down ... They just got in my way when I was going home."

In February 1944, Major Don Sapp of VMF-222, whose score had stood at four since November 17, 1943, suddenly found himself plowing fertile ground. After a month in Australia, the squadron was back in combat on February 3, 1944, escorting SBDs and TBFs in the same major effort against the Rabaul area in which Bob Hanson was flying his last mission.

Something was different this month for Sapp. Maybe it was that the skies over Rabaul were so crowded, after it had been the opposite over Bougainville at the end of 1943. Whatever it was, the result was a clean slate for Sapp, who filled it with a victory over a Zero to become an ace at last.

After the frustration of two probables in the intervening days, Sapp scored his sixth confirmed victory, another Zero, on February 11 while escorting USAAF bombers exiting a raid on Vunakanau airfield.

The morning of February 17 saw VMF-222 flying low cover for SBDs striking Japanese shipping in Rabaul's Simpson Harbor. The Japanese interceptors began piling on over Blanche Bay south of Rabaul and a rolling, running gun battle ensued. Don Sapp, leading one of the squadron's two divisions that day, returned having downed a pair of Zeros.

On March 12, VMF-222 dispatched eight Corsairs for a low-level fighter sweep across the airfields of eastern New Britain. As they passed over Tobera, Sapp saw four Zeros flying at just 200 feet using the ongoing antiaircraft barrage as cover.

Accepting this as a challenge, he went down to attack and came in on the tail of the Zero trailing at the end of the enemy formation. A two-second burst from his guns turned this Zero into a torch and Sapp quickly moved on to another.

The second Zero fell off into a diving turn from 250 feet. It was an impossible situation, but as no impact was observed, it was to be recorded merely as a probable.

Sapp accelerated and quickly slid up on the third Zero and opened fire. Just as pieces began flying off the wing of the Japanese fighter, they passed over the end of the Tobera runway and Sapp overshot the slower-moving Zero.

Meanwhile, Robert "Bobby" Wilson, who had been flying on Sapp's wing, crept up on the fourth Zero, gave him a three-second burst and watched him crash into the revetment area at the airfield.

When Sapp and Wilson climbed away from Tobera, they saw two more Zeros circling below as though in a landing pattern. Sapp dived on one, catching him from above as he was only 50 feet off the ground with his gear extended. A close-range burst sent him crashing into the trees. Adding two more that day brought Don Sapp's score, his final, to ten.

In his 1952 book, *History of Marine Corps Aviation in World War II*, Robert Sherrod erroneously listed Sapp with a score of 11. Sherrod enumerated Sapp's November victory twice because some reports came in from the field with dates reckoned in local time and others in Greenwich Mean Time. Such dates are a day apart because of the International Dateline.

When VMF-222 stood down and began making their way to Sydney on March 20, their total score stood at 49, with nearly half of these scored on the tour of duty just ended.

February 1944 was also the time when Phil DeLong of VMF-212 finally joined the ranks of the double-digit aces. On February 15, the squadron was flying top cover for Operation *Squarepeg*, the amphibious landings by the New Zealand 3rd Division on Nissan Island in the Green Islands, 150 miles east of Rabaul. The objective was to add to the number of AirSols airfields ringing Rabaul.

The Japanese naturally took exception to Allied plans, and vigorously attacked the invasion ships. For its part, VMF-212 downed six Aichi D3A Val dive bombers. Three of these, plus one probable, brought DeLong's victory score to 11.166.

This was his final number for *this* war, though he would add two more over Korea six years later. Two days later, the squadron's aviators would be boarding SCAT transports for Efate. DeLong would be the highest-scoring ace in VMF-212 history, just a hair above the 11 that had been scored by the immortal Joe Bauer back in 1942.

In the "ending of eras" that we mark in this chapter, perhaps the biggest milestone involved Rabaul, the infamous keystone of Japanese power. In Volume IV of *Army Air Forces in World War II* (1963), Captain Bernhardt Mortensen of the Air Force Historical Division wrote "everything began to turn sour for the Japanese in February, as concurrent [US Navy] operations in both the Southwest and Central Pacific made the Rabaul airbases untenable … The net was closing on Rabaul, and the Japanese knew it."

In February 1944, as the AirSols bombers and fighters were attacking Rabaul with routine 200-aircraft raids, USAAF Fifth Air Force bombers from New Guinea were conducting massive raids on the Japanese base at Kavieng on New Ireland, and Admiral Halsey's SOPAC forces were preparing to land in the Green Islands, only 115 miles from Rabaul. In the mid-Pacific, the Americans had become entrenched in the Gilbert and Marshall Islands.

Meanwhile, on February 17–18, the US Navy's Central Pacific Force (Fifth Fleet after April 1944) under Vice Admiral Raymond

Spruance conducted a devastating raid against Truk, another of Japan's great Pacific naval bases, located about 800 miles due north of Rabaul in the Caroline Islands. Attacked by aircraft from nine American carriers, the Japanese lost a dozen warships, nearly three dozen transports, and around 250 aircraft.

This defeat, against the backdrop of the other Allied advances, convinced Admiral Mineichi Koga, the commander-in-chief of the IJN Combined Fleet, to tighten his perimeter. He withdrew the Combined Fleet headquarters back to Japan proper, then ordered all operable aircraft still at Rabaul to be withdrawn to Truk.

In fact, the withdrawal of Japanese aircraft from Rabaul had already begun. On February 16, one particular G4M had been part of the air exodus making this flight. This aircraft happened to be carrying a half-dozen heavily bound Allied prisoners. Among them was Major Greg Boyington, who had been in captivity in Rabaul, beneath the rain of AirSols bombs, for six weeks.

According to a postwar summary prepared by Lieutenant Colonel Sakuyuki Takagi of the IJA, "the only aircraft remaining in Rabaul were about 30 damaged fighters, a few Navy utility types, and four Army reconnaissance planes." Don Sapp's March 12 final aerial victory was among the last to be scored over Rabaul. He was awarded the Navy Cross.

The great Japanese citadel had been the focal point of Allied air strategy for a year, and it had naturally been assumed by both sides that the climax of the campaign would be an Allied amphibious invasion to capture Rabaul—but a different script was in play.

The climax had already come and gone. Rabaul, no longer an offensive threat, would simply be allowed to "wither on the vine."

Inside Fortress Rabaul, an enemy force, unaware that it was about to be bypassed, waited for the Allied invasion that would never come. As William Manchester wrote in his biography of MacArthur, "their officers' war diaries leave the impression that they felt themselves the victims of a monstrous injustice. Here they were, commanding an army larger than Napoleon's at Waterloo or Lee's at Gettysburg—or Wellington's or Meade's, for that matter— which was spoiling for a fight ... Crack troops, designated to launch counterattacks, lurked in huge bunkers behind concertinas of barbwire. And there they remained, in an agony of frustration, for the rest of the war."

Though AirSols bombers would continue to occasionally attack Rabaul through the end of the war, they would no longer be challenged by airpower.

The momentous turn of events in February 1944 was best summarized by Mortensen when he wrote that "although the men of AirSols had no way of knowing it, they had won the air battle of Rabaul; the Japanese would never come back."

PART IV

Countdown to Victory

29

Second Acts

Major Joe Foss concluded his 1943 autobiography by saying that "I want to be in there again somewhere, shooting those good .50-caliber guns and working the controls of a hot military airplane. That's the life for me till this war is over."

He assumed that this would come sooner, rather than later, but the Marines had other ideas. Most Marine aviators were rotated out of combat after two or three six-week tours, and all the services were reticent to see Medal of Honor recipients—especially America's then-ace of aces—back in harm's way.

After several months on the "Dancing Bear" circuit of recruitment and war bond rallies, Foss took command of VMF-115 at MCAS Goleta near Santa Barbara in July 1943, and mastered the F4U Corsair. It was expected that the new squadron would go overseas, but there was no urgency. Foss still found himself called away to Hollywood or elsewhere to make occasional public relations appearances. Celebrities such as Bing Crosby, Bob Hope, and Gary Cooper became friends. When VMF-115 needed an insignia, Foss met personally with Walt Disney, who put his creative team on the task.

As Foss would recall in his 1992 autobiography, life in balmy Santa Barbara was quite pleasant. He and his wife June rented a spacious hillside home from the actor Ronald Coleman "for peanuts." Then the legendary aviator Charles Lindbergh came calling. Lindbergh was now a free-lance consultant to United Aircraft, the parent company of Vought, who made the Corsair, and Pratt & Whitney, who made its R-2800 engine. He had been sent to Santa Barbara as part of an effort to develop methods of extending the range of the Corsair. Foss invited him to become a long-term house guest, and the two men became lifelong friends.

VMF-115, officially named "Joe's Jokers," finally shipped out for SOPAC in January 1944 aboard the USS *Copahee* (CVE-12). After many weeks of Corsair familiarization and flight training operations out of Turtle Bay on Espiritu Santo, the squadron finally reached its duty station on May 3. How far the war had progressed geographically is illustrated by the fact that VMF-115 was based at an airfield recently completed by the SeaBees on Emirau Island off the north tip of New Ireland, 475 miles northwest of the AirSols base complex at Torokina on Bougainville, and 240 miles northwest of neutered, bypassed Rabaul.

An entirely new roster of island names now filled the Marine air target lists. Missions were now datelined in islands such as Djaul (Dyaul), New Hanover, and Selapiu across the Bismarck Archipelago north of New Britain. The Japanese base complex at Kavieng on the north tip of New Ireland became the "new Rabaul," the nexus of numerous missions. These sorties included strafing attacks against Japanese barges and ground positions, as well as flying escort for PT Boats and SBD and TBF bomber strikes.

Yet there was no reason to protect the bombers from enemy interceptors. The air forces of both the Japanese Army and Navy had conceded the once vigorously contested skies to AirSols. The daily entries in the squadron war diaries were punctuated with phrases such as "sightings negative" or "no sightings" or other ways to say the same thing. Joe Foss never got another crack at aerial combat.

Toward the end of May 1944, Charles Lindbergh showed up on Emirau. Foss had once told him that "you can fly with me any time," and the "Lone Eagle" had come to collect on the offer. He flew several strike missions with Foss and VMF-115.

After nearly two months in Australia, VMF-115 returned to Emirau at the end of July 1944, and stayed through November. Joe Foss, however, was gone by that time. The malaria that had laid him low a year and a half earlier returned with a vengeance. Barely able to walk, he departed SOPAC for the last time on September 21.

Major John King, the executive officer, took over VMF-115 as it departed SOPAC for the island of Leyte to begin operations on December 3 in the Philippines campaign.

Most of the Marine aviators from that first generation who became aces over Guadalcanal in the fall of 1942 had seen the last of their aerial combat. As with Joe Foss, even those who returned to the Pacific would not again share the skies with Japanese aircraft.

John L. Smith, who led VMF-223 over Guadalcanal, was America's leading ace when he went Stateside in October 1942 to receive the first Medal of Honor awarded to a living Marine aviator. In April 1943, he traded a Washington desk job for assignment to Marine Air Group 32 at MCAS Cherry Point, North Carolina. In November 1944, now a lieutenant colonel, he finally returned to the Pacific as executive officer and later commander of MAG-23.

He passed through Emirau two months after Foss departed and spent the remainder of the war in the Philippines. In March 1945, MAG-23 was joined with MAG-24 in Marine Air Groups Zamboanga (MAGSZAM), flying SBD dive bomber missions under the operational command of George Kenney's Far East Air Forces.

Bob Galer, who had led VMF-224 in the Solomons during the early months of the Cactus Air Force in 1942, became a staff officer with the 3rd Marine Aircraft Wing, which was stationed at MCAS Ewa in Hawaii from April 1944 through the end of the war.

Marion Carl, the number two ace in VMF-223, had gone back to the Solomons in time to score a pair of aerial victories in December 1943 and bring his score to 18.5. He returned from Australia in February 1944, fully expecting to resume command and lead VMF-223 back into battle. It was not to be. In his words, "the roof fell in," as he was kicked upstairs to a desk job on the staff of MAG-12.

During the summer of 1944, when MAG-12 relocated its headquarters from Efate to Emirau, Carl got to know Joe Foss, and flew a few missions with VMF-115. Carl even flew a sortie over Kavieng with Charles Lindbergh when the legendary airman was at Emirau.

In October 1944, Carl called on Major General Claude "Sheriff" Larkin, commander of the 3rd Marine Air Wing, the parent organization of MAG-12, to request a leave. With Larkin having roots in a small Oregon town near where Carl had grown up, the two were practically neighbors, so the veteran ace received a favorable response. By the first week of November, Carl was at Pearl Harbor, phoning his wife in New York and telling her to meet him in Los Angeles.

———

Another VMF-223 ace from the Guadalcanal days was Loren "Doc" Everton, the "pharmacist aviator" from Nebraska, who was badly injured back in October 1942. He had recovered, had taken command of VMF-113 at MCAS El Toro, and had deployed the squadron to MCAS Ewa in Hawaii in September 1943. As Everton later recalled in a 1966 conversation with US Navy ace Eugene Valencia, the operations officer for Major General Lewie "Griff" Merritt's 4th Marine Air Wing recruited VMF-113 to join the 4th as it deployed to the Central Pacific.

The Marine 1st Amphibious Brigade had captured Enewetak Atoll in the Marshall Islands from the Japanese early in 1944, and plans were being made to use the airfield on Engebi, Enewetak's largest island, as a base for operations against Ponape (now called Pohnpei) 870 miles to the southwest in the Caroline Islands.

The Japanese were using the airfield on 129-square-mile Ponape to base long-range reconnaissance aircraft to monitor American operations in the Central Pacific, and had even used Ponape as a base for bombers to attack Engebi. They had brought in fighters to protect their Ponape base, and Corsairs were needed to escort bombers against Ponape. Everton calculated that Corsairs could make the round trip between Engebi and Ponape and still have 15 to 20 minutes to engage the enemy fighters.

The mission kicked off before dawn on March 25, 1944, with the VMF-113 Corsairs escorting USAAF B-25Gs, each armed with a nose-mounted 75mm cannon for attacking the Japanese aircraft on the Ponape airfield. About 200 miles south of Engebi, Everton's Corsair developed an oil leak, so he had to turn back. At about 1100hrs, he learned that the bombers had been intercepted by Zeros over Ponape—but the Corsairs were not with them.

As Everton explained to Valencia, he soon learned that the USAAF had changed the mission plan, and had "sent four planes in 30 minutes ahead of the main force ... and they got jumped by Zeros ... So when the main force came down with my fighter escort, no airplanes, no Zeros, nothing." When the Corsairs showed up, the Zeros laid low.

The next day, March 26, they ran the mission again, this time with the lead force of four bombers escorted by four VMF-113 Corsairs—led by Everton personally.

The strike force came in under 1,500 feet of heavy cloud, passing through a valley which Everton described as having "an 800-foot ridge on one side and a mountain that went up into the overcast on the other." Here, they were intercepted by 14 Zeros. None of the Japanese fighters survived the ensuing dogfight.

Doc Everton claimed two aerial victories that day to bring his own final score to 12. These would be VMF-113's only victories scored in the Central Pacific, but the job had been done. When the main strike force reached Ponape, there were no Zeros left to challenge it. "We never had any problems after that," Everton recalled. "In fact, there wasn't a thing left when we got through ... And so my reward out of that for [being] the first Marine to shoot down a Japanese in the Central Pacific was a case of whiskey from the Wing Commander, which was put to good use."

Several other double-digit aces had a second-round career in the Pacific, but added no further aerial victories. Jack Conger, who had scored ten with VMF-223 and VMF-212, returned to the Pacific with VMF-114 on Peleliu in the Central Pacific later in 1944. After a Stateside stint training replacement pilots with VMF-524, Don Sapp came back in May 1945 to take command of VMF-122 at Peleliu. Manny Segal deployed to the Philippines with VMF-115 in 1945, flying ground attack missions.

Finally, there were four double-digit aces, Gus Thomas, Jim Swett, Archie Donahue, and Ken Walsh, who would run up their scores in 1945, and two single-digit aces, Bill Snider and Herb Long, who became double-digit aces in the final months of the war. For each of them, it was a case of wrapping up unfinished business.

30

Unfinished Business

When 1945 began, Marine air operations entered a new phase which would allow double-digit aces whose careers had begun in the Solomons campaign to round out their careers in operations over the heartland of the Japanese Empire.

In a sense, Marine air operations in World War II came full circle. Before the war, Marine fighting squadrons had trained for carrier operations—though only rarely deployed aboard flattops. Exigent circumstances had put them ashore in the Solomons in 1942, but new circumstances put them back on carriers in 1945.

Back in the fall of 1942, when the land-based Marines had been the first line of air defense in the Solomons, the US Navy's aircraft carriers available for combat could be counted on the fingers of one hand with fingers left over. Two years later, the Navy had four dozen carriers, hundreds of F6F Hellcats and a growing roster of naval aviator aces.

By mid-1944, as the air campaign in the Solomons had wound down, and the noose around the Japanese Empire had tightened geographically, the role of Marine fighting squadrons had changed dramatically. The days of target-rich skies and clouds of Zeros were gone—at least in the South Pacific.

As the strategic focus moved north into the islands of the Central Pacific, from the Gilberts to the Marianas, the air war became a Navy show.

When MacArthur returned to the Philippines with the landings at Leyte in October 1944, General George Kenney's USAAF airmen led the way overhead. Once he had run his Fifth Air Force on a shoestring, but now he also commanded the Seventh and Thirteenth and had more than 1,200 fighters and America's top aces at his disposal. Marine air units that participated in the Philippines campaign did so primarily in an air-to-ground role.

Yet as 1945 began, a new chapter was in the offing. The idea of actually deploying Marine fighting squadrons to the Pacific aboard aircraft carriers had long percolated among strategic planners, but finally the time was right. Marine airpower was being reimagined, and the man doing the reimagining was Major General Francis Patrick Mulcahy.

A Marine aviator since he flew combat missions in World War I, Mulcahy's command credits included the 2nd Marine Air Wing in the Solomons and the Cactus Air Force itself. In September 1944, he was chief of staff at AirSols when Marine Commandant General Alexander Vandegrift summoned him to assume command of Aircraft, Fleet Marine Force, making him the top Marine aviator in the Pacific.

Just as Mulcahy was stepping up, a new threat was emerging in the western Pacific which called for the established expertise of Marine fighting squadrons.

This peril flowed from Japanese desperation. For two years, Japanese airpower had been subjected to a battering attrition at American hands. This had resulted a critical shortage of both quality aircraft and qualified pilots. Desperate times then led to desperate measures, and for the Japanese these measures included turning aircraft into flying bombs, and marginally qualified pilots into suicide bombers. This grisly project was known as *kamikaze* (divine wind), named after the thirteenth century typhoons which had saved Japan from Mongol invasions. The *kamikaze* attacks, which began during the Philippine operations, proved very costly to the Americans.

Mulcahy now began implementing plans to intensify carrier training for Marine aviators and to embark Marine air groups, consisting of fighting and bomber squadrons, aboard US Navy carriers and escort carriers. One of the first such air groups was Carrier Air Group 4 (CVG-4) aboard the USS *Essex* (CV-9), which included VMF-124 and VMF-213.

The Corsairs, which had been problematic for carrier operations when first introduced, had by now been refined and tweaked and were ready for prime time. The type had evolved into the faster and improved Vought F4U-1D and Goodyear FG-1D variants with water-injected R-2800-8W engines and provisions for external fuel tanks. The one-piece "blown Plexiglas" bubble canopies, originally introduced in the F4U-1A, afforded much better visibility. For ground attack missions, the new Corsairs added multiple five-inch High Velocity Aircraft Rockets (HVAR) to their arsenals.

On January 6, 1945, when the Allies landed at Lingayan Gulf on the main Philippine Island of Luzon, Marine fighting squadrons from the *Essex* were flying combat air patrols above. Through February and into March, CVG-4 flew missions from Indochina to Okinawa, and were even over Tokyo itself. During the Battle of Iwo Jima, CVG-4 aircraft were conducting ground attack missions.

The aviators of VMF-213, including the squadron's leading ace, Wilbur "Gus" Thomas, flew from the USS *Essex*. Even with *kamikazes* lurking about, air-to-air combat was rare for CVG-4 during this time, but VMF-213 scored eight victories. Two of these belonged to Thomas, who brought his final score to 18.5 in February. He was awarded the Navy Cross, the second highest decoration for valor awarded to Marines.

Meanwhile, the USS *Bunker Hill* (CV-17) sailed westward under the Golden Gate Bridge on January 24, 1945 destined for service as the flagship of Vice Admiral Marc Mitscher's Task Force 58. Aboard was CVG-84 with VMF-221, commanded by Major Edwin Roberts, and VMF-451, commanded by Major Hank Ellis. They were accompanied by bomber squadrons VB-84 and VT-84.

Within the Solomons-seasoned VMF-221 were two veteran aces, both now promoted to captain, who had not seen combat since the end of 1943. James Elms Swett, awarded a Medal of Honor in October 1943 for downing seven Japanese aircraft on April 7, 1943, was still the squadron's second highest-scoring ace with a total of 14.5 aerial victories in the Solomons. William Nugent Snider had just five.

VMF-451 was a newcomer outfit, but like VMF-221, it had two Solomons aces within its ranks. Major Archie Glenn Donahue had scored nine victories with VMF-112 in the Solomons, and Major Herbert "Trigger" Long had six with VMF-122. However, both had been out of combat since the summer of 1943.

Long had been assigned to Joe Foss's VMF-115 before they went overseas, but Hank Ellis had brought him over to VMF-451 as squadron executive officer when that unit was formed in 1944.

February 16, 1945 found the *Bunker Hill* off the coast of the main Japanese island of Honshu, and its aviators taking off for operations over Tokyo. Where once the target list was headed by Kahili or Rabaul, it now included the very capital of the Chrysanthemum Empire. Bill Snider flew a combat air patrol that first day, and along with Don MacFarlane, downed an IJNAF G4M bomber. It was the squadron's only score for the month.

Late in February, the *Bunker Hill* worked its way south to the Advance Base Fleet Anchorage at Ulithi Atoll, where the US Navy had established a naval repair and staging facility. Located 1,700 miles south of Tokyo and 1,300 miles south of Okinawa, Ulithi hosted more than 600 ships and was buzzing with activity in preparation for the upcoming invasion of Okinawa.

By March, the *Bunker Hill* had returned to Japan to begin operations against Kyushu, the southernmost of Japan's four main islands. VMF-221 Corsairs were back in combat on March 18, with one contingent flying ground attack sorties using HVARs against the Kiyasaki airfield, while Bill Snider led a group of ten Corsairs in a fighter sweep across Kyushu, hoping to lure enemy fighters into combat.

Snider's men crossed the east coast at 1630hrs, coming over the airfield at Tomitaka at 23,000 feet. They continued westward to Kumamoto and turned south. Still encountering no opposition, they descended to 13,000 feet and turned back to conduct a HVAR strike on the airframe plant at Kumamoto. They later reported that as they launched their rockets at a range 2,000 feet, huge fires erupted from the plant.

Passing back over Tomitaka, the Marines were intercepted by an estimated 25 Japanese fighters. These included both IJNAF Mitsubishi A6M Zeros and IJAAF Nakajima Ki-84 Hayates, code-named "Frank."

In the aircraft action report for the day, the VMF-221 aviators agreed that the Japanese pilots "did not use their natural advantages to any extent; even their turns were wide and sloppy. Their speed and dives were inferior." This circumstance, clearly an indication of how badly Japanese flight training had eroded by 1945, was very costly that day.

In the lead, Bill Snider was attacked head on by a Frank. The two enemies traded fire until nearly point-blank range. The Japanese fighter burst into flames just before they collided.

An inexperienced Japanese pilot in a second Ki-84 attacked Snider from approximately seven o'clock below, but took no evasive action when Snider returned fire. The stricken aircraft banked to the right as it burst into flames and the pilot bailed out over the water offshore from the Kyushu coastline. Snider then observed a Zero attacking a Corsair and destroyed it from four o'clock above.

Recounting minor damage to just one Corsair, VMF-221's aircraft action report claimed 13 enemy aircraft downed, though a list in the same document details only 11. Snider brought his total to 8.5 with his three confirmed victories that day.

VMF-451 was also in action on March 18 over Kyushu, conducting two fighter sweeps and a photoreconnaissance escort sortie. Both Archie Donahue and Trigger Long were leading divisions on the second sweep, which took off at 0945hrs. Making landfall near Miyazaki, they proceeded inland to attack the airfields at Hitoyoshi and at Sadohara with guns and HVARs. As the Corsairs returned eastward, passing back over Miyazaki, they reported "no remunerative targets remained due to the previous sweeps and strikes over the target."

However, a lone Zero was observed above at 10,000 feet, so Long led his division to attack. He opened fire at seven o'clock astern and the enemy aircraft promptly burst into flames. His first victory since July 1943 brought Long's score to seven.

By the last week of March, the *Bunker Hill* was offshore from Okinawa for the beginning of several days of air-to-ground strafing and rocket attacks in preparation for the Allied invasion on April 1. The Corsairs ranged up and down the island, shooting up the airfields at Kadena and Yontan, and attacking barges and small boats offshore. One after-action report mentions a midget submarine being attacked, while another from VMF-451 mentions strikes on the "largest buildings in towns along SE coast of Okinawa."

For VMF-451, both Donahue and Long led divisions on nearly all of the squadron's sorties during this period, while at VMF-221, Snider led relatively few missions, and Jim Swett's name does not appear in the flight roster until mid-April.

On April 3, Long was leading a combat air patrol over the island of Kikai, near Amani Oshima, about 150 miles northeast of the beaches where the Okinawa invasion had begun two days before. It was here that they intercepted 15 *kamikaze* aircraft coming south from Kyushu. The Marines managed to down eight of them, including two claimed by Trigger Long.

Three days later, 18 of VMF-221's Corsairs "went on a search for enemy shipping, extending to Kyushu coast," but they found Japanese fighter aircraft as well. One division, led by Major Edwin Roberts, the squadron commander, tangled with IJNAF A6M5-52s, the most advanced Zero variant, and downed three of them, plus a Ki-46 reconnaissance aircraft.

When Bill Snider's division crossed paths with the IJAAF, he claimed a Ki-61 Tony, while Stan Bailey downed a Ki-43 Oscar. The squadron downed 13 that day, but one aviator, Jarvis Carpenter, never came back.

April 12, 1945 belonged to Archie Donahue, who had not scored an aerial victory since his ninth back in June 1943. After an early-morning patrol by VMF-451 yielded no enemy contacts, Donahue's later patrol intercepted a large strike force consisting of D3A Val dive bombers and B5N Kate torpedo bombers, escorted by Zeros.

In the ensuing dogfight, the Marine Corsairs brought down ten Vals, four Zeros, and a Kate. Of these Donahue himself destroyed three of the Vals and pair of Zeros, making him the first Marine flying from a carrier to become an "ace-in-a-day." These five victories brought Donahue to his final score of 14 aerial victories.

By mid-April the mission for *Bunker Hill* VMF-221 shifted back to Okinawa and flying combat air patrols to protect the Allied fleet offshore from the intensifying intimidation of the *kamikazes*. April 16 was a day on which the Japanese mounted a major *kamikaze* assault on the ships off Okinawa.

Both Jim Swett and Bill Snider were in the air together that day, and each was leading a division. Swett saw no action, but Snider intercepted and shot down an IJAAF Ki-44 Tojo and an IJNAF Zero to establish himself as a double-digit ace with a final score of 11.5.

Meanwhile, VMF-451 also saw action during the April 16 onslaught. That afternoon, Trigger Long was leading a patrol that was orbiting over the Pacific between Amani Oshima and Okinawa waiting for *kamikazes*. Two D3A Vals were spotted preparing to go into their attacks when the Marines pounced, taking out both of them. One of these became Long's tenth aerial victory. For both Snider and Long, April 16 saw them making their final scores.

Through April and into May, massed *kamikaze* attacks were a daily scourge for the Allied fleet off Okinawa, and the results had been deadly. During the campaign, nearly 400 Allied ships were damaged, while 36, including a dozen destroyers, were sunk. The US Navy alone lost nearly 5,000 personnel killed. On May 4 and again on May 9, the British carrier HMS *Formidable* took major hits that sent black smoke and flames billowing into the sky. On May 11, there came the grim turn of the USS *Bunker Hill*.

Jim Swett was leading a combat air patrol that morning, attempting to shield the fleet from the *kamikazes*. It proved fruitful in that three of the seven aviators on the patrol managed to down a kamikaze. One of them was Swett, who took out a Nakajima B6N torpedo bomber before it did any damage on its one-way strike mission.

His May 11 aerial victory, the only one scored by Swett on his 1945 cruise, was his last. Though he survived the day unscratched, his world was suddenly upended, bringing his combat career to an abrupt and unexpected finale.

While Swett's patrol was out, the *Bunker Hill* took two deadly strikes from a pair of *kamikaze* Zeros 30 seconds apart. This turned its wooden flight deck into an inferno and killed 393 men, including 11 VMF-221 ground crewmen. Swett and his men managed to land successfully aboard the USS *Enterprise*.

Badly damaged, the *Bunker Hill* survived and made its way Stateside by way of Ulithi under its own power. It was still undergoing repairs when the war ended. For VMF-221 and VMF-451, World War II had come to an end on May 11. Swett's final score was 15.5. His last victory was the second to last to be scored during World War II by a double-digit Marine Corps ace.

31

Victory Achieved

The final aerial victory by a Marine double-digit ace came on June 22, 1945 more than a month after the USS *Bunker Hill* was knocked out of commission by *kamikazes* on May 11.

Captain Kenneth Ambrose Walsh had come a long way, having begun his career as a Marine aviator when he was still an enlisted man. He had gone on to become the first Marine Corsair ace while flying with VMF-124 in May 1943. During the summer of 1943, his actions resulted in him being written up for the Medal of Honor, which was personally bestowed on him by President Roosevelt in February 1944. He was the second Marine, after Joe Foss, to reach an aerial victory total of 20. As he arrived on Okinawa in June 1945, he was tied with Don Aldrich as the fourth highest-scoring Marine of the war.

Despite the general reticence of the top brass when it came to sending Medal of Honor recipients back into combat, Walsh was assigned to VMF-222. Having been held in reserve in the Green Islands through the second half of 1944, the squadron was sent to the Philippines in January 1945 to conduct ground attack missions.

By the latter part of May, most of Okinawa was under American control after one of the bloodiest battles yet seen in the Pacific. As the island was a prefecture of Japan proper, the Japanese had mounted a tenacious defense. Gradually, though, the airfields of Okinawa were captured. By June, they were being rebuilt, expanded, and put into service to support Operation *Downfall*, the invasion of the main islands of Kyushu and Honshu. Among the units that were assigned to these airfields was VMF-222.

When the flight echelon of VMF-222 received its formal orders to depart Clark Field in the Philippines on June 7, the ground echelon had already been setting up tents and getting things "squared away" at Kadena airfield on Okinawa for about a week.

The squadron flew its first combat air patrol on June 13, but had its first and only contact with enemy aircraft on June 22. Floyd Thompson and Robert Rause each shot down a Ki-43, and Ken Walsh claimed a Zero.

With this, his twenty-first aerial victory, he became the fourth highest-scoring Marine ace of all time behind Joe Foss, Greg Boyington, and Bob Hanson.

When VMF-222 formally concluded its final combat tour on July 15 and sailed for the States by way of Midway, there was no way of knowing how soon the war would end. The aviators of more than 30 active Marine fighting squadrons fully expected to see combat in the skies over the home islands of Japan through the end of 1945 and into 1946 and beyond.

The fact that these expectations proved so soon and suddenly to be wrong was the cause of celebration at Marine airfields from Kadena, Okinawa to Cherry Point, North Carolina.

It took the two nuclear strikes against his dominion to convince Japan's Emperor Hirohito that continuing the war was a fool's errand, and on August 15, 1945, he ordered the IJA, the IJN, and their respective air forces to stand down. The formal surrender was signed on September 2 in Tokyo Bay.

———

When victory finally came, and the VJ-Day celebrations commenced, few of the double-digit Marine aces were still overseas. Ken Walsh, the last to see combat over a prefecture of Japan, had just departed. Archie Donahue, Trigger Long, Bill Snider, and Jim Swett, whose tour of duty aboard the USS *Bunker Hill* had been interrupted in May, now breathed the sigh of relief that came with knowing they'd not be going back to hostile skies.

John L. Smith, the one-time Marine "ace of aces" with 19 victories in 1942, was in the Philippines as the commander of Marine Air Group 32, which had been flying ground attack missions as part of Marine Air Groups Zamboanga (MAGSZAM) since March 1945. Along with MAG-24, MAG-32 had flown 8,842 combat missions.

Don Sapp greeted VJ-Day on the island of Peleliu, a thousand miles east of the Philippines, where he had been deployed as commander of VMF-122 since May.

Most of the double-digit men were Stateside when the war ended. Some were on the cusp of leaving the Marines for a civilian life, others preparing for a postwar career in the Corps.

Joe Foss greeted VJ-Day at MCAS Goleta near Santa Barbara preparing VMF-115 to go overseas for the final battle over Japan. He had come back from the Pacific in September 1944 stricken with malaria for the third time and weighing just 150 pounds. He spent half a year at the Marine Barracks in Klamath Falls, Oregon where the US Navy's Bureau of Medicine and Surgery had set up a special installation for the care of malaria patients.

As L.T. Coggeshall wrote in an article later published in *The American Journal of Tropical Medicine and Hygiene*, the now forgotten Klamath facility was considered important because the majority of malaria patients "were having repeated clinical breakdowns [and] it was considered an ideal opportunity to assemble these malarial patients in one place for observation and study."

For the infirm ace turned guinea pig, the stay was not one of stark, chilled wards. Oregon's lieutenant governor lent him a well-furnished house in town, where he was joined by his wife June and their infant daughter Cheryl.

For Marine aviators, relief and jubilation were tempered by thoughts of those who were not around to hear the news. Among the double-digit aces, the list of those not coming home numbered six.

Two were confirmed to have been killed Stateside. Bud Shaw died in a crash at MCAS Mojave in July 1944, and Hal Spears at

MCAS Al Toro in December 1944. Four were lost overseas: Joe
Bauer went down in November 1942, Bill Marontate in January
1943, Greg Boyington in January 1944, and Bob Hanson one
month later in February 1944.

However, Greg Boyington was about to become a personification
of Mark Twain's maxim about reports of his death being greatly
exaggerated.

Picked up by the Japanese submarine *I-181* on January 3, 1944
a few hours after being shot down, Boyington had been taken to
nearby Rabaul. Here, he spent six weeks in a filthy jail cell, enduring
interrogations, suffering from malaria, and listening to the crash
of American bombs. The thunder of American ordnance followed
Boyington when he and a small cadre of prisoners were flown to
Truk on February 16—where they happened to land in the midst
of a US Navy bombardment.

On March 7, 1944 Boyington had been flown north to Japan
and thrown into the infamous Ofuna POW camp at Kamakura. It
was one of the most brutal in Japan, where beatings were common,
and where prisoners were each kept in solitary confinement.
Conditions were harsh, with inmates losing a third of their body
weight because of starvation diets.

Ofuna was never officially acknowledged to the International
Red Cross which distributed food and other goods to incarcerated
prisoners, so its existence was not known to the Allies until after
the war. As such, the names of its inmates were never revealed to
the outside world. In addition to Boyington, well-known inmates
included Olympic distance runner Louis Zamperini, who had
been shot down in 1943 as a USAAF B-24 crewman. His wartime
memoir, *Unbroken*, became a best-seller in 2010.

Ofuna was run by the IJN as an interrogation facility, where
extracting information was the primary function. Many of the
interrogators were American-educated and spoke flawless English.

Because of his loquacious nature, Boyington responded well to having someone to talk to in his native tongue. Though he tried to portray himself as just an average aviator with little useful information to divulge, it was hard for him to keep a low profile. Since he had been shot down, Boyington's notoriety in the American media, especially surrounding his Medal of Honor recommendation, had only grown. He was mentioned in numerous national magazines, from *Time* to *Colliers*, and even *Cosmopolitan*.

When this media buzz became known to the Japanese, he became the object of special interest. Though he was punished by the Japanese for lying about himself, among the prisoners, he became somewhat of a celebrity.

In April 1945, he was transferred to the Omori POW camp near Tokyo. Once again, Boyington felt the reverberation of American bombs as the raids on Tokyo by USAAF B-29s—an aircraft that Boyington had never before seen—intensified. In July, Boyington and other Omori prisoners became part of a slave labor detail being used to dig tunnels and stockpile supplies underground in caves, presumably for use during the anticipated Allied invasion that would never come.

"The day hostilities ceased I was lying ill with yellow jaundice on my straw mat," Boyington wrote of August 15 in his memoirs. A guard told him that the war was over, but there was no official announcement.

That night, some of the prison guards got drunk and threatened to kill the POWs. Other guards handed out hammers and nails so that the prisoners could secure their quarters against the onslaught. According to Boyington, no prisoners were killed and no guards committed ritual suicide, though many had said they would. The next day, clean uniforms and vitamin tablets were issued, and gradually the inmates took over the asylum.

As American aircraft started being seen flying low and slow overhead, and no longer dropping bombs, the prisoners painted "PW," for "prisoners of war" on the roofs of buildings to identify themselves, and soon food parcels were being dropped. Someone painted a message that "Pappy Boyington" was at Omori, and the news that Boyington was alive quickly made its way to the outside world.

By August 29, as US Navy ships entered Tokyo Bay, the prisoners made their way to the nearby seawall with handmade flags, and soon Higgins Boats had been sent to evacuate them to a hospital ship.

The following day, Boyington, now aboard the destroyer escort USS *Reeves* (DE-156), was one of a dozen men interviewed by Julius Adler of the *New York Times*. A media sensation was about to be born.

When American transport aircraft began repatriating liberated prisoners, Boyington was among the first to go. A September 8 Associated Press wire photo showed him at Pearl Harbor wearing a thin, dapper mustache, and being greeted by his old friend and patron, Major General James "Nuts" Moore, now the commander of aircraft for the Fleet Marine Force, Pacific. Moore had asked for and received authority to formally promote Boyington, with a regular Marine commission, to lieutenant colonel.

By the time that he reached San Francisco four days later, Boyington had begun to realize how big a celebrity he really had become. His homecoming, like those of other high-profile former returning veterans, was seen as a symbolic underscoring in headlines of personal victories for all who would see battle no more.

September 12, 1945 marked two years to the day since Boyington had climbed into his Corsair to lead his Black Sheep to the airfield in the Russell Islands that would be their first home of their first tour of duty. It had been nearly three years since Boyington had last been in the States.

"At San Francisco I was given a most fantastic reception by the American public and press," he wrote in his memoirs. "More fantastic than I had ever dreamed possible, even in my drunken dreams."

The Marine Corps public relations machine, which had been crafting the images of aces since they had put John L. Smith and Marion Carl on the "dancing bear" circuit in 1942, took over.

A photo op was arranged in the form of a reunion for the returning hero with several members of the Black Sheep Squadron. The gala party at the posh St. Francis Hotel was covered by *Life* magazine. The *Seattle Post-Intelligencer* picked up the tab to fly Grace Hallenbeck, Boyington's mother, in from Okanogan along with two of his children for an exclusive photo op of their own.

"It was truly fantastic; the legend of bravery and idealism that had been concocted during those twenty months since I had last been seen going down in a ball of flames," Boyington later recalled. "And, on top of it all, the majority of all this had been released from Marine Corps Public Relations. There was no question in their minds that my watery grave would hold me, and that I would never return to disgrace them or haunt them, or, one thing for certain, they would never have let those releases out of their hands."

Enter Major Frank Walton. He had been the VMF-214 air combat information officer who had carefully crafted the Boyington legend back in 1943. He had also made Boyington's claim of six AVG victories—instead of the AVG reckoning of two—part of the official Marine Corps record.

He arrived on the scene in San Francisco just as Boyington was describing his having scored *three* aerial victories on the day he was shot down—instead of just the one that was witnessed by other VMF-214 aviators, thus further adding to his number of victories.

Walton's assignment was to escort Boyington on a victory bond and publicity tour around the United States. They began with "Welcome Home" appearances in Seattle and Okanogan. They passed through Chicago and on to Washington, DC, where President Harry Truman personally awarded Boyington's Medal of Honor, along with a number of others, on the South Lawn of the White House on October 5.

In the meantime, Walton had stopped in at the Navy Department to amend the record of Boyington's final mission, officially bringing the 26 victories that had been in the headlines for two years to 28.

Less than two months after walking out of a squalid prison, Boyington was on the top of the world with an image to match. Everyone, from his adoring public to Frank Walton, wanted to keep him there.

"How happy I was that I'd decided to be a dignified character behind a mustache, and how fortunate I was that liquor was no longer an obsession, so I wouldn't louse up the act," Boyington wrote in his memoirs. "But I was soon to find that carrying on with this act wasn't going to run as smoothly as I had planned, for I found that my drinking past was waiting back home, to pick up where I left off, whether I wanted to or not."

The reunions and the tour made good press, and for a brief moment, the carousing drunk that inhabited Boyington's dark side seemed sealed away like a caged bear. Even Boyington himself was amazed, because he knew that this monster still lurked.

For that brief moment, lasting barely three weeks, Boyington's story was what everyone wanted to believe for all such valiant homecomings and for the fulfillment of a hard-won victory. But such things are almost always more complicated than they first appear.

PART V

Postwar Lives

32

In War and Peace

VJ-Day did not bring a blanket of peace down upon the Far East. War and conflict continued even as the guns of World War II fell silent. John L. Smith and Jim Cupp were among the first Marine aviators to experience this first hand.

Even as the Japanese war machine in China laid down its arms, the long simmering civil war in that country between Chiang Kai-shek's Nationalist government and Communist insurgents was already heating up. The 1st Marine Air Wing was dispatched to Tientsin (now Tianjin) in October 1945. The Marines took neither side, merely flying reconnaissance patrols.

Among the units assigned to the 1st MAW were John L. Smith's MAG-32, which was based in the Philippines at the time. Coincidentally, MAG-32 contained the observation squadron VMO-6, now commanded by fellow double-digit ace Jim Cupp.

Cupp's presence was a monument to his herculean willpower. He should not have been there at all. He should not have escaped from his Corsair, its cockpit engulfed in flame, as he was shot down two years earlier in October 1943. But he had.

He should not have survived the severe second and third degree burns to both his legs, his right arm and hand, and his head and face. But he had. His doctors assumed that he would never walk again, but after many long months at the Oak Knoll Naval Hospital in Oakland, California, he proved them wrong. He even managed to resume flight duty.

When Smith's MAG-32 finally returned to MCAS Miramar near San Diego in June 1946, Cupp's VMO-6 remained in China as part of MAG-25 until January 1947, mainly aiding in the evacuation of American citizens from the war zone.

———

Joe Foss, who was at MCAS Goleta near Santa Barbara on VJ-Day, preparing to take VMF-115 overseas again, considered remaining in the Marines. However, he had only a reserve commission and was considered too old at the time of enlistment to get a regular commission.

He had already made up his mind to leave the service when he was called to Washington in late 1945 and asked to stay. It was here that he learned that Secretary of the Navy Frank Knox had already given him a regular commission, but that the paperwork informing him of this had been lost in the mail while he was overseas. Nevertheless, he was on the retired list by Christmas 1945.

Ken Walsh, the fourth-place Marine ace with 21 victories—and the recipient of a Medal of Honor and *seven* Distinguished Service Crosses—did remain in the Corps, and stayed on in Okinawa as assistant operations officer for MAG-14 of the 2nd Marine Aircraft Wing during the initial stages of the occupation of Japan. In March 1946, as the wing was preparing to rotate Stateside, Walsh was assigned to a desk job in Washington, DC. He later flew with several Marine transport squadrons.

Don Aldrich, with 20 wartime victories and a Navy Cross, remained a Marine fighter pilot when the war ended and was stationed at MCAS Cherry Point in North Carolina. He was on temporary duty at Quantico in 1947 when he was given leave to visit family in Chicago. On May 4, he was inbound to NAS Glenview near Evanston, north of Chicago, when he encountered engine trouble about 25 miles from his destination. He attempted an emergency landing at Ashburn Airport, not realizing that it was closed. He was killed when his Corsair crashed.

There were two wartime squadrons in which there had been a trio of double-digit aces. One was VMF-213, where the leading men were Gus Thomas (18.5), Bud Shaw (14.5), and Jim Cupp (12). Their stories each ended in tragedy. After Cupp's terrible ordeal, Shaw was killed in a Corsair crash at MCAS Mojave in July 1944. Thomas flew one of the Corsairs that escorted the transport that carried Shaw's body home for burial in Spokane, Washington.

After the war, Thomas flew a Grumman F7F Tigercat in the Marine Corps "Victory Squadron," and he was at the controls of a Tigercat when it crashed into a southern California mountain during a storm in January 1947. Thomas and Aldrich were not the last of the double-digit aces to die in postwar Stateside crashes. Ken Frazier went down in an FJ-3 Fury jet fighter in 1959.

The other squadron with a trio of double-digit men was VMF-221. These aces were Jim Swett (15.5), Manny Segal (12) and Bill Snider (11.5)—though Segal and Snider scored their final victories with VMF-211 and VMF-221 respectively. Swett, whose combat career ended abruptly with the crippling of the USS *Bunker Hill* in May 1945, went on to command VMF-141 in California after the war. Both Segal and Snider left the service in 1945. Aviation historian Barrett Tillman, who knew Segal in later years, commented to this author, "Lord, what a character. He dressed like a Vegas lounge lizard with leisure suit and jewelry. He 'never met a stranger.'"

Archie Donahue, whose final total reached 14, was, along with Bill Snider, one of only two Marine aces from the Solomons to score another five or more while flying from a carrier. Like Snider, Donahue did not pursue a postwar career in the Marines.

Doc Everton—like Aldrich, Cupp, and Thomas, a recipient of the Navy Cross—did not return to his prewar career as a pharmacist, but remained with the Corps in a series of posts that included a stint as an intelligence officer at Marine Corps headquarters in Washington. Nevertheless, at the time he retired from the Corps in 1967, his pharmacist's license was still current, though he had not used it in decades.

Marion Carl's extensive and distinctive postwar career began in
January 1945, even as the final chapter for Marine aces in the Pacific
was about to be written in the skies over Japan and Okinawa. He
came home in November 1944 anticipating a routine assignment,
but with the new year came orders posting him to the Naval Air
Test Center (NATC) at NAS Patuxent River (better known as
"Pax River") on Chesapeake Bay, 50 miles south of Annapolis,
Maryland.

His new job would be to evaluate new types of aircraft for carrier
compatibility, but the Navy was anxious to start its own test pilot
school at Pax River—and Carl was selected as part of the initial
cadre designated as "Class 0."

Carl was now in what was, in many ways, a pilot's dream job. He
flew a variety of new and experimental aircraft. He was especially
fond of the F8F Bearcat, the ultimate fighter in the lineage of
Grumman monoplane, single-engine prop fighters that began
with the F4F Wildcat, which Carl had flown in the Solomons.
He also became one of the first Marine aviators to gain extensive
experience of jet fighters. These ranged from a captured German
Messerschmitt Me 262 to the McDonnell FH-1 Phantom, the first
operational jet fighter used by the US Navy and Marine Corps.

In August 1947, Carl set a world speed record of Mach .85 in the
Douglas D-558-1 Skystreak research aircraft—two months ahead
of US Air Force test pilot Chuck Yeager, who became the first man
to break the sound barrier.

Marion Carl commanded VMF-122, the first Marine jet fighter
squadron, and in early 1949, he helped found and originally
led a VMF-122 aerobatic display team. Flying five FH-1s, they
were known as the "Marine Phantoms" and made a memorable
appearance at the Cleveland National Air Races in September 1949.
Loren "Doc" Everton, late of VMF-223 and VMF-113, took over
leadership of the Marine Phantoms and led them through their
final performances in the summer of 1950.

In late 1949, Carl returned to the Test Pilot School at Pax
River and was involved with a number of new aircraft programs,
including the Douglas XF3D-1 Skyknight and carrier trials for the

North American Aviation AJ-1 Savage medium bomber and the AF-2S/AF-2W Guardian series of submarine hunters.

Though Marion Carl was not among World War II's double-digit aces to fly during the Korean War, he would be back in action over Vietnam.

—————

Among the Marine aviators who served in the Korean War were several double-digit aces from World War II—Jim Cupp, Phil DeLong, Bob Galer, John L. Smith, and Ken Walsh.

After the Soviet-backed North Korean People's Army (KPA) swept into South Korea on June 25, 1950, overwhelming the woefully undermanned South Korean Army and the US Army 24th Infantry Division, a United Nations Command (UNC) was organized under the leadership of US Army General Douglas MacArthur to stem the tide. Gradually, the UNC was greatly expanded by American reinforcements, and the tide was turned. Before the conflict was suspended with an armistice on July 27, 1953, the US Marine Corps would play a major role, with Marine aircraft flying 10 percent of all UNC combat sorties.

Marine Air Group 33, incorporating VMF-214, VMF-323, VMF(N)-513, and VMO-6, arrived in August 1950, and for the first time since 1945, Marine Corsairs were flying ground support missions in the Far East. John L. Smith, the leading ace of VMF-223 over Guadalcanal, came to Korea in 1953 to command MAG-33 in its final months in the conflict. Ken Walsh, meanwhile, flew cargo aircraft with VMR-152 during the first year of the war.

Colonel Jim Cupp went to war as the air operations officer with the 1st Marine Division, coordinating air attack operations in support of ground troops. The division famously spearheaded the Inchon landing in September 1950, which outflanked the KPA in South Korea and liberated Seoul, the South Korean capital. A month later, the division landed at Wonsan, behind enemy lines on the east coast of the Korean peninsula, and pushed north.

In November, when China intervened in North Korea, the 1st Marine Division was suddenly outnumbered four-to-one. The Marines found themselves surrounded at the Chosen Reservoir (now called Lake Changjin or Lake Jangjin), 120 miles north of Wonsan and were forced to fight their way out. This painful, two-week operation would not have been possible without air support, and Jim Cupp received the Bronze Star for his role in coordinating this air support.

In 1951, Captain Phil DeLong became the last of the double-digit Marine aces from World War II to score aerial victories. He deployed to Korea in July 1950 with VMF-312 aboard the USS *Bataan* (CVL-29) and flew his first mission a month later.

On April 21, 1951, DeLong and his wingman, Lieutenant Harold Daigh, were flying F4U-4 Corsairs on a patrol mission over the Yellow Sea off the west coast of North Korea when they detected other single-engine prop aircraft in these enemy skies. Momentarily thinking they were US Air Force F-51s, the Marines then realized they were the enemy—when the Yakovlev Yak-9 fighters opened fire.

Remembering the days of Zeros over Rabaul, DeLong turned to face them. Taking a few hits from the Berezin 12.7mm machine guns, DeLong tore into the enemy flight, outmaneuvered the Yaks and destroyed two in the space of three minutes, while Daigh downed a third. These were the first Marine aerial victories of the Korean War.

DeLong, whose final aerial victory score now stood at 13.166, was awarded the Silver Star for this action. When he later rotated out of the war zone after 125 mainly air-to-ground attack missions, he took home three Distinguished Service Crosses to add to the pair he earned in World War II.

Colonel Bob Galer, who commanded VMF-224 on Guadalcanal a decade earlier, arrived in Korea in March 1952 as assistant chief of staff for the 1st MAW, and served with it until May, when he took command of MAG-12 at the K-6 air base near Pyongtaek, south of Seoul.

Though the Corps frowned on Medal of Honor recipients doing so, Galer flew a number of combat missions over North Korea. On

August 5, 1952, he was leading 31 Corsairs on a strike mission to Wonsan when he was shot down 100 miles behind enemy lines. He later told Elaine Woo of the *Los Angeles Times* that he had done "a dumb thing … We were bombing and when we finished, I went back to take a picture. And this anti-aircraft gun, he nailed me."

Braving enemy fire, Lieutenant E.J. McCutcheon flew a Sikorsky HO3S-1 helicopter in to pick up Galer, who lay wounded and incapacitated with broken ribs and a damaged shoulder.

His combat career over, Galer returned Stateside to serve on the staff of Fleet Marine Force, Pacific at MCAS El Toro. He graduated from the Air War College in 1953 and served as assistant director of the Navy Department's Guided Missile Division in Washington.

No mention of World War II Marine aviators in Korea is complete without a nod to John Franklin "Jack" Bolt. One of the Black Sheep of Boyington's VMF-214 at Vella Lavella during World War II, he had scored six aerial victories in that conflict. In 1951, while in the United States, he became involved in the "exchange program" under which the US Air Force invited aviators from other services to fly with their squadrons and vice versa. Here, he gained experience in the North American Aviation F-86 Sabre, the only American jet that was superior to the MiG-15s flown by the enemy in Korea.

In 1952, Bolt went to Korea to fly Grumman F9F Panther jet fighters with VMF-115, but when he had completed 100 missions and VMF-115 rotated back to Japan, he stayed on. The US Air Force exchange program was going strong, and Marine aviators were now flying combat missions in Sabres. He finally managed to land a slot with the 39th Fighter-Interceptor Squadron, where he had a chance to fly with Lieutenant Joseph McConnell, the leading American ace of the Korean War.

On May 16, 1953, Jack Bolt was leading a 39th FIS combat air patrol over MiG Alley in northwestern Korea when the enemy attacked. He found himself with a MiG-15 in his sights and shot it down. With this, Bolt's first aerial victory in a decade, the stars aligned. Between June 22 and July 11, he downed five additional MiGs, the last two in the space of five minutes.

Jack Bolt, formerly a Black Sheep, took home a Navy Cross and the distinction of being the only Marine aviator to down more than five enemy aircraft in each of two separate wars.

A decade later, as the American involvement in the long-running war in Southeast Asia began to escalate, most of the double-digit Marine aces who had previously remained with the Corps had retired.

The majority of those from all the services who had tasted combat in World War II would not be on the front lines in Vietnam. But there were exceptions, and one of these was Brigadier General Marion Carl. He'd had a stellar postwar career. From his role as a test pilot, he had progressed to flying McDonnell F2H-2P Banshee photoreconnaissance aircraft over the Chinese coastline during the tense moments of the stand-off between the People's Republic of China and the exiled Nationalist Chinese government on Taiwan.

In November 1954, he had taken command of the 1st Marine Photo Squadron (VMJ-1) at Pohang in South Korea. They were flying routine patrols over the east coast of North Korea, helping to monitor the ceasefire that had suspended the Korean War in 1953.

In May 1955, VMJ-1 was relocated to Taiwan to fly patrols over the contested waters of the Taiwan Strait, where the People's Republic of China was threatening an invasion of the small Nationalist-controlled islands of Quemoy and Matsu.

On May 12, Carl tangled with fighters of an opposing air force for the first time in a dozen years. He was leading four flights of F2H-2Ps at 40,000 feet. Carl had argued against flying missions so high because contrails formed at that altitude and made it impossible to obscure the presence of the reconnaissance aircraft. As might have been expected, a pair of Chinese MiG-15s appeared, shadowing Carl and his wingman.

Though the "Photo Banshees" carried no guns, Carl instinctively turned into the MiGs and made a head-on pass, indicating that he was unintimidated. Followed by his wingman, Carl then went into a steep descent, pulling out low over the Chinese coastline before heading back to Taiwan.

After this experience, VMJ-1 was assigned armed F2H-2 Banshee fighters to escort the reconnaissance aircraft, and Carl flew one of these. He also convinced the US Navy Seventh Fleet, which ran the operation, to let VMJ-1 fly below contrail altitude. Subsequent missions went off without incident.

After a year at the Air War College and a stint as Director of Marine Corps Aviation in the early 1960s, Carl received his promotion to brigadier general and became chief of staff of the 1st Marine Brigade at MCAS Kaneohe in Hawaii in 1964.

In March 1965, as the Marines landed at Danang, marking the first large-scale commitment of American ground combat units to Vietnam, Marion Carl made several visits in-country before becoming the deputy commander of the 3rd MAW at Danang in August.

Having previously become qualified in the McDonnell F-4B Phantom II, Carl lost little time calling on fighter attack squadron VMFA-542, with whom he flew his first of many Vietnam combat missions, an air strike near Hue, in early September.

Though a general, Carl also flew numerous combat missions in armed Bell UH-1E Huey helicopters, including five medevac missions in the space of five days in November 1965. Early 1966 found Carl doing the dangerous task of flying armed Hueys to escort Sikorsky H-34 transport helicopters flying missions in and out of US Army Special Forces outposts.

In March 1966, Carl flew his first mission in an F-8E Crusader strike fighter, dropping 260-pound fragmentation bombs and doing some strafing with the Colt Mk 12 20mm cannons. The following day, he was approached by his boss, Major General Lew Walt, the commander of the III Marine Amphibious Force (MAF) and the 3rd Marine Division. He showed Carl a memo that had just come down from General Wallace Greene, the Commandant of the Marine Corps. It explicitly forbade general officers from flying combat missions. When Walt told Carl that this applied especially to him, Carl reminded Walt that he had been at the front just as often.

Though Marion Carl was the only Marine double-digit ace to fly combat missions in Vietnam, he was not the only one to set foot officially in that war-torn place. Don Sapp, now a colonel, served on Lew Walt's staff at the III MAF at Danang. He retired in 1968, changed his surname to "Stapp," and passed away the following year at the relatively young age of 50.

Pappy Boyington even made a cameo appearance at Danang in 1965, having been sent there by his then-employer, the Electronic Specialty Company. Many of the aircraft used by the Marines and the US Air Force at Danang used the company's avionics systems, but Boyington's visit was in large part a publicity tour. Any interaction between him and either Sapp or Carl, if such even occurred, would have been minimal.

Boyington did not linger long at Danang. The current incarnation of his old Black Sheep Squadron, now VMA-214, a ground attack squadron, was based Chu Lai, 50 miles down the coast, so he hitched a ride down there. The aviators, less than half his age but well aware of his reputation as a fighter pilot, welcomed the chance to meet him, and he savored the opportunity to look over the Douglas A-4C Skyhawks that this new generation of Black Sheep were flying.

The scene, aviators living in tents on sandy beaches beneath palm trees and a muggy tropical sky—reminiscent of the South Pacific of yore—certainly inspired a feeling of nostalgia in the 53-year-old. An invitation for barbecue and beer was naturally extended and just as naturally accepted.

Marion Carl left Vietnam in May 1966, having logged more than 40 hours flying aircraft from Hueys to Phantoms—though in his memoirs he wrote that he wished he could have taken a Crusader up into North Vietnam to hunt MiGs.

33

The Black Sheep and the Governor

Greg Boyington and Joe Foss were two of the three highest-scoring Marine Corps aces of World War II, and they probably had more newspaper ink devoted to them during—and especially *after*—the war than any other pair of Marine aviators.

Bob Hanson, the third man in that top tier, did not, of course, have a postwar career to parallel Foss and Boyington through decades of headlines. Unlike Boyington, who disappeared only to return from the dead, Bob Hanson was never seen again. His parents, the Methodist missionaries to India who spent the war years in Massachusetts, returned to India. Here, they would be remembered for their work with the Lodhipur School in Punjab—far from the world suggested by that of the nickname of their son, "Butcher Bob" Hanson.

However, Bob's name would be memorialized in India. The sports complex at the Woodstock School in Landour, near Mussoorie in the Himalaya foothills, which he attended, is known to this day known as Hanson Field.

Hanson's siblings, meanwhile, also had notable postwar careers far from his wartime image. Earl had a four-decade career as an award-winning biologist and educator, serving for a time on the faculty at Yale. Edith, who was only four when Bob was lost, became an actress and moved to Japan in 1960 to be a television presenter. Half a century on, she was still living there.

In paralleling the lives of Foss and Boyington, we see two celebrated, high-profile Medal of Honor recipients who both came home as heroes and lived lives that were at the same time similar, and very dissimilar.

Boyington's star burned brightly in October 1945 as he collected his Medal of Honor in Washington and as he and Frank Walton traveled on to New York for a ticker tape parade.

Though he was delighted with the attention and thrilled by the applause, the pace of the tour gradually exhausted him, and his bright star began to dim. He continued to believe that after the long months of enforced sobriety in Japan he had his drinking under control, but it would not take long to realize he was wrong.

By his own reckoning, the Boyington victory tour finally went off the rails in Portland a couple of weeks after his ticker tape parade. He took the stage visibly drunk—his memoirs mention "five or six" glasses full of scotch and soda. Things went downhill from there.

"Good evening, ladies and gentlemen ... I shall not keep you long. You came here to be entertained by some sideshow freak," he began, according to his own recollection. "I would like to inform you of the only reason you should be here. It is not to pay homage to a so-called war hero ... because he would have been helpless without the financial assistance of slobs like you. So ... I'm going to remind all of you slobs to continue to invest in War Bonds. ... Good night."

As he remembered, "there wasn't one single clap of hands. The guests filed out of the private dining hall with bewildered expressions on their faces. None of them ganged up at the speaker's table to shove and shake my hand as they usually did. The committee members were dumfounded and probably hoped that the whole thing was nothing but a bad dream."

Realizing how badly Boyington had embarrassed the Marine Corps, Walton cut the tour short and they retreated to Walton's home in Los Angeles. Here, the two men made substantial progress on Boyington's autobiography, which would not be published for a decade.

"I do not know what Lazarus found when he returned from the dead," Boyington later observed, "but as for me I found myself and my earthly affairs in one hell of a state of confusion, and maybe Lazarus had found them that way too. Naturally, mine happened to be all of my own making."

High on his list of "confused early affairs" were his finances. "I was still broke," he wrote. "The reason I had not received any money or back pay is that before going away in the Pacific I had all my wages put into a trusteeship for my three children. I had done it through a reputable law firm and a bank in San Diego. But arrangements like this take more than a reputable law firm and bank, for they can't do anything about an alcoholic's friends. Anyhow, my friend (female) had taken care of things until her alcoholic buddy [Boyington] was missing in action, then things ceased being carried out as planned."

The "friend" was a beautiful brunette named Lucy Malcolmson. She was a still-married previous love interest with whom he still professed to be in love, despite her clumsy handling of his money and her marital status. A plan took shape by which she would establish a brief residency in Nevada, get a quickie divorce and marry Boyington, though Boyington admitted to Walton that he did not want to be married, and told Lucy as much.

The plan derailed after Boyington met Frances "Franny" Baker, a Hollywood starlet, who convinced him to break things off with Lucy. To make a complicated story short, he dumped Lucy and married Franny in the space of a day. With Frank Walton and his wife Carol in attendance, the wedding took place in Las Vegas on January 8, 1946, the same day that Lucy's divorce decree was to be issued, and the day *she* had planned to marry Boyington. The tabloids devoured the scandal of the hard-drinking war hero, the jilted "other woman" and the beautiful blonde interloper whom they described as a "former actress."

The confusion in Boyington's affairs only intensified. Lucy kept the money, went to the media, and hired a lawyer. Grand theft charges were filed against her, but eventually dismissed. The press seized upon this juicy story, and as Boyington's public image crashed, that glorious future, his for the taking in September 1945, disappeared forever.

The drunkenness continued, intensified, and cost him his relationship with Frank Walton. Boyington was in and out of Navy hospitals with various ailments, some related to wartime injuries, others to his heavy consumption of alcohol, caffeine, and cigarettes. Finally, the Marine Corps washed their hands of him, placing him on the retired list in August 1947.

Even Boyington's travails at rock bottom would pale by comparison to those of another of the Black Sheep. Christopher Lyman McGee, the cousin of poet John Gillespie McGee and a nine-victory ace with VMF-214, had a colorful but tragic postwar career. In 1948, he was hired by Israel to fly as a fighter pilot in the Arab-Israeli War. He checked out in the Avia S-199, the Czech-built variant of the Messerschmitt Bf 109, and made it to Israel, though he flew no combat missions.

Back in the United States, McGee fell in with a gang smuggling liquor across state lines, and eventually turned to bank robbery. In 1955, while Boyington was scratching out a living as a Southern California beer salesman, McGee was robbing a bank in Cicero, Illinois. He pulled two more jobs before he was caught in 1957. Two years later he began serving eight years of a 15-year sentence in federal custody.

In South Dakota, Joe Foss also found that fame opened doors, and he was luckier that Boyington in that they did not slam shut on his fingers.

He reconnected with his boyhood pal, Duane "Duke" Corning, who was back in Sioux Falls after flying PB4Y-1 Liberator patrol bombers for the US Navy in Britain. Much to the consternation to Foss's wife June, who had just given birth to their second daughter in September 1945, Joe and Duke spent much of their first months out of the service on out-of-state hunting and fishing trips, or shooting craps at local dives.

When they finally settled down, the two friends started a Packard-Studebaker dealership called Foss Motors and the Joe Foss Flying Service, so named to capitalize on the household name. The services offered at the latter included charter flights, contract maintenance, and even a flying school. Through the years, they bought and sold a number of single and multi-engine general aviation aircraft.

In 1947, as Greg Boyington was getting out of uniform, Joe Foss was getting back in. He was approached by the commander of the South Dakota National Guard to take command of the 176th Fighter Interceptor Squadron, the recently established Air National Guard contingent in the state. Thus the retired Marine major became a lieutenant colonel in the Air Force-affiliated Air National Guard (ANG). Interservice rivalry being what it was, this move was met with a great deal of displeasure from his fellow Marines. Nevertheless, Foss plunged into the project with enthusiasm, and even formed an aerobatic team with the squadron that was known as the "Red Devils."

During the Korean War, Foss, now an ANG colonel, was recalled to active duty with the US Air Force's Air Defense Command. He lobbied for the Air Force to send him into combat, but his request was denied because of his Medal of Honor—despite the fact that fellow ace Bob Galer, who also had the medal, was flying combat missions.

In 1948, Foss began to be encouraged by various Sioux Falls civic leaders to get into politics. Though initially disinclined, he was talked into running for the South Dakota House of Representatives on the Republican ticket, and he won. "Most of those guys had backgrounds as shallow as the Missouri River," he wrote in his memoirs of the politicians he had known. "When I thought about it, I figured I could do at least as well as they did."

However, her husband's new avocation did not sit well with June. It was partly his absence from home while the legislature was in session, and according to Foss in his memoirs, they did not see eye-to-eye on his small-government political philosophy. This began to drive a permanent wedge into their relationship.

In his memoirs, Foss also admitted to having had a wandering eye. In July 1951, when he was at an ANG training session at Williams AFB in Arizona, he met a woman named Donna "Didi" Wild, who operated an event facility at a Phoenix hotel. As Foss recalled, "our lighthearted friendship might have developed into something more serious except I was still married."

Didi put a stop to it in 1951, but they would meet again.

Meanwhile, politics had become an obsession for Joe Foss. Elected to two terms in the legislature, he decided "without consulting anyone," that he would run for governor in 1954. Though the state Republican party already had another man in mind, Foss easily won the primary contest, and went on the campaign trail, flying throughout the state at the controls of his own aircraft.

When he won by a comfortable margin, newspaper headlines called him a "War Hero, Family Man, and Humanitarian." The latter was a reference to his longtime support for the National Society for Crippled Children, better known as the Easter Seals Society. He had become involved in this charity because his daughter Cheryl had been diagnosed with cerebral palsy.

In his memoirs, he admitted that "June took exception to the 'family man' description, given our situation at home."

At least the family was united at the Governor's Mansion in Pierre. The new governor burnished his "down home" image by walking to and from work every day, and by carrying a duck call with which he communicated with waterfowl on the pond near the capitol.

His policies included increasing employment through encouragement of new businesses and business expansion. He even began sponsoring a celebrity pheasant hunt each year to promote South Dakota tourism.

Foss promoted merit-based pay raises for state employees. As he wrote in his memoirs, "I tried never to lose sight of the fact that government existed for the good of the people, and sometimes I needed to remind people in government of this."

Nevertheless, he found himself wrangling with local jurisdictions over state policy, and with President Dwight Eisenhower, a fellow Republican, over federal agriculture policy.

In 1956, June threatened to leave him if he ran for reelection, but he did and she did not—at least not yet.

In 1958, when term limits prevented another reelection bid, Foss decided to run for the US Senate, but he lost to state legislator— and 1972 Democratic presidential nominee—George McGovern.

With his political career now over, Foss fielded a number of private sector offers, including one from World War I ace-of-aces Eddie Rickenbacker, who owned Eastern Air Lines.

He had worked for a few months at Raven Industries, a maker of high-altitude research balloons, when he was offered the post of commissioner of the American Football League (AFL), recently created to compete with the established National Football League (NFL).

In January 1961, after his first season as AFL commissioner, Foss contacted Pete Rozelle at the NFL with his idea for a "World Playoff" between the two leagues. Joe Foss's idea of a "big game" bounced around for six seasons before finally becoming a reality in January 1967 at the end of the 1966 season as the first Super Bowl.

While Joe Foss was pursuing his political career and working his way toward the reality of the Super Bowl, Greg Boyington and his wife Franny had made their home in Southern California, though one would hesitate to use the phrase "settled down."

Boyington, who had now embraced the nickname "Pappy," still made headlines, but not the ones that would find a place in the scrapbook. On October 13, 1951, for instance, United Press reported that Pappy "was jailed today on a drink charge. The police said he was picked up driving erratically." Given his continuing battle with the bottle, this was not the only time he was picked up on the charge, and not all the incidents were without damage to other cars.

Despite his troubles, Boyington managed to find employment and earned enough that he and Franny bought and sold at least two homes which he fixed up himself—even to the extent of adding rooms. "I'm getting a kick out of that," he told the Associated Press in 1955. "Might even become a contractor."

He never did.

His day job was as a salesman for the Eastside branch of the Los Angeles Brewing Company, which had become the West Coast flagship plant of Pabst of Milwaukee, one of the largest brewing companies in the country. He also dabbled in side jobs, such as being a referee for small-time professional wrestling matches.

"I could spend about three evenings a week at it, have a hobby, get exercise, fun and pick up some dough," he explained in his 1955 Associated Press interview. "Then arenas began closing and they'd chase you from San Diego to Bakersfield for jobs and there wasn't much money so I quit."

Boyington's drinking and brawling strained their marriage so badly that Franny, no teetotaler herself, convinced him to see a psychiatrist. He also tried Alcoholics Anonymous for a while and it helped keep him on the wagon as often than not.

He had virtually nothing to do with his children, though Janet lived nearby, married to a middleweight boxer. In 1955, Greg Junior had managed to get into the Air Force Academy on the coattails of his father's Medal of Honor.

After more than a decade out of the cockpit, Boyington got his pilot's license in the late 1950s and worked freelance flying charter flights in light general aviation aircraft out of the Lockheed Air Terminal (now Burbank Airport), which was just a five-minute drive from his home. This led to his being hired by Coast Pro-Seal, a company that manufactured sealants for the aircraft industry.

He even picked up the autobiographical manuscript that he and Frank Walton had started a decade earlier and decided to try to get it published. For the first time since he had blown his chance to cash in on his returning hero image in 1945, Pappy Boyington was in the right place and at the right time. G.P. Putnam's Sons in New York bought the manuscript. They only lightly edited the coarseness of his writing style, which turned out to be the right choice.

Cashing in on the still resonant cache of the Black Sheep squadron, the memoir was named *Baa Baa Black Sheep* and published in the summer of 1958.

"Putnam, playing it close to the vest, ran off a small first printing and undertook virtually no promotion," wrote columnist Gene Sherman of the *Los Angeles Times* in October. "This nettled Pappy who, with characteristic directness, decided to promote it himself. He has since appeared on 50 or more television shows and has been interviewed by any number of previously skeptical critics."

Baa Baa Black Sheep received rave reviews from leading publications across the country. The book reached the top spot on the *Los Angeles Times* best-seller list, and hovered around number three on the *New York Times* reckoning for months, selling 100,000 copies in its first year. Boyington bought a sports car and a Cessna, and embarked on a nationwide publicity tour.

Talk of a movie deal murmured through Hollywood for the next couple of years, with gossip columnist Hedda Hopper even reporting that Burt Lancaster might be cast as Boyington.

Joe Foss had also been courted by Hollywood. Only a year earlier, director Hall Barlett had flown Foss out to the Coast and introduced him to John Wayne, suggesting that the "Duke" might be a good casting choice to play Foss himself. Foss and Wayne got along well, and, as Foss later recalled in his memoirs, the scheme was "going along slicker than butter on a hot pan—until I read the script."

Realizing that the narrative of his character "had little to do with my experiences," Foss himself pulled the plug, walking away from the promised high six-figure payday.

For Boyington, his movie project faded the way so many Hollywood projects do—in the echoing silence of unreturned phone calls. Nevertheless, the project brought Boyington to Riverside, California one day in 1959 to talk to a pilot named Carson Shade about sourcing vintage aircraft for use in the film.

Here, Boyington inconveniently met and fell in love with Shade's wife, magazine cover model Delores "Dee" Tatum.

Like Franny, Dee was a former actress, though slightly more successful. Dee had appeared in several films earlier in the decade, such as *Fingerprints Don't Lie* and *Mark of the Dragon*, albeit not with top billing.

Things moved quickly. Dee divorced Carson Shade in Alabama, and Boyington's divorce from Franny was granted in Los Angeles in October 1959. She took half of his net worth, including proceeds from *Baa Baa Black Sheep*, but left him his sports car and airplane. Pappy and Dee wound up in an apartment on Colfax Avenue in North Hollywood.

Boyington and his third wife were married three times. The first wedding was in Colorado on October 27, 1959, but his divorce did not become final until February 1960, so they had a second wedding in Las Vegas just in case. In December 1960, the *Los Angeles Times* reported that "they did not want to depend on the second because it took place after she had filed for a California divorce from Shade but before the decree became final [so] they tightened their matrimonial ties ... with a third knot."

It didn't last long.

He began flirting with other women, and was drinking heavily again. In February 1964, he moved out of the North Hollywood apartment and the fireworks got serious. He and Dee began suing one another for an annulment. She claimed that he beat her and fractured her spine, while he claimed that her Mexican divorce from her husband *before* Carson Shade was not valid. Amazingly, they reconciled in 1964, though they finally divorced in 1973.

———

At exactly the same time as Greg Boyington was going through his second divorce, Joe Foss's first marriage was on the rocks. As Foss recalls in his memoirs, it was in November 1959 that he and his wife June "began going separate ways."

In 1962, Joe Foss, now a brigadier general, attended an Air Force Association meeting in Arizona. While there, he ran into Didi Wild, the woman with whom he had almost had an affair back in 1951. Again, a mutual attraction blossomed, and this time they agreed to a "long-distance courtship" while Foss proceeded to get a divorce. Joe and Didi were married in 1967.

In the meantime, Foss finally had his chance to go before the cameras. During his time spent in New York with the AFL, he had come to know a great many people associated with the broadcast media. One of them was Tom Moore, president of the ABC television network. In 1963, Moore was one of the bigwigs who Foss had invited to the annual celebrity pheasant hunt in South Dakota that Foss still sponsored. Moore enjoyed himself and mused that it would be great to get the hunting experience on air.

From this conversation there came the idea for *The American Sportsman* program, which aired on ABC for more that two decades. Hosted by Foss himself in its early years, the program was an ancestor of the "outdoorsman" reality television shows that are still popular in the twenty-first century.

34

Final Flights

In later years, many of the double-digit Marine aces remained active in aviation circles. Archie Donahue, who had studied engineering at the University of Texas before the war, returned to the Lone Star State and was active in the warbird community for many years as an aviator with the Confederate (later Commemorative) Air Force organization.

Phillip DeLong retired to Sumter County, Florida, where he was involved in fundraising for local schools and veteran families. A former wingman restored a Corsair and DeLong was honored when his name was put on the side.

Jim Swett went to work at his father's industrial machinery company in San Francisco. He wound up running the company for 23 years before turning it over to his son in 1983. In his 2009 obituary, he was noted for his frequent presentations to school groups and civic organizations. A computer video recreation of his 1943 Medal of Honor battle, with him providing the voice-over, appeared on the History Channel's "Dogfights" series in 2006.

Bob Galer was one of many wartime aviators to find a postwar career in the aviation/aerospace industry. After retiring from the Corps in 1957, he went to work for Chance Vought Aircraft of Dallas, Texas—the company that built the F4U Corsair—which was soon absorbed into the Ling-Temco-Vought (LTV) conglomerate.

He later worked in the real estate component of the petroleum industry services company owned by Harvey "Bum" Bright, the one-time owner of the Dallas Cowboys football franchise.

John L. Smith was another former Marine who went on to work in the aerospace industry after his retirement in 1960. His latter years in the service, however, had been increasingly troubled. In December 1959, he had finally asked to be admitted to Bethesda Naval Hospital to be treated for depression.

Because it was a short-staffed holiday period, the decorated colonel fell through the cracks. As recalled by Robert Mrazek, writing in the August 2012 issue of *Naval History* magazine, Smith was "placed in a locked psychiatric ward" for 12 days. Reviewing Smith's records, Mrazek observed that the former aviator had a series of short sessions in early 1960 with "a flight surgeon doing temporary work in psychiatry while pursuing a career in space medicine ... a clinical board summary—based solely on the flight surgeon's diagnosis—said: 'He has now received maximum benefit of hospitalization and further treatment is not indicated at this time.'"

Considered unfit for duty, Smith was discharged in September 1960, but found work with Grumman Aerospace, the company that had built the F4F Wildcat in which he had achieved his fame. He soon moved to California and took another job with the Rocketdyne Division of North American Aviation (later Rockwell International) in Canoga Park.

Quoting Smith's daughter, Caroline, Mrazek reported that his job was in "marketing," but "more often it was mere glad-handing [and Smith] bristled at being trotted out to play golf with potential customers and being introduced as 'John L. Smith, our Medal of Honor winner.'"

Medal of Honor recipients consider the decoration to have been "earned," not "won."

In 1972, Smith was 57, still relatively young, when Rocketdyne laid him off after a decade of service. He tried unsuccessfully to find another job, and on June 10 of that year, Smith went into the back yard of his home in Encino and shot himself.

He was buried in Arlington National Cemetery beneath a stone marked only with his surname, though a city park in his home town of Lexington, Oklahoma has a granite monument with a short overview of his life. His wife, Louise Maddox Outland Smith, returned to her native Virginia, and passed away in Virginia Beach in 2007. Sadly, she outlived not only her husband, but also their son, John L. Smith, Jr., an attorney with the US Navy Judge Advocate General Corps, who died in 1993.

Greg Boyington, whose own troubled life had marinated in the ruin of alcoholism for years, suffered his own suicide tragedy in 1971. This involved the mysterious death of his daughter Janet, whose own life had been crippled by drugs and alcohol. By this time, Boyington had left Los Angeles and was living in Fresno, suffering from the after-effects of lung cancer surgery, going in and out of the Veteran's Administration Hospital, and waiting for his divorce from Dee Tatum to become final.

As bad as things got for him, Boyington's self-destructive life had always been punctuated by moments of amazing good fortune. In 1975, he got a call from Frank Price, the head of Universal Television, and the man behind such series as *Columbo*, *Kojak*, and *The Six Million Dollar Man*. Price had just read *Baa Baa Black Sheep*. He liked it—*and* he had put it in front of producer Stephen Cannell who had created *The Rockford Files* for Universal.

As Joe Foss had his time in front of the cameras with *The American Sportsman*, Boyington was about to enjoy his own moment of televised glory. The movie deal for *Baa Baa Black Sheep* had faltered and faded twenty years earlier, but suddenly, it was full steam ahead with an action comedy in the spirit of contemporary World War II television shows such as *Hogan's Heroes* and *McHale's Navy*.

The man picked for the lead role, that of Boyington, was Robert Conrad, who had achieved stardom in such television series as *Hawaiian Eye* and *Wild, Wild West*. Incongruously, Conrad's dashing, leading man good looks were just the opposite of Boyington's appearance—often described by the adjective "bulldog." Nevertheless, the "chemistry" gelled. Boyington and Conrad got along well during filming. The actor submerged himself in the role, while people on the set became enraptured with Boyington's rough charisma.

A pilot episode, called "Flying Misfits," was filmed and a contract for a 22-installment season was issued. As the first season of *Baa Baa Black Sheep* began on NBC in September 1976, the *Washington Post* sarcastically described the show as a "war-is-swell series [for] anyone who remembers World War II as a rousing, blowsy, fraternity turkey shoot."

Among those who did *not* remember the war in this way were members of Boyington's own Black Sheep Squadron. They objected to the significant inaccuracies, especially the portrayals of themselves as screwballs and miscreants lacking in professionalism. Frank Walton was especially outspoken in his criticism.

Joe Foss had once pulled the plug on a lucrative movie deal because of the script being erroneous, but Boyington seemed not to care.

The second season of the program was canceled because of staff changes at NBC, then reinstated, albeit with only 13 episodes. When the last installment of *Baa Baa Black Sheep* aired in April 1978, Boyington was once again a household name, and generally seen in a positive light by those untroubled by the sort of technical and historical flaws that are generally accepted in television comedies.

Boyington self-published a new edition of his book and became a fixture at air show tents, hawking his product and spinning his own version of reality for a postwar generation.

Within his circle of acquaintances in Fresno, as he toppled in and out of Alcoholics Anonymous, Boyington met Josephine "Jo" Moseman. They had a lot in common. Both were divorced and both were trying hard to put the bottle behind them, though she was more successful than he was. They were married in 1978 and stayed together, as his body slowly deteriorated, until his death ten difficult years later.

Loren "Doc" Everton, who achieved fame with VMF-223 and commanded VMF-113, passed away in 1991, but his name became the center of a curious story that occurred more than two decades later.

In 2014, Keith and Ellen Littlefield of Annandale, Virginia, decided to visit an "antique roadshow" event at the Stafford County Museum. They had heard that someone from the National Museum of the Marine Corps would be there, and they wanted to share a mystery object that Ellen had found while digging in her garden in the 1990s. It was a brass bracelet with the name "Major L.D. Everton, USMC" on one side and the phrase "Dale from Dolores" on the reverse. They had researched the names, but amazingly had *not* found an L.D. Everton. According to the National Museum's own account, it took their curators a while to discover that the people mentioned were Doc and his wife Dolores Miller Everton, whom he had married in 1942.

Having consulted the Everton family, the Littlefields donated the bracelet to the Museum. Though Doc was stationed at the Pentagon, a few miles away, in the 1950s, it is still a mystery how the bracelet wound up buried in the Annandale garden.

In May 1973, after three years as Inspector General of the Marine Corps and 35 years in the Corps and more than 13,000 hours of flight time, Marion Carl retired. Until 1980, when they moved to Oregon, he and Edna remained in Virginia, where they had lived during his final years in the service. As with Joe Foss and South Dakota, Marion Carl saw the mountains of Oregon's Coast Range as an ideal place to indulge his interest in the outdoors.

After decades of impermanent base housing situations, Marion and Edna finally moved into a home in Roseberg on the meandering South Umpqua River, landing 150 miles south of where he had grown up. As Joe Foss published his postwar memoir, *A Proud American*, in 1992, Marion Carl's *Pushing the Envelope*, coauthored by aviation historian Barrett Tillman, was published two years later.

It all came to an end for Marion Carl on June 28, 1998 in a home invasion robbery, as he was killed by a shotgun blast to his head while trying to defend Edna from an attacker. She was wounded. The assailant got away but was later apprehended and convicted.

The 82-year-old Carl was laid to rest at the Arlington National Cemetery, where he was joined in July 1998 by Ken Walsh. Walsh had had a heart attack while preparing to attend the Experimental Aircraft Association's annual air show in Oshkosh, Wisconsin. Greg Boyington, Herb Long, Jack Conger, and Joe Foss were also interred at Arlington.

Through the latter decades of the twentieth century, Joe Foss had kept busy, spending much time in Washington and New York as a lobbyist for Royal Dutch Airlines (KLM), and later as president of the National Rifle Association (NRA). Eventually, though, he and Didi decided that they "really like[d] the West" and they put the cities behind them to divide their time between a new home in Scottsdale, Arizona and a summer place on Sand Creek near the Wyoming-South Dakota state line.

In this book of stories of individual lives and individual battles, we conclude with one from the closing days of the life of Joe Foss.

It was January 11, 2002, 59 years to the week since he had completed the tour of duty that had earned him the Medal of Honor. On this day, the 86-year-old ace had that very medal, awarded by Franklin Roosevelt personally, in his pocket as he was about to board another aircraft, the jetliner that would take him east, where he was scheduled to speak to cadets at the US Military Academy at West Point.

As Foss moved toward his flight, the security checkpoint metal detector at Phoenix Sky Harbor Airport shrieked and Foss was beset by zealous screeners. Only four months had passed since the infamous terrorist attacks of September 11, 2001, and the security people were nervously anxious. They searched him vigorously, finding and seizing the offending artifact.

As explained to this author by Barrett Tillman, who knew Joe Foss, "the guardians were not with the Transportation Security Administration, which was still getting started, but airline employees filling in. Joe asked why the 'security' wanted to confiscate the medal and was told with its beveled edges 'You might hurt somebody.' Now, Joe was a bone-deep gentleman but he could get spooled up. He exclaimed, 'Hurt somebody? Why do you think they gave me the medal?'"

Ricardo Alonso-Zaldivar reported in the *Los Angeles Times* on March 11 that "Security relented and Foss was allowed to board with it. 'Nobody takes that medal,' Foss said."

Foss later said that the Medal of Honor "represents all of the guys who lost their lives—the guys who never came back. Everyone who put their lives on the line for their country."

He was one of those who *had* put his life on the line. He was one of those Few who had prevailed in the desperate and dangerous skies over the South Pacific six decades before.

Appendix

Folded Wings

Joseph Jacob Foss (1915–2003)
Robert Murray Hanson (1920–1944)
Gregory "Pappy" Boyington (1912–1988)
Kenneth Ambrose Walsh (1916–1998)
Donald Nathan Aldrich (1916–1947)
John Lucian Smith (1914–1972)
Marion Eugene Carl (1915–1998)
Wilbur Jackson "Gus" Thomas (1920–1947)
James Elms Swett (1920–2009)
Harold Leman Spears (1919–1944)
Edward Oliver "Bud" Shaw (1920–1944)
Archie Glenn Donahue (1917–2007)
Robert Edward Galer (1913–2005)
William Pratt Marontate (1919–1943)
Kenneth DeForrest Frazier (1919–1959)
James Norman Cupp (1921–1984)
Loren Dale "Doc" Everton (1915–1999)
Harold Edward "Murderous Manny" Segal (1920–1998)
William Nugent Snider (1918–1969)
Phillip Cunliffe DeLong (1919–2006)
Harold William "Coach" Bauer (1908–1942)
Jack Eugene Conger (1921–2006)
Herbert Harvey Long (1919–2001)
Donald Hooten Sapp (1918–1969)

Abbreviations and Acronyms

A6M Mitsubishi Zero	(IJNAF fighter)
AirNorSols	Allied Air Forces, Northern Solomons
AirSols	Solomons Air Command
ANG	Air National Guard
AO	USN oiler
AVG	American Volunteer Group (the "Flying Tigers")
B-17 Boeing Flying Fortress	(USAAF bomber)
B-24 Consolidated Liberator	(USAAF bomber)
B-25 North American Aviation Mitchell	(USAAF bomber)
B5N Nakajima "Kate"	(IJNAF torpedo bomber)
BB	USN battleship
C-47 Douglas Skytrain	(USAAF transport)
CA	USN heavy cruiser
CENPAC	Central Pacific Area (Part of POA)
CINCPAC	Commander in Chief, Pacific
CL	USN light cruiser
ComAirNorSols	Commander, Allied Air Forces, Northern Solomons
ComAirSols	Commander, Solomons Air Command
CV	USN aircraft carrier
CVE	USN escort carrier

CVG	Carrier Air Group
D3A Aichi "Val"	(IJNAF dive bomber)
DD	USN destroyer
F4F Grumman Wildcat	(USN/USMC fighter)
F4U Vought Corsair	(USN/USMC fighter)
F6F Grumman Hellcat	(USN/USMC fighter)
F7F Grumman Tigercat	(USN/USMC fighter)
F8F Grumman Bearcat	(USN/USMC fighter)
FEAF	Far East Air Force (of the USAAF, 1941–43)
FEAF	Far East Air Forces (of the USAAF/ USAF, 1944–45, 1947–57)
FG	An aircraft like the F4U, but manufactured by Goodyear
FIS	Fighter-Interceptor Squadron
G3M Mitsubishi "Nell"	(IJNAF bomber)
G4M Mitsubishi "Betty"	(IJNAF bomber)
HVAR	High Velocity Aircraft Rocket
IJA	Imperial Japanese Army
IJAAF	Imperial Japanese Army Air Force
IJN	Imperial Japanese Navy
IJNAF	Imperial Japanese Navy Air Force
Ki-43 Nakajima "Oscar"	(IJAAF fighter)
Ki-49 Nakajima "Helen"	(IJAAF bomber)
Ki 61 Kawasaki "Tony"	(IJAAF fighter)
KIA	Killed in Action
MAF	Marine Amphibious Force
MCAS	Marine Corps Air Station
MIA	Missing in Action
NAS	Naval Air Station
NATC	Naval Air Test Center
P 38 Lockheed Lightning	(USAAF fighter)
P-40 Curtiss Warhawk	(USAAF fighter)
POA	Pacific Ocean Areas (includes CENPAC and SOPAC)
POW	Prisoner of War

R4D Douglas Skytrain	(USN/USMC transport)
RAAF	Royal Australian Air Force
RAF	Royal Air Force (United Kingdom)
RNZAF	Royal New Zealand Air Force
ROTC	Reserve Officer Training Corps (US Army)
SBD Douglas Dauntless	(USN/USMC dive bomber)
SCAT	South Pacific Combat Air Transport Command
SOPAC	South Pacific Area (Part of POA)
SWPA	South West Pacific Area
TBF Grumman Avenger	(USN/USMC torpedo bomber)
TF	Task Force
USAAF	United States Army Air Forces
USMC	United States Marine Corps
USN	US Navy
USS	United States ship
VB	USN Bombing Squadron
VF	USN Fighting Squadron
VMA	Marine Attack Squadron
VMB	USMC Bombing Squadron
VMF	USMC Fighting Squadron
VMF(N)	USMC Night Fighter Squadron
VMJ	Marine Photo[reconnaissance] Squadron
VMO	Marine Observation Squadron
VMR	Marine Transport Squadron
VMS	Marine Scouting Squadron
VMSB	USMC Scout Bombing Squadron
VMTB	USMC Torpedo Bombing Squadron
VT	USN Torpedo Squadron

Bibliography

Note: A chief source of material for this project, and a highly recommended source for further reading on the topics herein, is the monthly War Diaries and the Aircraft Action Reports compiled in the field by the Marine fighting squadrons that are mentioned throughout this book.

The originals are in the collection of the US National Archives and Records Administration (NARA). Page-by-page scans are viewable online at the Fold 3 site maintained by Ancestry.com. These are highly recommended for minute, day-by-day detail of the actions of the squadrons and all of their individual aviators.

Boyington, Gregory. *Baa Baa Black Sheep.* New York: G.P. Putnam's Sons, 1958.

Brokaw, Tom. *The Greatest Generation.* New York: Random House, 1998.

Carl, Marion with Barrett Tillman. *Pushing the Envelope: The Career of Fighter Ace and Test Pilot Marion Carl.* Annapolis: Naval Institute Press, 1994, 2005.

Condon, John. *Corsairs and Flattops: Marine Carrier Air Warfare, 1944–45.* Annapolis, Maryland: Naval Institute Press, 1998.

Condon, John. *US Marine Corps Aviation: 75th Year of Naval Aviation.* Washington, DC: Deputy Chief of Naval Operations (Air Warfare) and the Commander, Naval Air Systems Command, 2017.

Coonts, Stephen. *War in the Air: True Accounts of the 20th Century's Most Dramatic Air Battles by the Men who Fought Them.* New York: Pocket Books, 1996.

Craven, Wesley Frank and Cate, James Lea. *The Army Air Forces in World War II, Volume 4. The Pacific: Guadalcanal to Saipan, August*

1942 to July 1944. Washington, DC: Office of Air Force History; Chicago: University of Chicago Press, 1950.

Crowder, Michael J. *United States Marine Corps Aviation Squadron Lineage, Insignia & History, Volume One: The Fighter Squadrons.* Paducah, Kentucky: Turner Publishing Company, 2000.

De Chant, John A. *Devilbirds: The Story of United States Marine Aviation in World War II.* New York: Harper & Brothers, 1947.

Doll, Thomas. *Marine Fighting Squadron One-Twenty-One.* Carrollton, Texas: Squadron/Signal Publishing, 1996.

Foss, Joe (as told to Walter Simmons). *Joe Foss, Flying Marine: The Story of His Flying Circus.* New York: E.P. Dutton, 1943.

Foss, Joe. *A Proud American: The Autobiography of Joe Foss.* New York: Simon and Schuster, 1992.

Gamble, Bruce. *Black Sheep One: The Life of Gregory "Pappy" Boyington.* New York: Random House, 2000.

Gamble, Bruce. *The Black Sheep: A Definitive Account of Marine Fighting Squadron 214 in World War II.* New York: Random House, 1998.

Hammel, Eric. *Marines at War—20 True Heroic Tales of US Marines in Combat.* Pacifica, California: Pacifica Press, 1999.

Hollister, John N. PhD. *The Methodist Church in Southern Asia.* Lucknow, India: The Lucknow Publishing House of the Methodist Church in Southern Asia, 1956.

Hubler, Richard G. and Dechant, John A. *Flying Leathernecks: The Complete Record of Marine Corps Aviation in Action 1941–1944.* Garden City, New York: Doubleday, Doran & Co., 1944.

Johnson, Edward C. *Marine Corps Aviation: The Early Years 1912–1940.* Washington, DC: History and Museums Division, Headquarters, US Marine Corps, 1977.

Mersky, Peter B. *US Marine Corps Aviation—1912 to the Present.* Annapolis: The Nautical and Aviation Publishing Company of America, 1983.

Morison, Samuel Eliot. *History of United States Naval Operations in World War II: Volume V: The Struggle for Guadalcanal, August 1942–February 1943.* Boston: Little, Brown & Co., 1958.

Morison, Samuel Eliot. *History of United States Naval Operations in World War II: Volume III: The Rising Sun in the Pacific.* Boston, Little Brown & Co., 1984.

Mortensen, Bernhardt. Various articles in Craven, Wesley Frank and
Cate, James Lea. *The Army Air Forces in World War II, Volume 4.
The Pacific: Guadalcanal to Saipan, August 1942 to July 1944.*
Washington, DC: Office of Air Force History; Chicago: University
of Chicago Press, 1950.
Okumiya, Masatake and Fuchida, Mitsuo. *Midway: The Battle that
Doomed Japan; The Japanese Navy's Story.* Annapolis, Maryland:
Naval Institute Press, 1955.
Rottman, Gordon. *US Marine Corps World War II Order of Battle—
Ground and Air Units in the Pacific War, 1939–1945.* Westport,
Connecticut: Greenwood Press, 2002.
Sherrod, Robert. *A History of Marine Corps Aviation in World War II.*
Washington, DC: Combat Forces Press, 1952.
Sims, Edward H. *Greatest Fighter Missions.* New York: Harper & Row,
1983.
Stavisky, Samuel. *Marine Combat Correspondent.* New York: Ballantine
Publishing, 1999.
Styling, Mark. *Corsair Aces of World War 2.* Oxford: Osprey Publishing,
1995.
Tillman, Barrett. *US Marine Corps Fighter Squadrons of World War II.*
Oxford and New York: Bloomsbury Publishing, 2014.
Tillman, Barrett. *Wildcat Aces of World War 2.* Oxford: Osprey
Publishing, 1995.
Tregaskis, Richard. *Guadalcanal Diary.* New York: Random House,
1943
Walton, Frank E. *Once They Were Eagles: The Men of the Black Sheep
Squadron.* Lexington: University Press of Kentucky, 1986.
Western Province Assembly. *Recorded and Transcribed Oral Stories of
Wartime Participants.* Gizo, Western Province (Solomon Islands):
Western Province Assembly, 1998.
Yenne, Bill. *Aces High: The Heroic Saga of the Two Top-Scoring American
Aces of World War II.* New York: Berkley/Caliber, 2009.
Yenne, Bill. *MacArthur's Air Force: American Airpower Over the
Pacific and the Far East 1941–51.* Oxford: Osprey Publishing,
2019.
Yenne, Bill. *The Imperial Japanese Army: The Invincible Years.* Oxford:
Osprey Publishing, 2014.

PERIODICALS CITED

American Journal of Tropical Medicine and Hygiene
Aviation History magazine
Chicago Daily News
Collier's magazine
Cosmopolitan magazine
Esquire magazine
Life magazine
Los Angeles Times
Minneapolis Star-Tribune
Naval History magazine
New York Times
Saturday Evening Post magazine
Seattle Post-Intelligencer
Time magazine
Washington Post

Index

References to images and maps are in bold.